Praise for Lidia Yuknavitch

The Chronology of Water

2012 Finalist, PEN Center Creative Nonfiction Award
2012 Readers' Choice Award, Oregon Book Awards
2012 PNBA Award, Pacific Northwest Booksellers Association
2011 Best Books of the Year, *The Oregonian*
Top 10 Portland Books from 2011, *Willamette Week*
Best Portland Book Releases of 2011, *The Portland Mercury*
2011 Best Books of the Year, *The Nervous Breakdown*
Best books of 2011, *LitReactor*
The 10 Best Memoirs of 2011, *Flavorwire*
The 100 Great Nonfiction Books must-read works of narrative nonfiction and
    journalism, *The Electric Typewriter*
Canadian booksellers top non-fiction books of 2012, *Quill & Quire*: Canada's
    Magazine of Book News and Reviews

Flooded with light and incandescent beauty, *The Chronology of Water* cuts through the heart of the reader.

DIANA ABU-JABER, author of *Origin: A Novel*

This is the book Lidia Yuknavitch was put on the planet to write for us.

REBECCA BROWN, author of *The Gifts of the Body*

Reading this book is like diving into Yuknavitch's most secret places, where, really, we all want memoir to take us.

KERRY COHEN, author of *Loose Girl: A Memoir of Promiscuity*

This intensely powerful memoir touches depths yet unheard of in contemporary writing.

ANDREI CODRESCU, author of *The Poetry Lesson*

[I]mmensely impressive …

DAVID SHIELDS, author of *Reality Hunger: A Manifesto*

I'm also convinced that this bold and highly unconventional book – hot, gritty, unrelenting in its push to dismantle the self and then, somehow, put the self back together again – gets not just under a reader's skin but seeps all the way into her bloodstream.

DEBRA GWARTNEY, *The Oregonian*

Lidia Yuknavitch is my favorite new writer … It's so genius I'm not quite sure how she did it.

VALERIE STIVERS-ISAKOVA, *Huffington Post*

Simply stated: She is important. Read. Her. Now.

MARGARET ELYSIA GARCIA, *The Plumas Weekly*

Yuknavitch can write a really hot sex scene. It's super sexy, and it's never cheesy or over-the-top or too tame. It's perfect … Yuknavitch's memoir is one of the best books I've ever read.

CASEY REVIEWS, *The Lesbrary*

I find Yuknavitch's frankness about the emotional and physical experience of being a woman (in sex, in athletic competition, in childbirth) surprising. Not because it offends my sensibilities, but because it affirms them.

DANIELLE DEULEN, *Essay Daily*

This isn't for everyone. Some will read and be exasperated or disgusted or disbelieving. I get that. I get that chaos and promiscuity and addiction are ugly, messy, and life is too short to waste reading about someone else's tragedy and self-destructive behavior. But something about this story – the goddamn gorgeous language, the raw power of its brutality – gave me so much comfort and solace. In Yuknavitch's word embrace, I felt the magic of self-acceptance and self-love, and the crazy-wonderful beauty of life.

JULIE CHRISTINE JOHNSON, *Chalk the Sun*

Praise for Dora: A Headcase

Best Books of 2012, *Bust*
Best Books of 2012, *Daily Candy*
The Best Literary Heroines of 2012: An Alternate List, *Flavorwire*
21 Books Written by and About Women That Every Man Should Read, *Flavorwire*

Yuknavitch has wrestled with the force of her own convictions and given a powerful voice to a bad-ass character born on the literary landscape.

MONICA DRAKE, author of *Clown Girl*

Dora is too much for Sigmund Freud but she's just right for us – raunchy, sharp, and so funny it hurts.

KATHERINE DUNN, author of *Geek Love*

In these times there's no reason for a novel to exist unless it's dangerous, provocative, and not like anything that's come before. *Dora: A Headcase* is that kind of novel. It's dirty, sexy, rude, smart, soulful, fresh, and risky.

KAREN KARBO, author of *How Georgia Became O'Keeffe*

Lidia Yuknavitch casts a very special slant of light on our centuries and our lives. Put simply, the book is needed.

CAROLE MASO, author of *Defiance* and *The Art Lover*

Snappy and fun. I can pretty much guarantee you haven't met a character quite l like Ida before.

BLAKE NELSON, author of *Girl* and *Paranoid Park*

The world of *Dora* is not just possible, it's inevitable. It's revenge as the ultimate therapy.

CHUCK PALAHNIUK, author of *Fight Club*

Yuknavitch has written the best portrait of teen girlhood I have ever read. I loved this book – it's like a smart, fast, chick *Fight Club*. In twenty years, I hope to wake up in a world where *Dora: A Headcase* has replaced *Catcher in the Rye* on high school reading lists for the alienated. I'm pretty sure that world would be a better one.

VANESSA VESELKA, author of *Zazen*

Ida's narration is … a convincing voice …

SAM SACKS, *The Wall Street Journal*

It's a *bildungsroman*, but this is no *Portrait of the Artist as a Young Man* or *The Sorrows of Young Werther*.

JUDITH PULLMAN, *Art Watch*

The sustained voice of Ida is a narrative tour de force. It's angry, lonely, stomach-churningly ugly, and rings unwaveringly, perfectly true. But it takes a talented writer to make that kind of story palatable, much less amazing. Lidia Yuknavitch is that writer.

JOSEPH THOMPSON, *ForeWord Reviews*

Dora: A Headcase is a book for us – we lovelorn and clit-throbbing, we the bullied and bruised, we who kiss a picture of Kim Deal with our cherry lipgloss mouths, we, the punkettes with yellow caution tape wrapped around our wrists, our Rorschach blood spilling, we, the beautiful, the howling, the cuntgushing.

TASHA MATSUMOTO, *Quarterly West*

Clearly, Yuknavitch possesses a great well of empathy for misfits and a great passion for radical art. This has resulted in an enthusiastic, sometimes vexing novel that nevertheless will win over even the grumpiest lefty.

EUGENIA WILLIAMSON, *The Boston Globe*

It's a kind of fairy tale where history is given an opportunity to be set right, not unlike Quentin Tarantino's *Inglourious Basterds*.

PAUL CONSTANT, *The Stranger*

"I want to create new girl myths," Yuknavitch said of the book. It's about damn time someone did.

EMILY TEMPLE, *Flavorwire*

Totally bloody amazing. On par with Jonathan Swift's *A Modest Proposal*. Read it.

RENÉE E. D'AOUST, *The Collagist*

Like Salinger's Holden and Chbosky's Charlie and de la Pena's Sticky Boy and Green/Levithan's Will Graysons, Yuknavitch has written a frightfully insightful voice of youth, mimicking the language of our texters and status-updaters but with an angst and propensity for violence so explosive it puts Holden to shame.

J.A. TYLER, *The Rumpus*

Simply stated: She is important. Read. Her. Now.

MARGARET ELYSIA GARCIA, *The Plumas Weekly*

A Declaration: Lidia Yuknavitch has done more for "the body as art form" than anyone in recent memory. Read *Dora*, and if you haven't already, read *The Chronology of Water*.

SARA HABEIN, *Persephone Magazine*

If this had been published by one of the big ... publishers ... it could have easily have become a runaway bestseller, describable as a contemporary female version of *The Catcher in the Rye*.

CHRISTOPHER HIGGS, *American Book Review*

Library of Congress
Cataloging-in-Publication Data

Yuknavitch, Lidia.
The chronology of water : a memoir /
Lidia Yuknavitch.
p. cm.
ISBN 978-0-9790188-3-1
(alk. paper)

1. Yuknavitch, Lidia.
I. Title

PS3575.U35Z46 2011

813'.546–DC22 [B]

2010041860

Hawthorne Books
& Literary Arts

9   2201 Northeast 23rd Avenu
8   3rd Floor
7   Portland, Oregon 97212
6   hawthornebooks.com

Form:
Sibley House, Portland

Printed in China

Set in Paperback.

This book is for – and written through – Andy and Miles Mingo.

Acknowledgements

IF YOU HAVE EVER FUCKED UP IN YOUR LIFE, OR IF THE
great river of sadness that runs through us all has touched you,
then this book is for you. So thank you for the collective energy
it takes to write in the face of culture. I can feel you.

Energy never dies. It just changes forms. My beloved
friends and mentors Ken Kesey and Kathy Acker are in the space
dust and DNA and words.

Thank you Rhonda Hughes, editrix extrodinaire, as well
as all the people at Hawthorne Books for believing in my writing.
Bold Swimmers.

Thanks to Lance and Andy Olsen, my artheart heroes. And
to Ryan Smith and Virginia Paterson, through the miles.

To Diana Abu Jaber, thank you for saying to me twenty
years ago about a single story, "I think this might be a book." It
just took me a really long time to get it.

Thank you to the less than Merry Pranksters, particularly
Bennett Huffman: rest peacefully, Bennett, you were the best
among us, chaotic, beautiful stardust.

A great waterfall of thanks to Michael Connors for, well,
everything, and to Dean Hart, for making the everything possible. Thank you for mercifully loving all the me's I have brought
to your doorstep.

Thank you to the greatest writing group in the history of
ever: Chelsea Cain, Monica Drake, Cheryl Strayed, Mary Wysong,

Diana Jordan, Erin Leonard, Suzy Vitello, and Chuck Palahniuk. And Jim Frost.

Special thanks to Chelsea for writing the introduction, and to Chuck for inviting me in, and to Chuck and Chelsea for reading early versions of this manuscript and helping me to not lose my marbles. Well at least sometimes.

I would not be around to write this book had it not been for my sister going ahead of me. To Brigid who was Claudia: how to thank you for the lifeline of your enduring love. You have carried me well. Sister. Friend. Other mother. Poet of most tender thunder.

And though words suddenly seem remarkably puny, my pounding heart belongs to Andy and Miles – you make me able to be. Write. This love. Life. I didn't know.

The Chronology
of Water

Lidia Yuknavitch

 HAWTHORNE BOOKS & LITERARY ARTS
Portland, Oregon | MMX

Introduction
Chelsea Cain

LIDIA AND I ARE IN THERAPY TOGETHER.

That's what she calls it. Technically it is more of a writing workshop, at least that's what the rest of us would like to think. It works like this. We meet once a week. Some of us bring work. We all critique it. Then someone goes into the bathroom and cries.

Lidia joined two years ago.

Chuck Palahniuk brought up the idea of inviting her. "She writes this literary prose," he told us. "But she's this big-breasted blond from Texas, and she used to be a stripper and she's done heroin." Needless to say, we were impressed.

I already wanted her to sit by me.

There was more. Chuck told us that some really famous edgy writer – I didn't recognize her name, but I pretended that I did – had given a talk at a conference about the State of Sex Scenes in Literature and she'd said that all sex scenes were shit, except for the sex written by Lidia Yuknavitch. Maybe Chuck didn't tell us that. But someone in the group did. I don't remember. I think I was still thinking about the stripper thing. A real-life ex-stripper in our writing group! So glamorous.

Yes, we said, invite her. Please.

She showed up a few weeks later, wearing a long black coat. I couldn't see her breasts. She was quiet. She didn't make eye contact. She did not sound like she was from Texas.

Frankly, I was a little disappointed.

Where was the big hair, the Lucite platform heels? The track marks?

Had Chuck made the whole thing up? (He does that sometimes.)

How was he describing me to people?

Lidia had pages. That first night she came. She shared work. If you are a writer, or really a human at all, you will recognize how terrifying this is. You show up and sit down with a group of strangers and share your art, having no idea how they will respond, these assholes marking up your pages with their pens, judging you, leering at your tits.

She read us the first chapter of her novel *The Small Backs of Children* (due out with Hawthorne Books next year), while we all followed along with the copies she'd passed out. They say that alcoholics remember their first drink, that lightening feeling in your body that says yes-yes-let's-feel-this-way-all-the-time – well, I will always remember the first time I heard Lidia Yuknavitch read.

I thought, this is how writing is supposed to be. I thought, man oh man, she's good. I thought, I want that.

Literally. I wanted that chapter.

See the protocol at workshop is that we bring in pages, hand them out, read them out loud, and then go around the table for comments. After that, we collect the pages, which by then are theoretically covered with highly useful notes. Work does not leave the room. We never take home anyone's pages. They don't let scientists take home uranium in their pockets after a day at Los Alamos. That's the deal.

But I wanted that chapter. I wanted to take it home so I could read it again and again. I'd never felt like that about anyone else's work, ever.

I considered stealing it.

I could pretend to put it in the stack as the pages were collected, but then palm it off the table onto my lap and slip it onto the floor into my open purse. I didn't want to ask her for it. She already thought we were all perverts, the way we kept checking out her chest.

I decided to play it cool. We went around the table, all of us giving feedback, happy, exhausted, delighted that she didn't suck.

I tried not to blather, counting on the fact that there would be more, more writing, more Lidia.

It worked. She came back. The next week. Amazing!

She workshopped that book, and this memoir. And the more I've learned about her, the more in awe I am.

To start, she isn't really from Texas. She just went to college there, which is a totally different thing. She does have nice knockers. For the other stuff, you'll have to read the book.

I'm just looking forward to getting a copy I can keep.

Contents

THE CHRONOLOGY OF WATER

Tell all the Truth but tell it slant—
   —EMILY DICKINSON

Happiness? Happiness makes crappy stories.
   —KEN KESEY

Here lies one whose name was writ in water.
   —JOHN KEATS

I. Holding Breath

The Chronology of Water

THE DAY MY DAUGHTER WAS STILLBORN, AFTER I HELD
the future pink and rose-lipped in my shivering arms, lifeless
tender, covering her face in tears and kisses, after they handed
my dead girl to my sister who kissed her, then to my first husband
who kissed her, then to my mother who could not bear to hold
her, then out of the hospital room door, tiny lifeless swaddled
thing, the nurse gave me tranquilizers and a soap and sponge.
She guided me to a special shower. The shower had a chair and
the spray came down lightly, warm. She said, That feels good,
doesn't it. The water. She said, you are still bleeding quite a bit.
Just let it. Ripped from vagina to rectum, sewn closed. Falling
water on a body.

I sat on the stool and closed the little plastic curtain.
I could hear her humming. I bled, I cried, I peed, and vomited.
I became water.

Finally she had to come back inside and "Save me from
drowning in there." It was a joke. It made me smile.

Little tragedies are difficult to keep straight. They swell
and dive in and out between great sinkholes of the brain. It's
hard to know what to think of a life when you find yourself knee-
deep. You want to climb out, you want to explain how there
must be some mistake. You the swimmer, after all. And then you
see the waves without pattern, scooping up everyone, throwing
them around like so many floating heads, and you can only laugh

in your sobbing at all the silly head bobbers. Laughter can shake you from the delirium of grief.

When we first found out the life in me was dead, I was told the best thing to do was deliver vaginally anyway. It would keep my body as strong and healthy for the future as possible. My womb. My uterus. My vaginal canal. Since I had been struck dumb with grief, I did what they said.

Labor lasted 38 hours. When your baby isn't moving inside you, the normal process is stalled. Nothing moved my child within. Not hours and hours of a Pitocin drip. Not my first husband who fell asleep during his shift with me – not my sister coming in and nearly yanking him out by his hair.

In the thick of it I would sit on the edge of the bed and my sister would hold me by the shoulders and when the pain came she would draw me into her body and say "Yes. Breathe." I felt a strength I never saw in her again. I felt the strength surge of mother from my sister.

That kind of pain for that long exhausts a body. Even 25 years of swimming wasn't enough.

When she finally came, little dead girlfish, they placed her on my chest just like an alive baby.

I kissed her and held her and talked to her just like just like an alive baby.

Her eyelashes so long.

Her cheeks still red. How, I don't know. I thought they would be blue.

Her lips a rosebud.

When they finally took her away from me, the last cogent thought I had, a thoughtlessness that would last months: So this is death. Then a death life is what I choose.

When they brought me home from the hospital I entered a strange place. I could hear them and see them, but if anyone touched me I recoiled, and I didn't speak. I spent whole days alone in my bed in a cry that went to long moan. I think my eyes gave something of it away – because when people looked at me, they'd say Lidia? Lidia?

One day in their caretaking – I think someone was feeding me – I looked out the kitchen window and saw a woman stealing the mail from mailboxes on our street. She was stealthy like a woodland creature. The way she looked around – darted her eyes back and forth – the way she moved from box to box, took some things, not others – it made me laugh. When she got to my mailbox, I saw her pocket a piece of my mail. I belly laughed. I spit a mouthful of scrambled eggs out but no one knew why. They just looked worried in that uh oh way. They looked like cartoons of themselves. I said nothing of this, however.

I never felt crazy, I just felt gone away. When I took all the baby clothes I'd been given for my newborn and arranged them in rows on the deep blue carpet with rocks in between them, it seemed precise. But again it worried those around me. My sister. My husband Philip. My parents who stayed for a week. Strangers.

When I calmly sat on the floor of the grocery store and peed, I felt I'd done something true to the body. The reaction of the checkers isn't something I remember well. I just remember their blue corduroy aprons with *Albertson's* on them. One of the women had a beehive hairdo and lips red as an old Coca-Cola can. I remember thinking I had slipped into another time.

Later, when I would go places with my sister, who I lived with in Eugene, out shopping, or swimming, or to the U of O, people would ask me about my baby. I lied without even hesitating an instant. I'd say, "Oh, she is the most beautiful baby girl! Her eyelashes are so long!" Even two years later when a woman I know stopped me in the library to ask after my new daughter, I said, "She's so wonderful – she's my light. In day care she is already drawing pictures!"

I never thought, stop lying. I didn't have any sense that I was lying. To me, I was following the story. Clinging to it for life.

I thought about starting this book with my childhood, the beginning of my life. But that's not how I remember it. I remember things in retinal flashes. Without order. Your life doesn't happen in any kind of order. Events don't have cause and effect relationships the way you wish they did. It's all a series of fragments and repetitions and pattern formations. Language and water have this in common.

All the events of my life swim in and out between each other. Without chronology. Like in dreams. So if I am thinking of a memory of a relationship, or one about riding a bike, or about my love for literature and art, or when I first touched my lips to alcohol, or how much I adored my sister, or the day my father first touched me – there is no linear sense. Language is a metaphor for experience. It's as arbitrary as the mass of chaotic images we call memory – but we can put it into lines to narrativize over fear.

AFTER THE STILLBIRTH, the words "born dead" lived in me for months and months. To the people around me I just looked … more sad than anyone could bear. People don't know how to be when grief enters a house. She came with me everywhere, like a daughter. No one was any good at being near us. They'd accidentally say stupid things to me, like "I'm sure you'll have another soon," or they would talk to me looking slightly over my head. Anything to avoid the sadness of my skin.

One morning my sister heard me sobbing in the shower. She pulled the curtain back, looked at me holding my empty gutted belly, and stepped inside to embrace me. Fully clothed. We stayed like that for about 20 minutes I think.

Possibly the most tender thing anyone has ever done for me in my entire life.

I WAS BORN cesarean. Because one of my mother's legs was six inches shorter than the other, her hips were tilted. Gravely.

Doctors told her she could not have children. I don't know whether to admire the ferocity of her will for deciding to have my sister and me, or to wonder what kind of woman would risk killing her own infants – heads crushed by the tilted pelvis – before they could be born. My mother never believed she was "crippled." My mother brought my sister and me into the world of my father.

When the conventional doctors voiced their medical concerns to my mother, she went to another kind of doctor. An obstetrician/gynecologist who practiced alternative approaches to health. Dr. David Cheek was best known for his work using hypnosis on patients using their fingers to tell him the subconscious causes of emotional or physical illness. The process is called "ideomotor." Particular fingers are designated (by the doctor or the patient) "yes," "no," and "don't want to answer." When the doctor asks the hypnotized patient questions the relevant finger lifts in response – even when the patient consciously thinks otherwise, or has no conscious awareness of the answer.

In my mother's case, this technique was used to help her through cesarean labor. Dr. Cheek would say things to my mother during her labor such as: "Dorothy, do you have pain?" And she would answer with her finger. He would ask, "Is it here?" And stimulate the area. She would answer. He would ask, "Dorothy, can you relax your cervix for 30 seconds?" She would. "Dorothy, I need you to decrease the bleeding ... here." And she would.

My mother was an important case study.

Dr. Cheek believed we are imprinted with particular emotions even while in the womb. He claimed to have taught hundreds of women to communicate telepathically with their unborn children.

When my mother told my birth story, her voice took on a particular aura. As if something close to magical had transpired. I believe that is what she believed. My father's telling of the story was equally filled with reverence. As if my birth were other-worldly.

The morning I went into labor with my daughter the sun had not come up yet. I woke up because I didn't feel anything moving in me. I put my hands all over the world of my belly and nothing nothing nothing but a strange taut round. I went to the bathroom and peed and an electrical shock traveled up my neck. When I wiped there was bright red blood. I woke my sister. She wore worry in her eyes. I called my doctor. She told me it was probably fine and to come in when the clinic opened in the morning. In my belly there was an immovable weight.

I remember crying in great waves. I remember my throat locking up. Being unable to speak. My hands going numb. Child things.

When morning came, even the sun looked wrong.

In my body, birth came last.

Metaphor

I'M GOING TO TELL YOU SOMETHING THAT HELPS. NOT IN the usual way; this isn't in any textbooks or guidebooks. It has nothing to do with self-help or breathing or stirrups or speculums – god knows that territory has been done to death with its termi- nologies and systems – first second third trimester, quickening, lightening, labor, expecting, fetal heartbeat, uterus, embryo, womb, contractions, crowning, cervical dilation, vaginal canal, breathe – that's it, little short breaths, transition, push.

But what I want to tell you is away from this story. The truth of it is, the story of a woman having a baby is the fiction we make it. More precisely, a woman with bulging life in her belly represents – is a metaphor for making a story. A story we can all live with. The fertilization, the gestation, the containment, the production of a story.

So let me give you a tip. Something you can use in relation to this grand narrativity, this epic status, something you can live with when the time comes.

Collect rocks.

That's all. But not just any rocks. You are an intelligent woman so you look for the unimaginable inside the ordinary. Go to places you would not ordinarily go alone – riverbanks. Deep woods. The part of the ocean shore where peoples' gazes dis- appear. Wade in all waters. When you find a group of rocks, you must stare at them a long while before you choose, let your eyes adjust, use what you know of the long wait waiting. Let your imagination change what you know. Suddenly a gray rock becomes ashen or clouded with dream. A ring round a rock is luck. To find a red rock is to discover earthblood. Blue rocks make you believe in them. Patterns and flecks on rocks are bits of different countries and terrains, speckled questions. Conglomerates are the movement of land in the freedom of water, smoothed into a small thing you can hold in your hand, rub against your face. Sandstone is soothing and lucid. Shale, of course, is rational. Find pleasure in these ordinary palm worlds. Help yourself prepare for a life. Recognize when there are no words for the pain, when there are no words for the joy, there are rocks. Fill all the clear drinking glasses in your house with rocks, no matter what your husband or lover thinks. Gather rocks in small piles on the counters, the tables, the windowsills. Divide rocks by color, texture, size, shape. Collect some larger stones, place them along the floor of your living room, never mind what the guests think, build an intricate labyrinth of inanimates. Move around your rocks like a curl of water. Begin to detect smells and sounds to different varieties of rock. Give names to some, not geological, but of your own making. Memorize their presence, know if one is missing or out of place. Bathe them in water once each week. Carry a different one in your pocket every day. Move away from normal but don't notice it. Move towards excess but don't care. Own more rocks than clothing, than dishes, than books. Lie down next to them on the floor, put the smaller ones in your mouth occasionally. Sometimes, feel lithic, or petrified, or rupestral instead of tired, irritable, depressed. At night, alone, naked, place one green, one red, one ashen on different parts of your body. Tell no one.

Now.

After months of collecting, when your house is full and swollen, when you begin to experience contractions and dilation, after you check the color of the too red blood, after you use a timepiece to record the seconds, minutes, after you begin to regulate your breathing and abandon your thinking to the story you have been told about this, and, after your baby is born dead in the morning – which you cannot find in the story you were told – after you think of the words "born" and "dead" next to one another, turn to the rocks. Turn to the rocks and hear seas echoed from as far away as the Ukraine. Smell kelp and taste salt; feel that underwater animals have brushed near you. Remember parts of your body are scattered in water all over the earth. Know land is made from you. Lie all the baby clothes that have been given to you as scripts or gifts on the floor in lines. Sit with the tiny clothes and your rocks and think of nothing at all. Have endless patterns and repetitions accompanying your thoughtlessness, as if to say let go of that other more linear story, with its beginning, middle, and end, with its transcendent end, let go, we are the poem, we have come miles of life, we have survived this far to tell you, go on, go on.

You will see you have an underlying tone and plot to your life underneath the one you've been told. Circular and image bound. Something near tragic, near unbearable, but contained by your irreducible imagination – who would have thought of it but you – your ability to metamorphose like organic material in contact with changing elements. The rocks. They carry the chronology of water. All things simultaneously living and dead in your hands.

On Sound and Speech

IN MY HOUSE ONE OF THE CORNERS OF THE LIVING
room was called the crybaby corner. When you cried, you had to
go stand there facing the corner. The principle was one of shame.
My sister tells me that when she was sent to the crybaby corner
she would cease crying almost immediately. I can picture her
leaving the wall with a face as stoic as a nun's. Almost like an adult.

By the time I arrived in the family, eight years after my
sister, the laws of the house were in place. But none of them
seemed to work on me. By the time I was four, when I cried,
I wailed. Epically. And I cried all the time. I cried when I had to
go to bed. I cried in the night. I cried when people I didn't know
looked at me. I cried when people I did know talked to me.
I cried when someone tried to take my picture. I cried being
dropped off at school. I cried when new food was presented
to me. I cried when sad music played. I cried when we put the
ornaments on our Christmas trees. When people would open
the door to my "trick or treat" at Halloween. I cried every single
time I had to go to a public restroom. Or in bathrooms in anyone's house. Or bathrooms at school. Until I was in seventh grade.

I cried when bees came near me. I cried when I wet my
pants – in kindergarten, first, second, third, and sixth grades.
When I got any bruise or scratch or cut. I cried when they put
me to bed in the dark. When strangers spoke to me. When
children were mean, when my hair was tangled or ice cream hurt
my head or my underwear was inside-out or I had to wear

galoshes. I cried when they threw me in Lake Washington for my first swimming lesson. When I got shots. At the dentist. When I got lost in grocery stores. When I went to movies with my family – in fact, one of the more famous of my crying stories happened when they took me to see *Gone With the Wind*. When the little girl has the pony accident and Rhett leaves Scarlett my grief was inconsolable. For about a week.

I cried when my father yelled – but I also cried sometimes just when he entered the room.

When my mother or sister were sent to retrieve me, the victories were small. About the size of a child.

It was my voice that left.

In my house the sound of leather on the skin of my sister's bare bottom stole my very voice out of my throat for years. The great *thwack* of the sister who goes before you. Taking everything before you are born. The sound of the belt on the skin of her made me bite my own lip. I'd close my eyes and grip my knees and rock in the corner of my room. Sometimes I'd bang my head rhythmically against the wall.

I still cannot bear her silence while being whipped. She must have been eleven. Twelve. Thirteen. Before it stopped. Alone in my room I put a pillow over my head. Alone in my room I got my parka out of the closet and buried my skull in it. Alone in my room I drew on the walls – knowing the punishment – pushing the waxen color as hard as I could against the wall. Until it broke. Until I heard it stop. Until I heard my sister going into the bathroom. I would steal inside and hug her knees. My silent mother ghost would make a bubble bath. My sister and I would sit in it together. Voiceless, we would soap each other's backs and make skin pictures with our fingernails. If the picture was on your back, you had to guess what it was. I drew a flower. I drew a smiley face. I drew a Christmas tree that made my sister cry – but only into her hands. No one could have heard her. Only her shoulders and back moved. The red marks of a child's fingernails remaining even after the soap washes off.

When my sister left the house I was 10.

I didn't speak to anyone outside of my immediate family until I was about 13. Not even when called upon at school. I'd look up, my throat the size of a straw, my eyes watering. Nothing. Nothing. Or this: if an adult required me to speak, I'd hold one leg up stork like with one hand, and my other arm I'd put behind my head in an "L" shape, and I'd rock until I lost balance. Instead of talking. Little bird ballet. Little girl making an "L" for Lidia with her arm. Anything but speech. All those years with my sister in front of me I was silent. And after she left. Terror stealing the voice of a girl.

Sometimes I think my voice arrived on paper. I had a journal I hid under my bed. I didn't know what a journal was. It was just a red notebook that I wrote pictures and true things and lies in. Interchangeably. It made me feel – like someone else. I wrote about my father's angry loud voice. How I hated it. How I wished I could kill it. I wrote about swimming. How I loved it. About how girls made my skin hot. About boys and how being around them made my head hurt. About radio songs and movies and my best friends Christy and how I was jealous of Katie but also wanted to lick her and how much I loved my swim coach Ron Koch.

I wrote about my mother … the back of her head driving me to and from swim practice. Her limp and leg. Her hair. How gone she was, selling houses, winning awards into the night. I wrote letters to my gone away sister that I never sent.

And I wrote a little girl dream. I wanted to go to the Olympics, like my teammates.

When I was 11 I wrote a poem in my red notebook that went: In the house/alone in my bed/my arms ache. My sister is gone/my mother is gone/my father designs buildings/in the room next to mine/he is smoking. I wait for 5 a.m./I pray to leave the house/I pray to swim.

My voice, she was coming. Something about my father's house. Something about alone and water.

The Best Friend

WHEN I WAS 15 MY FATHER TOLD ME THAT WE WERE moving from Washington state to Gainesville, Florida because the best swim coach in the nation was there – Randy Reese, the coach of Florida Aquatic Swim Team.

I remember sitting in my room alone thinking what? Why would we leave our home out of the blue for something called F.A.S.T.? Why would we leave the trees and the mountains and the rain and the green of the Northwest for a strip of sand and alligators? We didn't know anyone in Florida. I'd never been there. The only things that mattered to me were at the pool – the only people I trusted or loved, the only time in my life I felt O.K., the only place I felt like something besides daughter. And why was he telling me we were moving for me? I didn't ask for that. Why would I?

I loved my swim coach. He was the only man I knew who was kind to me. He's the man that explained to me why there was blood running down my leg at swim practice and what to do about it when I thought I was dying of cancer. He's the man that I spent six hours a day six days a week with training to win. He corrected my stroke. He pushed me when I tired. He lifted me up in his arms when I won and put an arm around me and a towel when I lost. When I said, "What about Ron Koch?" My father, he said, "No one knows Ron Koch."

When I asked my mother her face creased with worry. She

pat one hand with the other on her thigh and said "Well, Belle, your daddy's been promoted. It's a lot of money."

When I asked her if she wanted to move to Florida, she said, "He says you deserve the best. Besides Belle, it's sunny!"

In reality, my father got promoted to lead architect for the southeastern coast. But that isn't what he told me. It was, as he put it, the sacrifice they were making for me.

Inside our house always smelled like cigarette. Back in my bed I thought about my best friend Christie. Who I'd known since I was five. Who I'd been eating lunch with everyday in the locker halls of high school. Who I'd sit by in Art class wishing every class was art class. Whose family I'd vacationed with, wishing they were mine. I cried so hard I chewed on my pillowcase until it ripped.

And so I left the water of one pool and slipped into another. Water, you'd think it would be the same everywhere. But it is not. The tap water in Florida tastes like swampshit. The water that comes out of the shower is weirdly slippery. The water that comes out of the sky is warm, and leaves behind a thick steam that chokes people who are not used to it. The ocean water is the temperature of urine, and the pool water is lukewarm even in December. Like a giant bath gone dull. Hurricanes go to Florida.

I hated it.

Randy Reese barely looked at me. There were Olympians on his team. I'd try to catch them, keep up with them, and sometimes succeed, but no matter how hard I swam or what my times were or my weight or place on the podium, I never felt like I was … his. When I did well, he'd show me my splits on a clipboard. Numbers. I'd stand there dumb and dripping, waiting for a hug. But he was not that kind of man. Before important swim meets? He'd make all the women swimmers weigh themselves. If you didn't hit your weight? You'd get "licks." A Styrofoam kickboard whack at the back of your thighs and ass. One lick for every pound of flesh. In this way the pool became a place of shame, and so there was nothing to distinguish it any longer from my home.

Whatever promise I may have carried in my swimmer skin, whatever hope I had in the water began to drown. At home the weight and rage of father took the air out of the rooms. At the pool a man yelled on the side and hit us with kick boards and never smiled.

At the State Swimming Championships my senior year our 200 yard medley relay had the best time in the nation. I stood on the podium with the three other girls and looked out into the stands. My father wasn't anywhere. My mother smelled like vodka – it seemed I could smell it all the way across the pool. Randy Reese didn't even look at me. Then Jimmy Carter took all little girl dreams of swimmer glory away from our bodies with a boycott Randy's famous pool full of winners included – anyway. There was no word left to belong to. Not athlete, not daughter.

I hated Randy Reese. I hated Jimmy Carter. I hated god. Also my math teacher, Mr. Grosz. I hated my father most of all, a hate that never left but just changed forms. My life had been ruined by men. Now even the water seemed to forsake me.

But I met a boy not like any other in the water.

In the pool with me. For those excruciating three years in Hogtown. A beautiful boy. With a long body and long arms and long legs and long eyelashes and long hair. And dark tanned skin. And dark eyes. And he had a secret in his skin too – not about fathers though.

This boy, my friend, was hands down the most talented artist in high school. That's an idiotic way to say it – he was more talented than ANY of the people in ANY high school; in fact, he was more talented than ANYONE in Florida who called them- selves "artists" by about 500 miles long and 160 miles wide. He painted. He sculpted. He drew. When he did, there was not any- thing that ever came out of his hands that was not astonishing.

When I'd first moved to the hellhole of Gainesville, he called our house the first week and invited me to float down the

Itchitucknee river on an inner tube. What a strange language coming through the phone holes. Itchetucknee? I had no idea on earth what he was talking about but I said yes.

The water of the Itchetucknee is ice-cube cold. And the river is not wide, but it is deep, and it has a current. Whitetail deer, raccoons, wild turkeys, wood ducks, and great blue herons can be seen from the river. And there are ... well, snakes. But there is a kind of beauty to it. The aqua blue crystalline Ichetucknee flows six miles through shaded hammocks and wetlands before it joins the Santa Fe River. I floated next to my friend the artist for three hours. He asked me questions about my life. I asked about his. We laughed. We basked in the sun like reptiles. We swam like swimmers do when they've been freed from laps. At the end of the float I felt I'd known him for years.

I think it might be true that we spent every single day together except Sundays for nearly three years. Much of the time we'd meet at school and I'd go to English and French and he'd go to the art lab and then we'd leave round about lunch. Or we'd spend the whole day in the art lab together. Or we'd go to his house and eat sandwiches and listen to Pat Benatar between swim practices. Or nap together. His skin had almost no hair and was soft as velvet.

I don't quite know how to describe how much I loved him. But it was a love I didn't have a wit's notion what to do with. I flirted as hard as I could, but he didn't seem interested in me sexually. Other Hogtown guys seemed to want into my pants on a regular basis, even at 7-Eleven, but him? Never. So I had sex with Hogtown men. And I continued to get all up in it with girl swimmers. But nothing between me and the artist.

And yet he made me the most gorgeous burgundy silk prom dress you can imagine, with a drop down back and tiny criss-crossing straps in the front and near my ass – NO ONE had a cooler dress. It's possible no one ever has. In any state.

And he made me a fetching short-waisted big-shouldered

women's 1950s blazer from a man's suit coat that everyone at school drooled over.

And he cut my hair in a bob that turned heads.

And he applied make-up on my face (the only make-up I'd ever worn) and took fashion photos of me.

So the love I had just got deeper and deeper for this man, but there was nowhere to put it. It just built up in me like sperm must in men who aren't getting any. Sometimes I thought I might faint in his presence, but he'd bake something and it would taste so good. He could make cheesecake, for christ's sake. All I wanted was to be around him. All the time. His skin smelled like cocoa butter.

Days and days and days and days and days. Perhaps the happiest of my life to that point. Just underneath how much I hated the Florida.

Then one day my drunk-drawled mother told Jimmy Heaney's mother in the Publix Grocery store aisle that she heard my artist was gay. What I'm saying is that my dumb ass mother outed my artist before he'd outed himself. He's homosexual. In a southern drawl.

And he stopped.

He stopped calling me. He stopped seeing me. He stopped having me in his life at all.

You know what it felt like to have a beautiful gay man stop loving me?

Like being dead.

Suitcase

SOMETIMES I THINK I HAVE ALWAYS BEEN A SWIMMER.
Everything collected in my memory curls like water around
events in my life. Or maybe everything that's ever happened to
me I understand better if I picture it in a great, aqua, chlorinated
pool. Not even Florida could kill the swimmer in me.

At my senior prom in Florida I armwrestled five boys about
to become men. I lost once. After the dance we all got drunk and
climbed the fence of the pool in Gainesville, Florida. We went
skinny dipping in a 50-meter competition pool – the same pool I
spent two hours every morning, two hours every evening in
swimming. My body was stronger than it has ever been in my life.
I looked like someone's son. The biceps of a son. The jaw. The
shoulders. My hair whiting out gender. Breastless. When it came
time for everyone to make out, I did laps.

That summer was long and wet differently for me than it
was for other people. The air got thick with more than heat. In
June, letters began to arrive in our mailbox. They were scholarship offers. For swimming. Exit visas.

In the evenings, I'd go out to the mailbox. My breathing
would jackknife in my lungs just before I opened the box, and
I'd shuffle through our idiotic mail waiting to feel the weight of
something different. Waiting for my leaving.

Five letters came.

The first scholarship letter was cool and weighted in my
hands. It was from Brown. The red and black logo of Brown

University on the envelope looked royal to me. I ran my fingertips across it. The envelop felt smooth – the paper announcing its
difference. I smelled it. I closed my eyes. I held it against my
heart. I walked it to the house almost believing in something.

Inside, I put it on the kitchen table. It sat there all through
dinner – which we ate in the living room watching TV. *Barney
Miller*. I could feel the blood in my ears.

After dinner, after *Taxi*, after my father smoked three cigarettes, he finally went into the kitchen. And my mother. And me.

We sat at the kitchen table like I guess families do. My
mother and I breathing. He opened the letter more slowly than
a retarded person. He read it silently. I watched his eyes. Blue
like mine. In my head I swam laps. My mother sat to the side of
me like a drunk lump patting her one hand with the other. I tried
not to bite my tongue off.

Finally, he spoke. A ¾ ride. At a Snob school. A snob school
for silver spoon girls and rich assholes. My mother looked out
the window into the Florida night. I stared at the paper with the
Brown logo on it. And my name. I knew it wasn't money. We had
money. It was what came out of his mouth next, his cigarette
smoke making shame swirls around my face. Did I think I was
special? Like someone squeezing my neck. In my throat I swallowed language.

The second letter came from Notre Dame. Again we sat at
the kitchen table, a mother, a father, a daughter. The cigarette
smoke nearly cinematic. I sat in silence, my very skin knew the
tyranny of speaking. My mother twisted a lock of hair until I
thought it would lift off of her head. Why did he say no? Because
he could.

The third letter came from Cornell.

The fourth from Purdue.

No.

At a kitchen table in Florida.

All the rooms of our house carried the weight of father. All
of them except one. My bedroom held the wet and dark of my

body. It smelled like my skin and chlorine and pot. The two windows in front had long been my portals to the night life of escaped girls. In July, on a night so thick with sweat lesser girls would have suffocated, alone in my bed I decided a leaving. I was leaving, and I didn't care how. I masturbated so hard that night I scratched my skin raw. Just before I went to sleep, I pictured a suitcase. The biggest one we owned. It rested silently in the garage behind my father's golf bag and boxes from former lives. Black and as big as a German Shepherd. Big enough to fit the rage of a girl.

At the preliminaries for State that year I sat in the locker rooms with Sienna Torres killing a fifth of vodka. If we'd been sons about to be men, I bet we would have taken one of our father's cars and headed for Canada. Or took our first punches at authority, not minding the black eye. Instead we sat on the concrete underneath the disgusted gaze of shaved and well-behaved athlete girls and drank.

Even loaded I qualified fifth for finals in breaststroke. At finals, a woman I didn't know with stringy blond hair and glasses thick as a Florida cola bottle came up to me after I got second in the 100 breast. I swam a 1:07.9. She looked like a stoner. She said she was the coach at Texas Tech, and that though she couldn't talk about it standing there like that, me dripping with water and underage rage, she would call me the next day to talk about a full ride. I didn't say anything. When my breathing stilled, I looked up at my drunk mother in the stands. She was sort of rocking. I hoped she'd stay up there. My mother: the only thing I knew of Texas sitting up in the stands, slurring her speech.

When the coach of Texas Tech called my home, my father was at work. I talked to the woman with the stringy hair and thick glasses on the phone. There was my mother's voice, its sweet southern drawl curling around my shoulders – like honey does to bees – and there was this woman's voice and there was me. Saying yes. Yes.

Wouldn't it be great if that's all there was to it? A mother's voice soothing the way for her daughter to leave. Blonde swimmer girl gets on a plane, bye bye y'all.

A week later, when the papers came to sign, my father was at work. My mother signed them. I remember watching her hand, a little stunned. She had beautiful handwriting. Then she put them in the envelope, grabbed her car keys, and told me *C'mawn*. In her southern drawl liquor voice. In her real estate station wagon. Driving to the post office with her and watching her drop my freedom into the blue metal mouth of the mailbox – I almost loved her.

All the rest of July he raged. And August. Every day when he came home from work he'd find another way to fill the house with rage, shake the walls with shame, while the little women took it and took it. Sometimes I thought he might kill one of us. But I was not afraid. In the palm of my bedroom I could feel the walls pulse.

Once that summer during a rage run my father threw a plate at the sliding glass door. I waited for the shatter but nothing happened. Another night he ripped my swim bag to shit, my suit and goggles flying into the air. Once he followed me all the way to my bedroom door. I could feel his words at my smoldering shoulders. He stopped in the doorframe. When I turned to face him, he was shaking with anger. Then he said, "This is control. I'm controlling myself. You don't know how far I can go." We stared at each other.

I thought: this is your daughter leaving, motherfucker.

But other nights he'd become the man whose desire had twisted up inside him. The closer we got to my exit. On an August night with rain as hard as drums he sat me down on our living room couch. He put his arm around my shoulders. He rubbed my far arm with his big thumb in creepy circles. His voice was more calm than is possible to make a voice. Then he narrated what boys would want to do to me, how they would put their dirty hands up my skirt and part my legs and finger fuck me. How they would reach inside my shirt and fondle my tits and grab my breasts. Suck them. How disgusting boys would be, their hands, their hot hips and breath, their wanting in and up. And what they would do with their dicks, me sitting there next to him on the couch feeling the heat of him touching his dick even without looking, my skin making pins, clenching my teeth inside my mouth, and him saying how I should say no, and how I could find the strength to say no by remembering I was his daughter, that he was the only man for me.

In my head: this is how you know he is insane. This is why to leave now.

I'd thought of leaving before. In the run away ways, but also the year my mother tried to commit suicide, my sister made a courageous return from the sanctuary of graduate school to see if I wanted to come with her. I was 16. Her coming and asking me – somehow it had been enough to get me through two more years.

I thought about the secrets I had stored up inside my body. How many times I'd crawled out my bedroom window to get in a car. The unstoppable fire between my legs. A fire not his. I thought about vodka. Nearly drowning. By the time he sat me on the couch to tell me I was his, I was miles away from daughter. A black suitcase making shape and story in my dreams. I felt like there was a muscle between us. The muscle was my sexuality. Not his.

Our filial showdown happened in our garage the week before I left, next to my mother's station wagon and my father's Camaro Berlinetta. I went there that night to get the black suitcase out of the garage. I planned to take it to my room and fill it and fill it. When I found it, I unzipped its mouth. It smelled like cigarette smoke. I opened it, and inside were two of my father's shirts from some trip. I stared at the shirts until my neck prickled with anger. I took a wad of cloth from one and shoved it in my mouth and bit it at hard as I could – so hard my head shook. Then I took them out and put them in the trash.

When I got back, I explored every compartment of the suitcase. A tube of Certs. Part of a wrapper from a pack of cigarettes. A comb. Two condoms. I picked it up and shook it. Finally it was empty of him. I zipped its mouth. I stood up to take the black suitcase to my room, and then there was my father. I heard him before I saw him, and when I turned to face him he was standing just underneath the lonely garage dangle of a bulb, his head weirdly illuminated. Then he began to yell, a slow nonsensical roll at first, but humming quickly into a roar. Like engines on Camaro Berlinettas do. He called me a slut, he named my sins, he listed all my mistakes and shortcomings and shameful behaviors – all the acting out that lived up and through me to bring me to this daughter moment.

Maybe they were all true. Maybe he was right. Maybe I would become the slut fuckup he said. But I was also a very good swimmer. And he was not.

He grabbed my arm at one point, and though I could feel the bruise forming, I never let go of the handle of the suitcase. I felt I could swing it into his head any time I wanted. Somehow that night my girl shame and fear were nowhere in the room. I thought the thought of somebody's son. You don't know how far I'll go, motherfucker.

I looked him in the eyes. Blue on blue.

I felt the width of my shoulders and the square of my own jaw. My adrenaline rushed up like before a race. Nothing he was saying was beating me down. I think maybe he saw that, because he shifted gears and began to rage about what I was doing to my mother – did it make me happy that it would kill her? My leaving? Just like my selfish shit of a sister? Is that the kind of person I was? A selfish bitch who wanted to kill my mother? You and your sister – such high and mighty assholes – you think you are so much better than anyone else?

My sister and I, we were selfish. We wanted selves. There was no rage or love that could stop us. That's what opened my mouth.

Fuck.

You.

Motherfucker.

I said it again, louder, and again, until I was screaming it, screaming with the lungs of a swimmer. Then I said get the fuck out of my way you fucking sadist, and I swung my suitcase back, and he drew up his full height of father and pulled his arm back and fisted up his hand until it white knuckled and his face went red and he clenched his teeth and those eyes, those rage filled father eyes ... so I did what I was born to do. I leaned in as close to his face as I could and said do it. Suitcase ready.

It was his voice I used.

It seemed we'd die in that moment. But all it took to leave that room was this body I had. Though I did hear him breathing – out of breath – at my mighty back. And I did consider what being punched in the back of the skull might feel like. I believed I could take it.

I carried the suitcase to my bedroom. I went in. I closed the door behind me. I took off my clothes. My skin smelled like chlorine and sweat. Summer heat snuck through the screen of my window. I put my head down on my pillow. I waited. I heard a car go by. I heard a dog bark. I could hear a shiver of wind in the shrubs outside my window. And Cicadas. And frogs. I waited and waited. And then I didn't. I put my hand between my legs. I parted my lips. The wet slid my fingers around and around and fast and hard. I closed my eyes. I thought about Sienna Torres shoving her fingers up my wide open cunt, as open as a mouth screaming motherfucker. I came so hard it shot out of me. I didn't know until that night a girl body could do that. Shoot cum.

The first things I put in the black suitcase were a flask and a box with what used to be my mother's hair.

Deliverance

TO BE BORN HAS MANY MEANINGS. HOW MANY TIMES WE leave a life, enter a new one. How it felt to fly out of the airport away from my family's home at 18: watch the airport grow tiny and then the land go smaller and then the strip of shitty sand that is Florida recede and disappear. Girl in the sky weightless as water.

Where I was going was Lubbock, Texas. When I got to Lubbock, whatever Lubbock was, I felt positively delivered. My own room my own friends my own food my own alcohol my own music my own sex my own money my own thoughts my own body my my my freedom to be whoever wherever however rose like a volcano in me – like something that had been pressed down so far in a body it had to explode. What all college kids feel. Though only some of us are carrying daughter rage secrets in our skin and bones. When the plane landed in Lubbock my swim coach picked me up at the airport. The woman who had paid for me.

It took about two weeks for the Lubbockness to set in.

Until May of 2009, Lubbock, my friends, was dry. Not arid. Though it's that too – arid enough to choke on. But it was Alco-holess. Except in bars and restaurants during certain times. To purchase "packaged" booze, you had to drive 25 minutes or more to a drive-through liquor barn type alcohol hut. Load up. Drive back. Stealthily sneak your load up at night through the side doors to the girl's dorm – carrying giant suitcases of beer up several flights of stairs, or bottles shoved down your pants.

The environmental extremes in Lubbock are stockyard cow shit smell so pungent it makes your eyes water as well as causing a special gagging reflex, and hot wind orange dust storms so thick you can't even see the hand in front of your face that also feel like you are being attacked by little Lubbock evil devil pins if you venture out.

Avenue Q, Buddy Holly Plaza. Big bronze Buddy Holly statue. Google it. Buddy, he's circled by a walk of fame including greats like Waylon Jennings and the venerable Mac Davis. Budfest takes place during the first week of September, Buddy Holly's birthday. During Budfest, drunk West Texans dress up like Buddy and his woman and ... holler.

Prairie Dog town. Picture a very large dirt area contained by a cement fence in the middle of nowhere. A cement fence about knee-high. And inside the cement fence? A great many holes in the ground. And in the holes? Prairie dogs. So if you were drunk and high and sitting on the cement wall in the middle of the night, the thing to do would be shine a flashlight and then throw rocks at all the heads. Like a grown up whack-a-mole. What's not to like?

Yeah. And when I say flat? I mean if you jump you can see Dallas.

Lubbock. Great place. Honestly you should save up.

By day I went to swim practice at 5:30 a.m. and breakfast at 7:00 a.m. and classes 10:00 a.m. through 3:00 p.m. and weight training at 3:30 p.m. and swim practice at 4:30 p.m. and dinner at 7:00 p.m. every day but Sunday with a pack of hot swimmer women and then the nights were ours.

All night. Every night. As much night as you could get in you before 5:30 a.m.

I was in love or something like it with my roommate within a month of meeting her. Maybe it was her drinking ability, or her swearing ability, or her rock and roll or her Bose speakers and kick ass stereo or her being from Chicago and thinking West Texans were cretins or her butterfly stud shoulders or her big tits or her bandana or her torn up jeans or her one-hit pipe. Maybe it was just her name. Amy. Amy, what you wanna do. I think, I could fall for you, for a while maybe longer if I do.

I don't know how much you know about swimmer partying but, well, it's formidable. College swimmers are nearly all on some kind of scholarship. That's money. There were the two British twins with spikey bleached hair. There were endless Barbie Texans with hairspray and drawls. There was a fantastic senior dyke and an amazingly beautiful boy-bodied Asian woman and mystical. Romanian. Of those with peckers, there was a tall lanky tow head with hair as white as mine whose last name was Creamer that I fell for like a blond brick house, there was a surfer So Cal king of Bruce Springsteen and Elvis Costello and beer dude, there was a two-stepping horn dog from Dallas, there was a guy from Amy's hometown who orchestrated the mandorm parties, and a whole pack of swimmer guys with rockets in their pockets and shaved skin in places regular guys didn't know about.

When I say we partied, I mean an epic poem.

About halfway through the year my days became swim practice at 5:30 a.m. big melon headed hangover and skip god-forsaken cafeteria shitty instant eggs breakfast at 7:00 a.m. and skip classes at 10:00 a.m. 11:00 a.m. 12 noon drink hair of the dog beer eat cold pizza and Haagen Dazs ice-cream and listen to Zeppelin get high take a test once every week or so and weight training at 3:30 p.m. and swim practice at 4:30 p.m. and fuck dorm dinners they taste like shit and you have to sit with a bunch of West Texan fuckwaddery lets go out early and drink lets hit the Rock-Z and dance and dance and dance and drink and barf and screw every day every night.

I lost my scholarship the second year. I flunked out the third.

Love Grenade I

I ALWAYS WANTED TO BE THE KIND OF WOMAN JAMES Taylor would sing: *I feel fine, anytime she's around me now* to. "Something in the Way She Moves." You know that song. Don't you wish someone wanted to sing that song to you?

Alas, my song would be Blood on Her Skin, Dripping with Sin, Do it again, Living Dead Girl. Yeah. By Rob Zombie. Because in college I was a living dead girl.

My first husband, beautiful boyman, reminded me of James Taylor. Of how exactly like his hands, exactly his voice, exactly his long lean body. Exactly his introverted acoustic guitar genius, exactly his artist eyes, exactly his ego underneath all that thin man. I shoulda been with Rob Zombie but I wasn't. For a few years, in Lubbock, Texas, where I'd come on a swim-ming scholarship, I was with a JT man named Phillip.

Me: Doc combat boots. Kohl – a LOT – racooning my eyes. Ripped to shit tights and plaid catholic girl skirt and black leather biker jacket. No hairspray, no fingernail polish, no purse. Utterly out of place in Lubbock, Texas.

Those years were filled with him painting and playing guitar and me listening and getting high and making love and oh yeah, going to school. Which by the third year I'd flunked out of. The only As I received were in Philosophy. And that was because the professor was high every class so we just sat around shooting philosophical shit until we all started coming to class high too. Going to school, sleeping with Phillip. Trying not to fall

in love with my roommate Amy. And swimming – though every
month of each year the swimmer in me drowned a little more in
alcohol and oceans of sex.

It was snowing the night of the first breakup in Lubbock.
Snow in Lubbock looks weirdly dumb – Lubbock is as flat as flat
gets. No mountains. No trees. No hills. When it snows in
Lubbock one must get drunk and drive around. Don't think badly
of me. Remember what I told you – Lubbock is dry. So a woman
gets ... thirsty. And there isn't much to "hit" in the dead of night,
and even if there was you would see it a mile away.

So it was a drive around night. After a while we stopped.
And I was drunk as a monkey, and I climbed up onto the
shoulders of the Buddy Holly statue in a cemetery-ish park.

The Buddy Holly statue isn't all that high, by the way. But I
was acting like I was king of the world.

The main event was Phillip. Phillip cut the fingertips out
of his gloves and played guitar at the base of the Buddy Holly
statue. He played the acoustic opening to "Wish You Were Here."
Which he'd picked out of the sky by ear. He played "Sweet Baby
James." Then he played "Suzanne." At Buddy Holly's feet. With
a drunk ass blonde lifting her shirt up to the 30 degree night sky
going "FUCK ALL Y'ALLLLLLL. EAT ME. WOOOOOOOOOOOO."
To no one in particular except Lubbock.

I'd been with Phillip for about a year. How I fell for him was
I heard his voice behind my head right after I walked past him
in the dorm hall. He had the deepest voice I'd ever heard on a
white boy. It was the kind of voice that curled around the top of
your spine and jaw and made your mouth open, wanting. In my
head was I am so far from my father I am so far from my father I
amsofarfrommyfatherIamsofarfrommyfather.

When I turned around, there he was. With shoulder-length
locks of hair, thick as shit eyelashes, Moccasin boots, and a guitar.

There he was that night, down in the snow playing "Suzanne." Singing the night wide open. Me perched atop Buddy

Holly sort of cross-eyed, looking at stars and drooling on Buddy's bronzed head. Even angry girls can be moved to tears.

There are two reasons for us going busto.

Reason one: I spent the entire year making poor beautiful Phillip break into strangers' homes at night to fuck on the floor. I don't know why. It did a real number on him, I can tell you. He'd get so terrified, but he'd do it, and I'd run and turn a light on and he'd nearly coronary leaping with his 6′3″ lanky ass body to turn it back off. I'd break into whatever liquor I could find and he'd try to fill the bottles back up with water and replace the lids and restore them to their sanctity. I'd scavenge the medicine cabinets and he'd chase me around in the dark trying to rescue little white pills.

And when we'd fuck I'd climb on top of him and ride the art of his cock as hard as I could, wishing I was his guitar and not some fucked up damaged girl so that his fingers would strum me to death, strum me clean, strum me calm, strum me into a woman he'd write a song for. My shirt off and my tits white moons and my head rocked back and my hair crazy. And he'd cum so hard I thought my spine might shatter – because those long and lean guys have huge cocks – and then we'd breathe and look at each other in the dark of a home we'd broken into and entered, and then he'd become terrified again and jump up and zip up faster than the speed of light, leaving me like sticky residue on a movie theater floor. Laughing the laugh of broken girls.

God. Poor Phillip. I wish I could go back and apologize. He was never cut out for a woman like me with a rage in her bigger than Texas. Although I've since learned that extreme passivity has its own power.

Reason two: he was too beautiful. Way more beautiful than me and way more beautiful than a beautiful woman. Have you met these men? His too beautiful voice and his beautiful hands and his beautiful cock. But the beauty went all haywire on the inside because he thought he was shit. And that thinking he was shit? It transformed him into the exact opposite of me – the most passive man on the planet. Particularly around any kind of high energy or conflict. Which was basically me, in the flesh.

And when my rage would come, he'd ... well, he'd fall asleep.

He's the only person I've ever met who would fall asleep in the middle of an argument, his chin on his hand, his eyes closing just as you are getting to the moment of victory. I never saw anyone do that but him. Drove me crazy. All my mighty energy with nowhere to go. I nearly imploded or spontaneously combusted dozens of times.

Phillip came from a big ass southern Baptist Christian family, all of whom sang. So there were a great many family Christian hymn sing-alongs on family front porches with family harmony rising and falling in their voices. And his father was the voice of god once removed, and his older brother was the voice of god twice removed, and the other three people besides Phillip were sisters, so that third removed god voice fell upon his slender shoulders. I mean how many goddamn times can you sing "I'll Fly Away" or the dreaded "Amazing Grace?" No wonder he was so tired.

And here's why the micromovements of a girl woman's sexual history matters. Phillip's older brother had already been through the reject god, leave home, become a pot smoking musician, have a family, return to the fold and take on the man mantle chapters. But Phillip had just hit the reject god, leave home, become a pot smoking artist and carry around a guilt bigger than Texas. He was the outcast son, unable to join the hymns on the porch.

And me, it was a secret shame I was carrying.

When Phillip wanted hand jobs instead of fucking and I couldn't do it and I couldn't do it and I couldn't do it, and when I wanted to suck his cock and he wouldn't let me wouldn't let me wouldn't let me, we met our wounds in each other's bodies. Guilt in the form of a beautiful gentle man and shame in the form of an angry girl became our sexuality.

The night he finally let me put my mouth on him we were

listening to "Comfortably Numb," which he'd played himself first until we got too high. In my mouth his cock made me feel forgiven. I don't know why. But once I'd turned him, he went anywhere I asked him to go with me.

There we were that night breaking up in the snow. A still shot of drunken rage looking down on gentle beauty. Well, I went a little wacko, which used to happen a lot back then, and I started a fight with him. I don't know why. I remember looking at the top of his head and thinking look, it's an angel, and my very next thought was, spit on his head. I told you, I don't know why. Why did I eat paper as I kid when I was scared? My panties were sopping and my head was spinning and it was cold and hot at the same time and it was so beautiful there in the snow and flat and quiet and music.

So I went in for the kill. I mean I snatched it out of the cold dark air as easily as he pulled songs from the sky and wrapped it in displaced rage and vodka breath and hurled it down at the top of his unsuspecting head until his neck nearly snapped. The way women in their twenties who are working out their ouch on everyone they meet do. Open wound girls. Swinging fist girls.

And we argued – or I did anyway – Phillip sort of ducked and growled – all the way to the car, a puke yellow beater mobile Pinto station wagon with faux wood paneling, and I kept it up inside the car, and he was having to drive with the window rolled down because we were too broke to get the windshield wipers fixed and it was snowing. In between trying to defend himself he had his head in and out of the window to see the road, but that didn't stop me, did it, I just got louder and bigger and hornier and more horribly chaotically blond. My father's rage and trespass in my voice and hands, in my very skin.

Phillip. Which means lover of horses. Or brotherhood. His voice was never meant for yelling.

That's when it happened.

At the crescendo of my rage opera. In the dumb ass Pinto. Near my anger orgasm.

He fell asleep.

The car sort of slowed and made a limp arc toward the curb, until it stopped, and his head fell gently forward onto the steering wheel.

I remember staring at him for a minute, dumbfounded by the moment, seeing – really seeing – how goddamn beautiful his face, his mouth, his long fingered mesmerizing hands … knowing I could never, ever keep a boy like that because the shear velocity of my anger and confusion would eat him alive … and feeling as sad as a girl who will never have a boy like that could feel … crying … a long mile of greenyellowred streetlights blinking us down … and then snapping out of it and yelling at the top of my lungs "WAKE UP MOTHERFUCKER!!!!!!!!!! YOU FUCKING FELL ASLEEP YOU COULD HAVE KILLED US!"

Then I leapt out of the car and slammed the Pinto door and ran down a snow alley behind a stranger's snow house in my Doc combat boots. Running and running thud-footed how you do in snow and kind of crying so that my Kohl melted down my cheeks and kind of laughing and reaching inside my black leather jacket for my vodka flask and never looking back at him in his beater mobile wood paneled Pinto station wagon, sleeping, or was he singing …

That's a great line, isn't it.

That's a great ending.

But lives aren't James Taylor songs, and girls like me don't just run off into the snow and go away.

I didn't break up with him that night.

When we really broke up, well, let's just say it wasn't a James Taylor song. And what we made between rage and love and falling asleep – what lived and died between us – haunts me still.

That dramatic ending was just the beginning.

In the end, I made that boy marry me.

The Other Lubbock

ONE OF THE RED RAIDER SWIMMER GUYS WAS A DEALER.
I don't think I ever saw Monty not high. His skin looked ashen –
even stretched as it was over athlete muscles. His eyes always
had rings around them. His face had little holes in it. He did not
live in the dorms. He lived with two other non swimmer guys in
a house. In his house, there was a basement. The basement door
had a marijuana leaf on it with a smiley face in the center. And it
was locked. To enter, you needed to know the knock.

Two.

Three.

One.

The first time I went down into Monty's basement I was
with Amy. When he opened up, we went in – we were the only
women that night. We were fishing for a little danger. Briefly I
felt weird. Then weirdly, I didn't. There were maybe four guys in
there besides us. One of those four was also a swimmer. When
I looked at him, I couldn't tell if his eyes were open or closed, but
he smiled and nodded and waved.

The room was dark – and not just because the walls were
painted black with all kinds of glow in the dark and neon shit all
over them. The carpet was dark red shag. One shit brown old
sofa, three lava lamps, three posters: Che and Jimi and Malcolm.
A fish tank with a bunch of tetras and a giant angel fish glowed
blue green in the corner. A small refrigerator, assorted glass

bongs, and a big ass coffee table upon which were a variety of items not so good to name. One Love in our ears.

Monty came over with pills in his hand and said, "Choose one, and I'll tell you what it does." I picked a capsule with a red cap on one side and a yellow cap on the other.

Amy passed, shaking her head, saying "Nuh uh, captain fantastic," reaching for a bong.

Monty looked at me and laughed a classic stoner laugh – huhuhuhuhuhuhuhuhuhuhuhuhow about you take two?"

"What's it do?"

"Don't you want to know what it is?"

"I just want to know what it does," I said, feigning bad-assery.

By that time in my collegiate athletic career I could give a shit about good citizenship. When I competed, I didn't even make the board. No one in the pool turned their head at the finish to see me. I was lucky I hadn't drowned. I'd become the kind of woman whose mouth was stuck in a permanent "yes" shape. All I wanted was experience – especially if it would numb the fuck out of my brain. My I don't know who the fuck I am-ism. My I don't know what's wrong with me. My couldn't someone, please, anyone, love me? I would have put anything in my mouths.

"Well, this particular little beauty will sedate your ass and make you dreamy."

I opened my mouth and ate it instantly.

$$\text{O}\diagup\overset{\text{H}}{\underset{\text{HN}}{\text{N}}}\diagdown\text{O}$$

He was right, I became sleepy, but not quite dreamy, so I asked for another. Two more women showed up. They didn't look like swimmers. Too skinny. Long stringy hair. Glitter nail polish. They wore tube tops and Levis and flip-flops and giggled. They ate acid tabs and danced.

Amy tried to get me to go back home that night but Monty

talked me out of it. "I'll walk her back, I'll walk her," He kept
saying.

The walk back was one of the funnier nights of my life.
Oddly, I remember it. 3:00, maybe 4:00 a.m. Black night. Warm.
We made a pit stop in the reflecting pool on campus where I
laid down with all my clothes on, laughing, laughing. I said,
"Look at me! I'm Ophelia!"

Monty said, "Am I Hamlet?"

"Fuck yeahhhhhhhhhhhhhhh!!!!!!!!!!!!!" I screamed, and
rolled around in 10-inch deep water illuminated by underwater
lights. Campus police showed up and wrote things on small
pieces of I'm not really a cop paper and handed them to us and
told us to go home. After they left we ate them. Then we bumble
fucked on the ground under a tree – my own pants were baffling
me and I was too gone to really get it on but Monty didn't seem
to mind. Then we played a game where we would run as fast as
we could and dive into shrubbery. The next day at swim practice
I was covered in shrub scrapes and scratches and my head felt
like cotton.

Again.

I wanted to do it again.

I wanted to eat all the colors and see what I felt. No.
I wanted to eat all the colors to get to the not feel. But even that
was not enough for a burning girl.

One night there were white lines on mirrors ready for me
when I entered. "Look," I said laughing, "I'm Dorothy in the
Wizard of Oz! Poppies!" Breathing in the white, breathing out
comprehension and emotion.

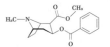

What I learned about Lubbock from the people in that
basement was a different brand of education. Someone's father
had been kidnapped and murdered. Police found him in
the stockyards under the hooves and shit of cows. Someone's

brother had O.D.'d and killed his girlfriend on the way under with
a shard of glass from a mirror. Someone's mother had murdered
his brother and sister – ages seven and 12 – because jesus told
her to. They were wicked, jesus had said into her ear. One woman's
uncle was a pedophile, but no one in the family was willing to
send him to the slammer, so they gave him an attic apartment.
Another woman's brother hustled coke over the border. One
guy's Mexican best friend had been found with his hands and his
dick cut off next to the train tracks – the severed items in a Glad
bag. Monty's half-brother was in the state hospital for repeatedly
raping a retarded girl neighbor.

I don't know how else to tell this but straight no chaser.
These dramas … these over the top horror stories seething with
blood and immorality … they made me feel better. Like television does. Less like a damaged daughter. A failed student.
A slut. An athlete gone to seed. And what was in the basement
helped feelings leave my body altogether, so I didn't need to
know who I was, or why, or anything at all.

Two.

Three.

One.

When I walked into the basement the second year, I was
nearly always by myself. I didn't care who else was there. I didn't
care what the room looked like. What posters were on the walls.
What the shit brown couch had all over it. What did interest me
was the set-up on the table. There sat a spoon and a tray with
cotton, a lighter and a syringe. I picked the spoon up and put it
in my mouth. Monty said "huhuhuhuhuhuhuhuhuhuhuhuhuhu
huh where do you want it?"

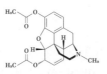

I said "Here," and slapped my arm hard enough to raise a
vein.

Zombie

FOR PART OF MY LUBBOCK LIFE I BECAME A ZOMBIE.
Not a flesh eating one. Gross. I'm no cannibal. No, I was of the
high functional type, like so many of the people around you right.
This. Second. We're everywhere.

In zombieland I met an M.D. one night at a club who
snorted enough to drop an elephant. His license plate read "DR
IS IN." I met a cop with chronic back pain from a gunshot
wound who smoked it rolled up in little brown cigarettes. I met
a Mexican sculptor who cooked it up with peyote. I met a
woman who took care of toddlers during the day and left reality
every night and came back to tend to children in the morning
with droopy eyelids. My creative writing teacher, two swimmers,
a football star, the owner of a popular restaurant, musicians,
artists, and oh yeah. Junkie zombies.

I liked the fang of the needle. I liked chasing the dragon. I
still like watching the action of a syringe in an arm. It actually
makes my mouth water. Even in movies.

30 seconds from being to nothingness.

And I liked how my life, and what it was and wasn't,
simply left.

When you enter zombieland, everything looks a little like
it is underwater. Slow motion and thick. Other people look a bit
cartoonish – their movements too quick, their mouths and eyes
sometimes taking on weird shapes, their arms and legs occasionally morphing into snakes or animal heads. Sometimes you

find yourself giggling at inappropriate times. Also, things are sleepy. Like in a lucid dream.

Actually, it's exactly like lucid dreaming. According to neurobiology, in a lucid dream, the first thing that happens is that the dreamer recognizes they are dreaming. When the area of the brain that is usually off during sleep is activated the recognition of dreaming occurs, the dreamer must be careful to let the dream delusions continue but be conscious enough to recognize them. It's a process some people theorize as the space between reason and emotion.

The zombie is also in this kind of space between reason and emotion – and more. Ask any high functional zombie – or a recovered zombie – and they will tell you right away that life was like a waking dream. Boy howdy. Though for some it is a nightmare beyond language.

In a general sense, for me it was cool in zombieland. For example, I could sit in one spot all day and look at light changes on the wall with absolute fascination until night fell. Another time I dipped my hand in blue paint again and again and covered a white wall of my apartment with hands. Though I admit at one point the hands became menacing and threatened to consume me, later they were again benign, even able to sing me to sleep through little mouths on their palms.

I guess now that I'm thinking about it, zombie state is also a good deal like hypnosis or meditation. In hypnosis or meditation, you shift awareness from the physical world and enter the deeper world of the subconscious. Sometimes this makes your regular body go numb. Neither zombies nor hypnosis/meditation folks are freaked out by this. In zombieland, when you are so relaxed your mouth feels lax as water and your muscles drop down into the warm flush, you are going somewhere important of the mind. Down and deep. Into the world of dreams.

But another tricky thing about zombieland is that in the dimension of dreams you might experience body distortions, vibrations, or weird shaking. The key was not to panic. It didn't mean you were turning into a Quaker. It was normal. It meant your body was ready to "go" where your mind was taking it. It meant you were going on the nod.

And there is no such thing as time. No past, no present, no future. Or else they are all there at once. So the slowing and slurring of language, the heaviness in your legs, the oddity of your hands turning to giant leaden balls that swing slowly from your arms, the big wad of pillowcase in your mouth, these are all body modifications needed to go where you are going. Though I distinctly remember things going better when I did not leave the apartment. I had, for lack of a better phrase, night blindness and dumb girl head out in the world. Plus there was the problem of legs and arms.

Or maybe I saw the world for what it was, no place for a girl like me. Why not ... leave?

There were other, not cool times. Like the time I woke up under an overpass with my face against asphalt in a pool of my own vomit with my pants down around my ankles. Or the time I woke up in some blond and blue-eyed Karate guy's bed with leather twine around my neck. Or the time I fell from a second floor balcony and cracked my head, the woman with the latex gloves touching my forehead in the ambulance saying, "Lidia, can you still see me? Stay awake for me, Lidia. Good girl." She looked like an underwater white octopus lady. Pretty though.

I'm a strong bodied person. And the thing of it was, the things I thought would kill me in my life, maybe even the things I wished had, didn't. What, I distinctly remember thinking, did I have left to lose? Crossing the blood-brain barrier. The mind body barrier. The reality dream barrier. All that euphoria filling up the hole of me. No pain. No thought. Just images to follow.

I was a zombie for a spell in Lubbock. In Austin. In Eugene. It wasn't epic compared to the other wounds in my life. Rehab and relapse and remember all start with the letter R.

What It's Not

THIS IS NOT ANOTHER STORY ABOUT ADDICTION.

It's not *The Heroin Diaries* and it's not *Trainspotting* and it's not William Burroughs and it's not a *Million Fucking Little Pieces*, OK? I'm not gonna be on *Oprah* and I don't have a series of meaningful vignettes to relate that can compete with the gazillion other stories of druglife. It's not *Crank* and it's not *Tweak* and it's not *Smack*. No matter how marketable the addiction story has become, this is not that story. My life is more ordinary. More like ... more like everyone's.

Addiction, she is in me, sure enough. But I want to describe something else to you. Smaller. A smaller word, a smaller thing. So small it could travel a bloodstream.

When my mother tried to kill herself for the first time I was 16. She went into the spare bedroom of our Florida home for a long time. I knocked on the door. She said, "Go away, Belle."

Later she came out and sat in the living room. I went into the spare bedroom and found a bottle of sleeping pills – most of which were gone. Alone in the house with her, I scooped up an armful of vodka bottles and pills and brought them to her in the living room, my eyes full of water and fear, my mind racing. She looked at me more sharply than I ever remembered, and more focused than I'd ever seen her. Her voice was weirdly stern and two octaves lower than the southern cheery slurry drawl I was used to. She said: "Stay away; this isn't anything for you. I'm not talking about anything." And she turned her gaze to the television. *General Hospital* was on.

I went straight into the bathroom and sat on the toilet and ate a wad of toilet paper. My face felt hot enough to ignite. I cried hard. That hard kind of cry that brings guttural grunting rather than sobbing. I muscled up my bicep and I punched the wall of the bathroom. It left a small crack. My hand immediately ached. How I felt was alone. Like I didn't have a mother. Or a father. At least not ones I wanted. When I came out of the bathroom I felt a little bit like a person who could kill her.

It scared the crap out of me. I didn't call my father. I didn't call an ambulance. I called my sister, who lived in Boston, where she was busy getting a Ph.D., trying to erase her origins. My sister told me to call an ambulance and then to call our father. My mother in the living room watching soaps.

I didn't know yet how wanting to die could be a bloodsong in your body that lives with you your whole life. I didn't know then how deeply my mother's song had swum into my sister and into me. I didn't know that something like wanting to die could take form in one daughter as the ability to quietly surrender, and in the other as the ability to drive into death head-on. I didn't know we were our mother's daughters after all.

My mother did not die. At least not that day. Eventually I did call an ambulance, and she went to the hospital, and they pumped her gut out. She was diagnosed with severe manic depression, and her doctor assigned talk therapy as part of her recovery. She saw a therapist five times. Then one day she came home and said, "I'm done." But when she came home she was a dead woman masquerading as a live one. Drinking. Slowly. Surely. What she did next, well, sometimes it's difficult to tell rage from love.

When I was 17 my mother signed me into an outpatient teen drug treatment center. She found dope in my pants pocket while doing laundry one day. The place I had to go to every day for eight weeks was a soft Khmer Rouge. I was told that "behavioral healthcare" is your "doorway to choice and hope." That was the motto. I didn't find choice and hope through the doorway. I found bibles and Christians with thick gator-mouthed drawls and skin cancer tans counseling me on self-esteem and a purposeful life. They fed me bible passages. I brought Mary Shelley's *Frankenstein* with me every day for moral support. They always made me put the book at the front counter, but I knew it was there. I knew it had my back. Not like my mother.

Through the doorway to choice and hope were the saddest girls I have ever met. Not because someone beat them or because someone molested them or because they were poor or pregnant or even because they put needles in their arms or pills in their mouths or weed in their lungs or alcohol down their ever-constricting throats. They were the saddest girls I have ever met because every one of them had it in her to lose a shot at a self and become her mother.

My rage became nuclear. But I did my time. I exited the program with a certificate. I wanted to punch my mother—my mother the puffy hypocrite, the woman currently putting away a fifth of vodka a day—in the face. But she was the same woman who would sign the signature on my scholarship papers a year later. So I did not punch my mother's mouth off of her face. I just thought this: get out. Hold your breath until you can leave. You are good at that. Perhaps the best. This woman's pain could kill you.

Later in life, after I flunked out of college, I lived alone in Austin in a crappy-ass efficiency off of the freeway. I got into some more trouble living on my own that led to another round of mandatory drug and alcohol counseling for six weeks in a very strange basement of a medical clinic serving underprivileged folks. Poor people, Mexicans, unwed mothers, African Americans, and me.

There, I was meant to "find meaning in life's traffic through clearing spiritual barriers." A different healing slogan. More self righteous hypocritical Christians. There was even a woman in my sessions named "Dorothy." My mother's name. Or *The Wizard of Oz*. I did my time there too, and left with yet another certificate.

Trust me when I say I definitely found "meaning in life's traffic."
Eventually.

So then this is not an addiction story.

It's just that I have a sister who walked around for nearly
two years when she was 17 with razor blades in her purse seeing
if she could outlive the long wait waiting to get out of family.

Her first round.

It's just that I had a mother who ate a whole bottle of sleeping pills at middle age with only her daughter the swimmer at
home to witness the will of it.

Her first round.

I know that will well now. It's the will of certain mothers
and daughters. It comes from living in bodies that can carry life
or kill it.

It's the will to end.

Crooked Lovesong

PHILLIP DID WRITE ME A SONG. HE DID. AND IT WASN'T about how my life was spiraling away from bold swimmer toward comfortably numb. It wasn't about the three abortions I'd had before I was 21. It wasn't even about how much money I'd won drinking Texans under tables. Or all the nights I made him break into other peoples' homes the way my father had broken into me.

The song he wrote for me was mostly instrumental. But you have to understand, and my archangel and his lover will back me up on this – he could play the acoustic guitar better than ... you know, James Taylor. So the song took on a rather epic quality. Way before Windham Hill. But there was one, small, tender refrain that would come out of nowhere, or rather, it would come from the very heart of the music, deeper than anything I'd known, and it went like this: Children have their dreams to hang on to. How they fly, and take us to the moon. They flow from you. They flow from you.

The first time I heard it? Sitting on a driftwood log at our wedding, which was on the beach of Corpus Christi, Texas. And it wasn't just me who couldn't breathe from the jesusfuckingchristknot in my throat and the salted water pouring out of my eyes rivaling the ocean. The whole posse of people there bawled. Nothing nothing nothing nothing about me deserved it. But very deep down in me, very tiny, very afraid, was a girl who smiled from within the cavernous place I'd hidden her.

Is that love? Was it? I still don't know. It's possible. But none of us are any good at naming it. It comes and then goes. Like songs do. I do know this: it's the kind of thing that happens in stories.

Phillip and I tried to make a go of it as something called "married." In Austin, Texas. I don't know how to explain why we went busto. OK, that's a big fat lie. I know exactly why we went busto, but I don't want to have to say it. Look, I'll tell you later. OK?

While we were trying to be married in Austin he got a job – the only job he could find – at a sign-making company. That's what happens to artists like him – a man with the talent of the most revered painters in art history has to go work at a sign factory. I got a job with ACORN. Yep, that ACORN. But I didn't give a shit about humanity or common cause or grass roots. By then, there wasn't much I gave a shit about. I'd so colossally failed athlete/student/wife/woman at that point I felt like something an animal puked up. A human fur ball.

This is something I know: damaged women? We don't think we deserve kindness. In fact, when kindness happens to us, we go a little berserk. It's threatening. Deeply. Because if I have to admit how profoundly I need kindness? I have to admit that I hid the me who deserves it down in a sadness well. Seriously. Like abandoning a child at the bottom of a well because it's better than the life she is facing. Not quite killing my little girl me, but damn close.

So I set to work destroying things.

The first thing I did was get drunk one night and punch Phillip in the face. Yep, I punched the most beautiful talented musician and painter I will ever meet in my life, also the most passive and gentle man I have ever met, right in the face. As hard as I could. Wanna know what I said? I said, "You don't want anything. You are killing me with your not wanting anything." Classy. Astute. Mature. Emotionally stunning. I am my father's daughter.

The second thing I did was get fired from ACORN. Which

is hard to do. But I hated it. I hated having to go out into the hot Texas sun and knock on door after door begging assholes for money when all they cared about was their next latte and what pair of jeans that cost more than my rent they were about to buy. I'd go to maybe 10 houses or so, enough houses to get beer money. Then I'd sit on curbs and smoke pot and drink beer. Then I'd fill in my canvassing sheets with made up addresses and names.

The third thing that happened is I got pregnant. I'm still not sure why, I took my birth control pills regularly. And more and more JT and I were not making love – shocker. But a seed went up and against all odds, in. Breaking my fucking heart.

Look here it is straight no chaser. The me I was if I leave Phillip out of it? Abortion. But something about him and something even deeper down inside me – like a hidden blue smooth stone – it all made that impossible for me to choose. And yet, there was no way to keep pretending the life we had together was anything but a sad ass country song, so as my belly bump turned into a hill, I did the only thing I could do, given the life I'd frankensteined. I called my sister in Eugene where she worked as a Professor of English at the University of Oregon and asked her if I could live with her. Across her leaving me as a child, across the waters of our age difference, across her life as a successful academic and my life as a reckless fireball. The fact was, we were both adult women now. Living adult women lives. Meaning we had something very deeply in common: the tyranny of culture telling women who they should be.

It's not possible to explain to you how quickly and profoundly she said yes. Maybe she was waiting for me to come back to her. Bringing my big as a house belly with me. To birth and raise a child together, to make a family outside the lines. Because it was the only story I could think of that might live. And though she'd left me to save her life, she somehow knew how to make a space for sister, child, self. But I know too that it was a sacrifice to bring a daughter in from the cold.

Phillip eventually followed me to Eugene. He lived on the

other side of town. We barely saw each other. He worked at Smith Family Bookstore, I went to school in English. Sometimes we'd run into each other, and lock eyes, and I wouldn't be able to breathe. I'd put my hand on my belly to feel what was there between us. It was all I had to give to him.

Here it is. What I didn't want to say before. It's me. I'm the reason we went busto. I could not take his gentle kindness. But neither could I kill it.

Family Drama

WHEN MY SISTER WAS 16 AND I WAS EIGHT, SHE'D MAKE me "do" things.

Like this: just hold this apple in your mouth by taking a partial bite out of it. Yeah, like that. Now hold it, hold it … her socking the apple out from between my teeth, sending it across the room, while my little blond head shot to the left with the momentum and my teeth clacked shut on my lower lip.

Or this: see this ashtray? Do this. Just blow in it. One, two, three.

Ashes going all up my nose and all over my face.

Or this: aren't the icicles hanging from the house cool? C'mere. Put your tongue on this one. It's pretty!

I would have done anything.

Lemme say from the get-go – I adored my sister to the point of going cross-eyed and fainting as a kid. I thought she was mythic. For one thing, she had the thickest, longest, most beautiful auburn hair I'd ever even heard of, better than the idiotic dolls my mother kept buying me with hair that you could pull out from the tops of their heads – Chrissy with the red-auburn hair and the shorter platinum blond Velvet. Whereas I had a kind of … Q-tip for a head. Chlorine bleached head fuzz. No matter how hard I tried, I couldn't pull any hair out of the top of my head.

For another thing, she could read and recite Shakespeare scenes by heart. She'd seen the R-rated "Romeo and Juliet" – she had the album. She could paint real paintings that went on walls. She had a black portfolio almost as big as me (that I was secretly convinced could be used as a sled). She could write poems, speak French, she could play guitar, recorder, she could sing, she could ice skate. I mean really, really well. Me? Eight years younger, if you discount swimming, about the best thing I could do was dress myself. It was a banner day if I didn't cry, pee, or rock back and forth like a little monkey.

And she had boobs.

Boobs were the magical thing women had. White and full and inexplicably mouthwatering.

But when I say I would have done anything, it isn't exactly these things. What it is: I took naïve pleasure in the small acts of humiliation, and I attached them to a feminine form. The things she made me do made my skin hot and prickly. Her beauty was stern and commanding.

As my sister neared adulthood, my father took a keen interest in her many talents. He'd brag. And put photos of her up in his office. Just her.

Her art teacher guided her more and more toward the world. Her watercolor paintings – giant, sexual looking flowers a little like Georgia O'Keefe's, her art teacher helped her to have them framed and entered into local art shows.

She played guitar and sang in her room with the door shutting out the word family, but out in the world her art teacher helped her and a friend perform together with microphones at local venues for money. When she learned how to make giant flowers from paper, her art teacher helped her sell those, too. Her art was making a path.

I'm not saying I figured all this out at eight. At eight, all I saw was how he looked at her hair. All I heard was his yelling every year of her development from girl to young woman, like a series of earthquakes pounding the life out of things, rattling the floors of daughter.

And anyway, maybe I have the ages wrong. Maybe I was 10. Maybe I was 6. Maybe I was 35 and getting my second divorce. I don't know how old we were as children. I only know my father's anger built the house.

Once in the entryway when she was on her way out of the door for school, he yelled "Christ you look like a bum with those jeans and that dumpy sack shirt – you trying to look like a man? You look like a goddamn man." Peering out from behind the door of my bedroom I saw he had his face close to hers. I saw her looking at the ground under a curtain of auburn hair. Then I saw her lift her head and meet his eyes, her literature and art books at her chest like a shield. They looked almost exactly like each other. It made the fact that I had to pee hurt.

When my sister was older, she started wearing this long, dusted gray-purple antique dress to school. And she went out sometimes with men named Victor and Park, both much older than her, men who would drive her away from our house for hours and hours, leaving my father to make a chain smoker's chimney of our living room. Watching *All in the Family*. Pounding the arm of the overstuffed sofa chair.

But the big event for me was that she moved down into the basement of the house, into some spooky bedroom we never used down there. There was nothing my father could do but watch, because my mother did it behind his back. My sister was smarter than my never-went-to-college mother by the time she was in high school, but my mother had survivor smartness. Like a savvy animal.

The move, to me, was unbelievable – my sister moved down into the belly of a haunted house. She wanted to. I couldn't even make it to the unfinished cement floors of the basement laundry room without an adult with me. Down the awful blue carpet stairs, down the treacherously dark and unfinished side-boards of the basement hallway. Through those unnamable smells. Those creepy dungeon sounds of knocking pipes and creaking wood. All the way to the other end of the house, into a room that I was sure I would pass out trying to get to. I remember asking my mother if someone could die from "hippoventating."

Sometimes I'd just stand at the top of the blue carpet stairs and look down into the throat of them wishing I could see her, and I'd lift my foot up to take a step and immediately feel VERTIGO, and then with a little wistful sigh and my throat knotting up I'd give up. Even if I ventured half way down the stairs solo, I'd start to get light headed and the skin on my chest would heat up. I'd hold the railing for dear life and say her name into space. Hoping she would come retrieve me.

If I made it down the stairs alone to the beginning of the horror hallway – a hallway with NO LIGHTS – the only way I could get to her was to close my eyes as tight as my fists, hold my breath, and sprint . . . always arriving at the light of her door letting out this sad little breathy MAAAARRRR sound. How I managed not to hit a wall I don't know.

But in her room. Being in her room was like being inside a painting. Our grandmother's hand-stitched quilts with the colors of the seasons spread out across her bed. Music and books and candles and wooden boxes with jewelry or shells or feathers in them. Incense and brushes and combs and dried flowers. Paint brushes and big squares of paper and drawing pencils. Velvet dresses and leather moccasins and jeans with legs shaped like big As. A guitar. A recorder. A record player. With speakers.

In her room you would never know the torture pit of the laundry room was three feet away.

She'd let me get in bed with her, and we'd move around under the covers, our body heat remaking a womb. "Watercolor covers," she'd say, and I'd nearly hippoventate with pleasure. Sometimes I held my breath or made little repetitive circles between my fingers and thumbs. Smiling like a giddy little troll. Girl skin smell making me high.

Getting back upstairs was nothing, because she'd escort me, and I'd be back in the upperworld of things.

What an imaginative leap she made to leave us and live

down there that year. How much I didn't understand where the
danger lived.

When my sister was in high school we got a phone call.
My sister was underneath a table in the Art Lab, telling her art
teacher Baudette very calmly but with complete certainty that
she was not going home.

Ever.

My parents had to go see the officials at the school, and
the art teacher, Baudette, who my sister had made into her better
family, explained to my ding headed mother that my sister
couldn't be around my father. That mandatory counseling sessions would happen. I thought her teacher's names were
magical. Mr. Foubert. Mr. Saari. Baudette. I sat in the corner of
the school office eating a little piece of paper trying not to cry.

I still remember the counselor's name. Dr. Akudagawa.
I remember how I had to stay with friends of my parents when
the three of them abandoned me for sessions. How my father
never went into the basement. How she rarely came up.

How my sister got closer and closer to the final act of leaving for college: exeunt daughter, stage left.

How my father's rage came to live in the house for good.

How I would be what was left of her, when she gave me a
piece of her hair as a keepsake.

How my father's eyes would turn.

This is Not About my Sister

THIS BOOK IS NOT ABOUT MY SISTER. BUT IF IT WERE,
I'd tell you again that for two years before she could leave
our Oedipal household she carried razor blades in her purse.

I'd tell you how her colon was irrevocably messed up –
how as a child I sat in the bathroom with her and held her hand
every time she tried to poo. How she squeezed my little girl
hand so tight I thought it might be crushed. Because it hurt that
bad to shit.

I'd tell you how she was born with a wandering eye, and
what the Dr. who later delivered me wrote about what that
might mean for infants like her – how to watch for it as a sign of
danger in a child. How fathers or uncles or grandfathers might
have had a hand in this particular kind of eye disorder – in
certain sexual abuse cases – a penis coming too close to the still
developing eyes of a child.

I'd tell you how, in the end, my sister replaced my mother
and father in my mind and heart, how we created a union of
survival that means we are both still alive.

If this book were about my sister, I'd tell you how she lived
past daughter.

And I'd show you a picture.

A Simca station wagon. Maybe white. Maybe wood paneling.

My father loved the Northwest. He loved to explore the
mountains and rivers and lakes. He loved to fish and camp and
hike. But his wife had a misshapen leg not good for walking and

he had two daughters instead of sons, so his disappointment always came with us everywhere we went. We could never hike far enough. Never carry enough weight. Never go as deeply into the wilderness. We couldn't fish right. We had to pee sitting down and we needed toilet paper. A crippled wife and two daughters. We couldn't even breathe right. Ever.

The Christmas I was four and my sister was 12 we drove and drove. From I-5 to Puyallup. Past Enumclaw. East on highway 7 to Elbe. Onto Highway 706 east through Ashford to Alexander's. Then there is the entrance to Mt. Rainier National Park. I have driven it many times as an adult. That's how I remember the path. Or so I tell myself.

But what I remember then is how bright the sun shone on the white – like an overexposed winter everywhere. How we got out of the car and made a snowman – my sister and my father and I. How we decorated the snowman with plastic Easter eggs that were in the car. How my mother laughed and wore her sunglasses and sat on the tailgate.

But too I remember my father's voice when we drove further, and I fell asleep, and my sister began to read a book: "What are you two doing, playing with yourselves? I bring you through the most beautiful scenery in the world and you are playing grab-ass? LOOK OUT THE GODDAMN WINDOW." So we did. Silently. The side of my sister's face looked as if it was made of stone. My ears burned.

We were dressed for our front yard – for maybe snowball fights with neighbor kids or going sledding. Running inside for new socks and hot chocolate. We had no food or water or blankets or radio or anything. Except a half finished plaid thermos of coffee. And matches. Both of my parents chain-smoked. My sister and I by this point were used to riding in the car like prisoners. Our father drove us to Mt. Rainier to get a tree. A goddamn tree. In the beautiful goddamn northwest.

The place we stopped to get the tree to me looked like the middle of nowhere. The "road" filled with more and more snow.

The drive became steep – switchbacks and a permanent tilt to the Simca station wagon that kept my head pinned to the back seat. The heater in the car blew full blast. On the sides of the barely there road enormous evergreens and firs rose up like giant snow covered sentries. Beautiful but vaguely ominous. To me anyway. I couldn't crane my neck hard enough to see the tops. Where he pulled over the trees were enormous. I remember wondering how we'd drag one back to our house ... with a giant rope?

Where my father pulled over and stopped the car, my mother said, "Mike?"

My father didn't say anything. He simply made ready to get out of the car. So the little women followed him.

My mother wore a wool lined long gray raincoat with a faux fur raccoon collar and gold metal fasteners. Pointy movie star sunglasses. Her hair in a bun wrapped and wrapped on her head. Red lipstick. My sister wore a light ski jacket and red pants and a white fake fur hat with snowball ties and cotton kid gloves and black rubber K-Mart boots. I wore red corduroy pants and a smaller brown version of my sister's hat with the pom pom ties and red galoshes and black cotton gloves – I remember our red pants because they stood out so in the snow. Like blood and urine do. And my mother made them. My father wore jeans and a fleece lined suede jacket and blond leather gloves. He pulled a handsaw from the back of the station wagon. And a rope. And my sister's hand.

My mother and I immediately got behind on the ascent up the snow-covered hill. Think about this – my mother's misshapen steps hobbling up and up. Me only four years old. Within five minutes the snow was up to my hips. Within 20 minutes up to my chin. My mother, again and again, pulled me out of a snow hole until I sunk into the next. The only way I experienced how cold it was happened in my mother's voice when she yelled up to the dots of my father and sister getting smaller and farther up the hill, "Mike! Lidia is blue!" That and my teeth clattering.

I remember seeing him turn and look down at us. I remember his yelling something I couldn't understand, then turning away from us. I remember him grabbing my sister's arm, and though I couldn't know this back then, I know now he wrenched her farther up with him.

"Well, shit." My mother's drawl made me laugh. But I was shivering and I felt wet. All over.

Somehow my mother and I made it back down the hill to the car, though I remember nearly drowning a couple times in snow past my head and my mother yanking me back to air and sky. So much sun I could barely keep my little blue eyes open.

In the car, my mother said "Belle, take all your clothes off." But I just sat there numb like a kid Popsicle. So she took all my clothes off. They were drenched. She placed the red weighted garments over the seats. She turned the car on. She blasted the heater and made me get on the floor where your feet go. She took off that weird coat with the raccoon collar and wrapped it around me like a tent. When I looked up at her, she said something I never forgot the rest of my life. She said, "Lidabelle. Pretend I am Becky Boone, and you are Israel Boone, and this is our adventure!"

I pretended immediately. Not only did I watch *Daniel Boone* all the time and love it, but I looked exactly like Israel. I laughed and smiled and forgot about how cold I was. I forgot my father was my father. Somewhere out there was Daniel Boone. A man. A big man.

My mother dug through her coat pocket and found butterscotch candies and we ate them. She made me drink coffee from the plaid thermos. It tasted like hot liquid dirt. But she said, "Remember, you are Israel Boone! You can do anything! When we get home I'll make you a buckskin shirt!"

It was a lie. A beautiful, stunningly creative, lifesaving lie.

When I felt better I looked out of the front car window to see if I could see my father and my sister. All I saw was the brilliant blue sky – all the sun and all the white made me have to squint. Plus the windows kept fogging up so I had to keep rubbing a see-through circle with my hand. My mother made me sing songs with her. I see the moon. You are my sunshine. The bear goes over the mountain.

I know what I felt at first. I felt ecstatic. To be alone with my mother. Singing. Wrapped inside her southern drawl, her raccoon coat, her story of us as Becky and Israel Boone. But even at age four my chest got tight after a while. I never lived a day without the squeeze of sister around my heart. Where. Was. She.

When my mother looked out of the car window and up the hill, her eye twitched.

Even at that age I knew how Christmas would be. My father would sit in a sofa recliner smoking and silent. Presiding. My sister would open presents looking like a girl doing chores. I would open presents with the know nothing glee of a kid and look around at them all. My mother would clap and laugh. Then something–nearly anything–would happen, and my father's anger would crush even the faintest tenderness, and my sister and I would be left alone in the living room with piles of wrapping paper to clean up. The smell of a fresh cut fir tree and cigarettes.

By the time I saw the blurry figures of a big man and a girl coming down the mountain I was sleepy. So they looked like dream people to me. My mother said, "Oh thank god," as they approached the car, but I could hear something else in her voice.

That's the picture I would show you – the way my sister looked through the window of the Simca station wagon. Her cheeks like apples. Her eyes puffy. My father had a hold of her arm. She looked like her legs didn't work right. My mother rolled the window down and I saw snot under my sister's nose. Was she crying? She did not make any sound. But she shivered. Then my sister looked straight at me. I bit my lip. Her eyes more cold than snow. That's the picture.

I remember the ride home. The long silence. To my knowledge, we did not bring home a tree. But we did bring home everything that was our family, laden. So laden.

Ash

DEAD INFANTS DON'T GET URNS UNLESS YOU PAY FOR them – and then they stuff crap in besides just ashes to cover the smallness. All those years ago? My daughter's ashes were in a small pink box – pink for girls – a box the size of a hacky sack ball that fits in the palm of your hand

I took my box to Heceta Head. The coast at Heceta Head in December is epic. Me, my first husband, my sister, and weirdly, my parents. Near strangers.

Pretending to be a family, we stumble-walked down over the rocks to the water's edge. The sound of ocean waves is large enough to stop your thinking. My mother closed her eyes and said a prayer in a southern drawl. Phillip sang *I See the Moon* – the lullaby my mother sang to me as a child – which made me feel a little like I might faint. My sister read "Ample Make This Bed" by Emily Dickinson, nearly killing us all. Then my father, the architect, pulled something out of his pocket. A folded up piece of paper. On it, he'd written a poem. Sort of. It rhymed. When he read it, his voice shook. The only time in my life I heard that.

It rained cold. Windy. Like Oregon is.

After that, Phillip and I took the little pink box which I had been clutching in my hand hard enough to nearly crush it and walked over to where the river joins the ocean. That's why I'd picked that spot. I could see river rocks leading into the sea and sand, and I smelled and tasted saltwater. I don't know if I was crying – my face was wet with ocean and rain. The lighthouse stood guard. All the waters of a life met at that tiny nexus.

Then I handed him the fragile little box. He took it in his hand. I said, throw it as far as you can. So he – there isn't another way to say this. He chucked it.

Yeah, so the thing is, that little riverway that leads to the sea? Right there at Heceta head? It has a mean cross-current. So while Phillip and I stood there watching the little box float nearly out of eyesight, we also stood and watched it … come the fuck back. Pretty much to our very feet. Knocking itself against his shoe.

I looked back over my shoulder to where the posse of sadness that was my idiotic family stood – they were far away, almost dots. I looked at Phillip. Then I said, try kicking it out. No, I don't know why I said that.

So he, um, kicked it.

This time it didn't go very far at all, it simply launched soggily into the air and plunked back down and circled back to us, just slower this time. Without being able to stop, I started laughing. And he started laughing. I mean hard. I said go get it, goddamn it. So he did.

By then the little box had begun to disintegrate. Cheap ass pink crappy cardboard. As I peeled the dumb paper away, I saw that the ashes were actually inside a little plastic bag. Almost like a pot baggie. I tried not to laugh but I couldn't help it, and Phillip went what? And peeked over my shoulder. We had giggles we couldn't stop.

I said goddamn it I have to stop laughing. It's not funny. It's pretty fucking far from funny. He agreed, but he couldn't stop either. I had snot all over my face. I was laughing so hard my stomach – former world – hurt. Finally I knew what to do.

I opened the little faux caul full of ash carefully with my teeth. Like animals do. Then I walked out into the ocean for real. I had a vintage red wool coat on. And brushed leather cowboy boots. Phillip tried to follow me in but I said no. I wave walked until I was up to my abdomen. The water felt ice cold on my stitches. Numbed the hurt there. I dumped the nearly weightless contents of my daughter into my right hand. Some of the ash blew into the air, but most of it didn't. It was wet. Like sand. And then I let my right hand lower into the water, and I let go. I closed my eyes.

My father told me later it was the bravest thing he has ever seen. I never knew how to take that.

When I walked out of the water back to my first husband, he held me close – we were already apart by then – but he did it anyway. Then I felt his shoulders shaking, and I thought he was crying, but nope, he was laughing again, so I said what? And he pointed to the side of my vintage red coat at the smear of ashmud there. I laughed again too and went I know. I know. Clutching each other.

My sister said from where they were we looked like we were sobbing.

Maybe we were sobbing.

I don't know.

I kept the plastic in my pocket like that for years. I still have the red coat – though if there is any trace of ash left, you can't see it.

II. Under Blue

Baptismal

A FAMILY ON THE BEACH AS IF WE WERE EVER A FAMILY on the beach.

When my sister and I were adults we visited my mother and father in Florida. We visited them because of guilt. We visited them because of shame. We visited them because of delusion. We visited them because grown women are idiots. I don't know why we visited them. I can't remember. I think my mother begged to see her daughters. Me 26. My sister 34.

My mother stayed with her shorter leg on the sand. A father and his two daughters waded into the ocean at the beach in St. Augustine. When we played in the ocean we forgot ourselves: sister, self, father, memory loss. The water in Florida is body temperature. The waves, unless there is weather, are calm. They roll a body gently. I heard a sound from the shore. I saw my mother running, lopsided. I followed her arm and finger to the father face down in the sea. I tasted salt on my own lips. When I finally reached him I could see the moles on his back at the surface of the knee-deep water. Running in water is like running in Jell-O. Almost funny. When I flipped him over, his face was distorted into a grimace – clenched teeth, bulging eyes, purple and white blotching his face. My sister then there. Us pulling his 220 pound of dead weight onto the shore, both screaming at him, "Daddy." The image of my mother: a tiny squawking penguin with a cane on the shore, too far from her daughters.

There are moments between years that surface with a great force when you do not expect it. My father almost dead in front of me. I'm going to say it plain: I could have killed him. I looked down into the flesh losing its color, the popping, staring blue eyes twinning mine, the animal teeth. His face so familiar I couldn't recognize it. I held his nose closed. I put my mouth to his mouth. I could feel his tongue, his teeth, spittle. His lips were warm but unresponsive. My sister pumped her fists into his chest. His swim trunks were half off. His sex hung harmless. I held my lips to his. I breathed air into his mouth until an ambulance came.

Hypoxia is suffocation in water that does not result in death. It may include brain damage and multiple organ failure. My father lost his memory from hypoxia.

I did not kill him. I did not save him. How do you live on land?

Swimming with Amateurs

YOU CAN TELL A LOT ABOUT A PERSON FROM SEEING them in the water. Some people freak out and spaz their way around like giant insects, others slide in like seals, turn over, dive down, effortlessly. Some people kind of tread water with big goofy smiles, others look slightly broken-armed and broken-legged or as if they are in some kind of serious pain.

I swam, once, with Ken Kesey. In a man-made reservoir up near Fall Creek. Puffy with drink, his bulk rounded and bulged around his former reputation. It was night swimming. Five people, I think. Totally, completely, unapologetically, rocket shot high.

The moon kept coming in and out of focus as the clouds moved around. And the water was warm yet, so it must have been late summer, but in my mind it has the crisp clarity of fall for some reason. If it had been fall we would have frozen our tits off. So sometime in late summer less than a decade before he died, we entered the waters. Man-made reservoirs smell like dirt and concrete mixed with algae.

I dove down into the black and opened my eyes. Looking into lake water at night is like looking into deep space while drunk. Black, and blurry. I resurfaced and strong-armed into a glide, went down, came up again, then took a look back, and saw his unmistakable head and burled broad shoulders. "Goddamn girl, what are you, some kind of mermaid?" he said. Spitting a stream of water. Yeah.

In the black reservoir water we swam around each other looking at the sky, treading water, floating on our backs and letting our feet break the surface. Sometimes Kesey's belly rose up like an island. We shot the shit, mostly he told stories ...

That's a bald faced lie. Just now I made it sound like we casually shot the shit out there, but really my brain was as numb as a wad of cotton and I couldn't think of anything interesting to say, so I just let him talk and I don't even remember what he said because my head was expanding and contracting like an idiot's.

And he wasn't really in the water with me.

He was on the shore.

But then he must have said something from somewhere that penetrated, because I opened my mouth, and it was nothing nothing nothing words until it wasn't nothing anymore, and I was listing all the horrible things people had said to me since my baby died.

Things like: "You know, it's probably better that she died before you got to know her." Or: "Well what you really want in your 20s is the freedom to party." Or my personal favorite, from my father's sister, fascist catholic: "The saddest part is that she'll go to hell, isn't it, since she wasn't baptized."

Then he was saying "When Jed died, everyone who talked to me said something asinine. Like the craziest crap you can imagine. No one understands death anymore. Death used to be sacred. Look at the Upanishads. Goddamn religion has killed death."

I had read the letter he wrote to friends Wendell Berry, Larry McMurtry, Ed McClanahan, Bob Stone, and Gurney Norman in the summer of 1984 in *CoEvolution Quarterly* when Jed died. How they built a box for his body themselves. How he threw a silver whistle with a Hopi cross soldered on it into the grave. How the first shovelfuls of dirt sounded like "the Thunderclaps of Revelation."

I held my breath. I thought about water. I thought about

the ashes of my daughter swimming in the ocean off the coast of Oregon. The deaths of our children swam in the water with us, curling around us, keeping us twinned and floating.

So if Ken said these things to me, does it really matter if he was in the water or not? If meeting Ken so close to a death brought writing into my hands, and if I cast that out as a dreamy lake front scene, who gives a shit if he was in the water? His big hearted wrestler's body. His irreverent mouth. His dead son. My hollowed out gut. Me in my better world. From the water I could see him on the shore, a little miniature Kesey doing his former Kesey thing, the smaller man within a man like a Russian doll.

That night I swam the lake and back trying to drown out voices.

Father

BEFORE MY FATHER'S HANDS MOVED AGAINST US HE
was an architect; lover of art.

Before my father was an architect he was a navigator in
the Korean War.

Before my father was a navigator he was an artist.

Before my father was an artist he was an athlete.

Before my father was an athlete he was an unhappy altar
boy.

That's the best I can do. I think.

Goddamn it.

Let me try again.

*Before my father's hands moved against us he was an architect;
lover of art.*

His hands. I remember his hands at work over great white
expanses of paper, rows and rows of pens and pencils and
sophisticated erasers, a T-square sliding up and down a wire on
the drafting table, his tall form bent over the territory of his
designs. I remember the sound of classical music coming from
his room, orchestral arrangements weaving up my spine, the
names of composers going into my head. I can still see the great
thick-paged architectural and art magazines on the coffee table.
This striking man teaching me how to draw, what is shadow,
what is light, composition, perspective. I walked with him
through the spaces of other men's buildings, and in place of bed-

time stories, I heard about Le Corbusier, Antonio Gaudí, Carlo Scarpa, Fumihiko Maki. The beauty of him speaking about art, slowly, a cigarette pointing toward heaven, swirls of smoke like curls of water around the sanctity of his speech. I walked with my father through Fallingwater.

Before my father was an architect he was a navigator in the Korean War.

I can only go to black and white photos here. When I hold them in my hand I suddenly have to face the fact of real war, and his body in it. The photos have barracks and rifles and uniforms. The photos have jeeps and helicopters and the landscape of the military. The photos are of my father with men I never met nor ever will, men who may be dead by now, men who went to war before I was born, before Vietnam.

There are two kinds of photos. In the first kind each frame is filled with an extraordinary architecture – Korean Buddhist temples and shrines.

The second kind carry men. There is a black man who reappears in several of the photos. When I hold the photos, my father isn't the abusive fuck. He becomes a different story, the one he and my mother and uncle and aunt told and retold about the lengths he went to concerning his best friend – a black man whose name I will never know. I can't remember it. I was a child when these stories were told.

But the stories are all about how my dad would sit out in the car with this guy when the other guys would go out to eat or drink or dance when they were on leave. How he'd go in and get food or beer and bring it out to the car or the curb or some vacant lot near whatever establishment and they'd sit and share it together.

I look at the black man in the photo. I wish I could talk to him. Ask him questions about my father then. Was he funny? Was he kind? Did he ever make a drawing for you? What things

scared him, or hurt him, or made him happy? What was my father
like during wartime? What is a man?

My father was handsome.

Before he was a soldier he was an artist.

Sometimes, when we were alone, I would ask my mother
questions about my father when they first met. She would
nearly always go into the spare bedroom, pull a shoebox down
from the closet, sit down next to me, and unfold a piece of
drawing paper. On the paper was a redbird. A beautifully drawn –
I mean artistically stunning redbird. She would smile, and
keep her eyes down, and say in her soft southern drawl almost
in the voice of a girl, "Your father won an art prize for this
drawing." In the same box, she would unfold a yellowed scatter
of pages filled with beautiful handwriting. "I won a prize for
this story."

And then she would carefully fold it all back up, put it back
in the box, return it to the closet.

When I hold photos of the two of them in my hands my
heart aches. My father looking all James Dean with his rolled at
the cuff denims and his white muscle tee with cigarettes tucked
in the sleeve and his mirror sunglasses. My mother in her 50s
dresses with wide skirts and her hair tied back, her lips that were
red as a coca-cola can looking black in the black and white
photos. They were gorgeous. Hollywood. She was smiling. He
looked like someone a woman would fall in love with.

There is another photo of him sitting at a picnic table. He
has khaki pants on and a white shirt. The way he is sitting? His
crossed legs and bad posture and long fingers running through
his thick hair? His other hand wrapped around his neck so that
his elbow folds softly in? He has the body language of an artist. I
know. I married three in a row.

Before my father was an artist he was an athlete.

I know how to tell this story. I know how to story over things.

His senior year. Bases loaded at a catholic school. Cleveland, Ohio, the gray of pavement and winter sealing fates. Nuns and Fathers in black, black coats and boots and hats on the bodies of family members. The boys on the field as beautiful as boys on a field are; strange angels. Breath making fog from mouths. Eyes keened in on plays and moves and the edge of things. Top of the ninth. The board wearing its scores, though no one needs to look. At the moment sweat is forming at his upper lip, and just as his arms uncoil to connect thick whack and send the little world out of the park, at that moment all the nuns and all the fathers look up, like faith. Right then the end of things rings in the boy like hope. He sees college. He sees leaving home. He sees a chance at inhabiting the word athlete. His arms surrender. His body shivers. A cheer rises up like a chorus. Everyone is a single voice. Except one. At that moment a man leaves. His back stopping the action.

The home run. The father gone. The boy turning into man – he must have looked ... beautiful.

That's it.

That's as far as I can go.

To go further into his story, it takes the air right out of my lungs as if I'd been swimming all night.

I do know his tongue was cut. When I look at my son and think of that I think I could kill a woman who would cut a boy's tongue.

Before my father was my father he was a boy.

Just a boy.

Before I hated him I loved him.

How To Ride a Bike

WHEN I WAS 10 TO CHEER ME UP FROM MY DESPAIR OF
my sister's leaving, my father brought home a hot pink Schwinn
with a banana seat and streamers coming out of the handlebars.
I saw him pull it out of the trunk of the station wagon. I saw him
wheel it up to the front porch. I saw him kick the kickstand and
let her rest. The window a membrane between us.

I thought it was perhaps the most beautiful thing I had
ever seen – except for my green metal toy army jeep. Still. Its hot
pink glory. Its streamers like hair. That big white banana seat. I
gasped.

The thing was, however, I did not know how to ride a bike.
Like at all. Scared of most things that required me to "do"
something besides swim, I'd even forsaken trikes, their three-
wheeling menace not something I'd ever mastered. With trikes
I'd flat foot the thing along, my failure disgusting my father
enough to hide it away in the garage. So when I came outside to
touch the hot pink ride, beautiful as she was, all I felt was terror.
When my father said, "It's time to learn to ride a bike," my legs
shook and my throat hurt.

He meant right then. He meant for me to get on and try
right that second.

My mother stood in the doorway saying "Mike, she doesn't
know howah" in her southern drawl, but my father meant
business.

"C'mon," he said, and wheeled the bike around to face the street.

I felt the immediate sting of tears but followed anyway. Between terror and drawing his rage, I chose terror.

My father kicked up the kickstand and held the handlebars and told me to get on. I did. He pushed us forward slowly and told me to put my feet on the pedals. But the pedals seemed like giant befuddlements to me, and they were going around in a way I couldn't understand, so my feet sort of interrupted them now and again like human clubs.

"Goddamn it, I said put your feet on the pedals."

Fear gripped my little chest, but fear of his anger again won. I put my feet on the pedals and tried to follow them round and round, looking straight down.

Still holding the handlebars, and walking us forward, my father said, "Now look up and put your hands on the handlebars. I put my hands near his – they looked like a doll's hands next to the meat of a father's. "I said look up, goddamn it, if you don't look where you are going you are going to crash."

Training wheels. Weren't there such a thing? Hadn't I seen them?

I put my hands on the handlebars. I looked up. My feet felt retarded – like heavy rocks going up and down. Then he let go of the handlebars and held on to the back of the bike. Briefly I wobbled and let go and tipped over. I fell knee first downward but he grabbed me by my shirt and lifted me upward. "Don't cry, for christ's sake," he said. "You better not cry."

Not crying, I could barely breathe.

We went through this routine up and down the street until the sun lowered. I remember thanking god for lowering the sun. Soon it would be dark, it would be dinner time, my mother would put plates out. I knew how to eat dinner.

But that was not what my father wanted.

On a pass close to the house, he turned me around and said, "Now we'll try the hill."

The hill was up the block from our cul-de-sac. I don't have any idea what the true grade was – but in the car coming home from swim practice my mother used the brakes. At the top of the hill was my beloved vacant lot. At the bottom was the right turn you had to make to get to our house.

My father had to push me up the hill. "Would you please pedal? For christ's sake."

When I say I thought I might vomit, I want to you understand. The vomit I was pretty sure I was about to spew felt like if it happened, my entire body would simply go inside out. That I'd puke so hard I'd puke my self. To this day I don't know why I wasn't crying at that point. I was silent. Just the breath of a girl pedaling up a hill.

At the top of the hill he turned me around on my beautiful bike and held the back of the seat. I remember shaking and staring down what looked pretty much like that moment on a roller coaster before the dive.

He said, "You back pedal to break it – little by little – as you pick up speed."

He said, "Down at the bottom you break enough to make a turn, and you turn. Left."

Incomprehensibly few words to me a girl.

Then I did the unthinkable. "Daddy, I can't do it."

My bottom lip kid quivering.

"You sure as hell can," he said, and pushed.

Psychedelic drugs put you in realms where language fails to describe emotion. I know this as an adult. What you think, what you feel, what happens to your body – your head, your arms and legs, your hands – goes into an alien dream. Your body disembodies. Your mind folds inward to the undiscovered geography of the brain. That's the best way I can describe the shape I was in when he pushed me down that hill. The endorphins of my terror induced an altered state.

At first I gripped the handlebars so hard my palms stung. I screamed all the way down. I backpedaled but it didn't seem to me like anything was slowing down. The possibility of stopping seemed like a lie. The possibility of turning right seemed like trying to ride to China.

Wind on my face my palms sting my knees hurt pressing backwards speed and speedspeedspeedspeed holding my breath and my skin tingling like it does up in trees terrible spiders crawling my skin like up high at the grand canyon my head too hot turnturnturnturnturn I am turning I am braking I can't feel my feet I can't feel my legs I can't feel my arms I can't feel my hands my head my heart my father's voice yelling good girl my father running down the hill my father who did this who pushed me my eyes closing my limbs going limp my letting go me letting go so sleepy so light floating floating objects speed eyes closed violent hitting objects crashing nothing.

I came to in my father's arms – he carried me into our house. I heard the worry in my mother's voice saying "Mike? Mike?" He carried me into my bedroom. She followed. He yelled "Get a flashlight." She yelled "What for? What's wrong?" He yelled "Get it goddamn it. I think she's hurt down there." She did. He laid me down on my princess canopy bed. I looked at the white lace. My hands between my legs. My mother returned with the flashlight. My father pulled my hands away and then pulled my pants down. My mother said "Mike?" I began to cry. Hurt where pee lives. My father pulled down my underwear. My mother said "Mike." My father spread my legs and turned on the flashlight and said, "She's bleeding." My mother crying my father saying "Dorothy go outside you are hysterical," my mother leaving. My father saying close the door goddamn it.

Weren't there things called doctors? Hospitals?

I'd crashed my bike into a row of mailboxes.

I'd ruptured my hymen.

My father's hands.

A flashlight.

Blood.

Girl.

The next day he made me get back on the bike after work. He made me go back to the top of the hill. It hurt so bad to sit on the bike I bit the inside of my cheek. But I did not cry. He said, "You have to get right back on and conquer your fear. You have to." Again he pushed me. Little girl not old enough to know her anger her fear her body sailing down the hill on her hot pink Schwinn, streamers flying.

Between terror and rage I chose rage.

Partway down the hill I thought of my father and how I hated the way his skin smelled like ash skin yellow cigarette stains on his fingers and his big architectural hands and his pushing me and I closed my eyes ... I closed them, I did, I let go of the handlebars and I put my hands out to the sides of my body. I felt the wind on my palms and fingers. On my face. My chest. Maybe blowing straight through my heart. I stopped breaking. My feet weightless.

I wiped out without making any turns toward our house. Though no bones were broken, I was scraped all over. My face. My elbows and arms. My knees and legs. My strong swimmer boy shoulders. All I was was my body. Bleeding. Bleeding.

But not crying.

For years and years, after that.

The Less Than Merry Pranksters

Bennett Huffman
Jeff Forester
Robert Blucher
Ben Bochner
James Finley
Lynn Jeffress
Neil Lidstrom
Hal Powers
Jane Sather
Charles Varani
Meredith Wadley
Ken Zimmerman
Lidia

Twelve last ditch disciples and me.

How I walked through the door of the 1988–89 collabora
tive novel writing workshop with Ken Kesey was that my writer
friend Meredith Wadley grabbed my hand and marched me into
the class without anyone's permission. Meredith seemed to
me like a cross between a gorgeous and complex Faulkner character with only the faintest hint of a southern drawl, and a
wealthy English equestrian champion. Meredith had a mane of
dark hair and even darker eyes. In her eyes there were electrical
sparks. On the day the "class" was to begin we were drinking
beers in her apartment. I admit it. I was jealous. Almost choke
on beer jealous. When it came time for her to go to the class, she

said, "Enough crappy things have happened to you. Come with me."

I said, "What? That's crazy. I'm not in the MFA program. I'm not even a grad student. They're not going to let me enroll."

If you look us up on Wikipedia it says the book we wrote was written collaboratively by Kesey and "13 graduate students." I was not an MFA student. I was an undergraduate sort of trolling in English and sleeping with lots of humans and riding the drug train and drinking drinking drinking. My athlete body was gone. I had grown big tits and something called "hips." I had a huge hunk of permed blond hair. I wasn't an accomplished writer. I wasn't an accomplished anything. The only thing I was good at was being a drunk or high cock tease, as near as I could tell. Why would they let me into their group? Why would Kesey?

"Bullshit," Meredith said, "Kesey is going to love you. Trust me. Plus you are a good writer. You already know half the people in the class. And anyway, you think Kesey gives a rat's ass about U of O rules?"

Blushing like an idiot, I let her march me down the road between the U of O and the Kesey house that would serve as the classroom for the year, and through the front door.

Sitting at a huge table were the disciples.

My throat shrunk to the circumference of a straw. I thought I might barf.

"Everyone, this is Lidia," Meredith said.

Great. Now I get to stand here like a moron and explain myself. I just stood there with a little ticker tape running inside my skull: thisiskenkeseythisiskenkesey. The books my father gave me. Sitting in a dark theater with my father watching the films. Paul Newman in *Notion*. *Cuckoo's Nest*.

Kesey, who was at the far end of the room, walked his barrel of a body straight over, pulled out a chair for me, and said, "Well HELLO. What do we have here? A triple A tootsie." It was the first time I'd seen him not in a photo or at some Oregon literary event. The closer he came, the more nauseous I felt. But when he got right up to me, I could see the former wrestler in his shoulders and chest. His face was moon pie round, his cheeks vividly veined and flushed, puffy with drink. His hair seemed like cotton glued in odd places on a head. His smile: epic. His eyes were transparent blue. Like mine.

My face got hot and the top of my head itched and all the others in the room looked like writers with special MFA badges while I felt like a human match. Like I might burst into a puny orange flame. While everyone was laughing about the tootsie remark he leaned down and whispered in my ear, "I know what happened to you. Death's a motherfucker."

In 1984, Kesey's son Jed, a wrestler for the University of Oregon, was killed on the way to a wrestling tournament when the team's bald-tired van crashed. My baby girl died the same year. Close to my ear, he smelled like vodka. Familiar.

He handed me a flask and we got along and bonded quickly the way strangers who've seen aliens can. That's all it took. No one ever questioned me, least of all Kesey. It was brilliantly incomprehensible to me. I loved it.

I was 25.

The first day of the collaborative novel writing workshop, Kesey brought out a brown cigar box and asked Jeff Forester to roll a joint. Jeff Forester had beautiful bleached brownblond curly hair and translucent eyes and tan skin. He looked like a surfer to me. But with a wicked vocabulary and mucho skill with words. Jeff didn't seem to bat an eyelash, he just rolled a perfect fattie, and Kesey began talking his Kesey talk, which began, "I've always hated sitting in a room with writers."

Bennett Huffman took a large toke from the christening joint and passed it. Bennett Huffman was tall and thin and light skinned. His quietness mesmerized me. While we were smoking in a round, Bennett closed his eyes, lost the color in his face, and fell to the ground – almost in slow motion. Passed out cold. I don't remember who expressed alarm. It was maybe a woman.

Like maybe we should call someone or do something. Beautiful Bennett there on the floor.

Kesey simply stepped over our comrade's body and kept talking, pausing only to say, "He'll be OK" Looking at us like don't you know that? It happens all the time. The distance between the 60s and 1988 was as wide as an ocean. You could tell by our clothes, the beer we drank, the I'm a U of O duck looks on our faces. There was no psilocybin, mescaline, or LSD glittering on the surface of our skin. There was no CIA-financed study on the effect of psychoactive drugs. To my knowledge, only one of us had been to rehab or jail, and I wasn't talking.

In my head I laughed my ass off while I sat and tried to write weird sentences so I wouldn't embarrass myself. I'd never been in any "class" like that in my life. But I'd failed several classes, and I'd flunked out of college before, and I'd been to institutional houses for bad behavior or instability already by then in my life, so this house seemed at least safe to me compared to the tyranny of others.

That first day we free-wrote in the house somebody – maybe Bochner – said, lamely, "I can't write on the spot like this." Bochner was sort of an aggressive hippie – the tree hugger with weaponry type. Kesey said: "Then write like a terrorist just busted in and threatened to kill you all – like you have a semi-automatic machine gun at your skull." And looked at us like we should already know that.

Kesey laid forth two rules: first, we could not talk the plot of the novel with anyone outside of the class; second, Kesey comprised 50 percent of the class. Later a third rule materialized: there could be no writing outside of class. Why? Because we'd do what Oregon writers do and become enamored with our individual voices.

Like with all cult famous folks, everyone in the collaborative novel writing class wanted to be the one Kesey liked best. But since we spent an entire year with him, that energy dissipated at least a little. We saw all the prescription medication he was on. We saw the true size of his gut. We saw how bad his allergies could get. We saw how much he slept. How he smelled. How little energy he seemed to have. How his eyes, when he drank, and he always drank, looked like swollen vodka marbles.

Still, his aura filled the room no matter what the room was. At a reading at U of O during that year he stood on a table and screaming into the microphone "Fuck You, god, Fuck You!" The crowd of about 500 burst into cheers. He believed in spectacle. In giving people the show.

In the fall of the year of Kesey I felt like an awkward jerkette most of the time. When we met as a group my ears kept getting hot and I'd make lines of sweat between my legs and sweat cups under each breast. I didn't know how to feel close to a group. My only model of group interaction was my dreaded Oedipal family death house. And swim teams. You don't talk to anyone when you are underwater. My distinguishing character- istics felt like tits and ass and blond. Sexual things. All I had.

I didn't feel like a terrorist was going to bust in and kill me, but I did feel like some kind of academic authenticity police were going to bust in and cuff me and say you, you don't belong here. You are not enrolled. You're not even in the writing pro- gram. Look at all that … hair. But it didn't happen. I just wrote things down on pieces of paper, like everyone else did.

I got the closest to Jeff and Bennett. Maybe that opening scene somehow imprinted on me – Jeff carefully rolling the joint. Bennett passing out like a reverse miracle.

The things I remember about everyone else are retinal flashes – how white Hal's hair was. How lithe Robert walked. How Jane's mind and sharp green stare intimidated me. How I wished Lynn had been my mother – a better more magnificent drinker than my own had been. How heavenly Meredith's ass, how Bochner became our Judas, how Charles became a cop and James had an impressive vocabulary to go with his blazing red hair, how Zimmerman appears elsewhere in this book.

In the winter of the year of Kesey we all went to his coast

house near Yachats together. A run down old place with wood paneling, a crappy stand up shower, a table with some chairs, and no heat. But the front windows looked out onto the ocean. And of course the rooms were filled with Kesey. We drank, we walked on the beach, we listened to Kesey stories. Look I'd tell you the stories but you already know them. And he'd say the same ones over and over again. We were, simply put, a pile of new ears. At the coast house we listened to stories about Tim Leary and Mason Williams and Jerry Garcia and Neal Cassady. At the coast house we got high, some of us fucked some others of us, we wrote in little notebooks. We slept on the floor in sleeping bags. We waited for something to happen.

I'm not sure if this is true; I'd have to call all 12 of them and take a poll. But I think we had a dumb hope the whole year. Our hope had nothing to do with the not very good at all book we were collaboratively writing. I think our hope was that Ken Kesey would write another perfect book. That he still had one in him and that we could somehow get it out. But all he kept doing was drinking. No amount of our getting high with him or walking the beach with him or listening to his stories could resurrect the man within the man.

Sometimes a Great Notion and *One Flew Over the Cuckoo's Nest* are on my bookshelf next to *As I Lay Dying*, *The Sound and the Fury*, and *Absalom, Absalom*. Some books take your breath away. Is it the books, or the writers? When I hold Kesey's books in my hands, when I open them, I can hear his voice. I can see him. Smell him. Feel him. But it's the words that take my breath. Isn't that enough?

In the spring of the year of Kesey, on Easter, we walked up Mt. Pisgah to Jed's resting place. Some of us were high on pot and some of us dropped acid and some of us ate mushrooms. And always Kesey drank from a flask. At the top the wind shuddered the leaves of trees. The mound of grass hill like one of Kesey's shoulders. I liked being up there. Jed underneath us. I felt most alive near death anyway. I just didn't talk about it much. Except a few times with Kesey. We embraced up there at one point.

Toward the end of the year of Kesey at his house in Pleasant Hill he showed all 13 of us video clips of Neal Cassady. I think Babbs brought them over. Some of us were high on pot and some of us dropped acid and some of us ate mushrooms. And always Kesey drank. Faye was in the kitchen, then she went to church. We sat on the floor we sat on old stuffed chairs we sat on a sunken couch.

When Neal Cassady came on the screen my chest filled with butterflies. He looked and acted exactly like a Kerouac sentence. The close up face of Neal Cassady ... all that random quixotic fantastic gibberish and eye shifting and head bobbing and facial tic-ery ... it was beautiful. Still though it seemed unreal, or surreal. We were nothing in the face of history but a bunch of waiting ducks. Someone could have picked us off one at a time in a pond. I sat there and wished our watching meant more.

I turned to look at Kesey watching Neal Cassady. The look on his face. Sitting there in the dark with the last ditch disciples. His smile was crooked – an inside joke kind of smile. His eyes narrowed. He chuckled once or twice. Then I saw him rub his forehead – no doubt a migraine – but in the glow of Neal Cassady it looked to me more like a man trying to rub out time.

The whole experience made me feel like Alice in Wonderland. How was it again I was in a room with Ken Kesey watching a video of Neal Cassady with a group of people who were "writers?" Who were we? After the video Ken talked a little and we asked him a few questions. Then he had to go to bed. It was 4:30 p.m. I felt like we'd failed at something but I had no idea what.

The end of the year of Kesey culminated in a reading and reception for the book in Gerlinger Lounge at U of O. We all wore 1930s vintage clothing to mimic the characters in the book. We drank peppermint schnapps one at a time from Kesey's flask, which sat up at the podium like a flag of his disposition.

We'd been interviewed by *People*. We'd had a photo in *Rolling Stone*. There were a few parties after that. I barely remember them.

My father actually flew up to Eugene from Florida to attend the reading. He sat in the audience in a $400 grey twill suit. He looked proud. Of something. In Kesey's presence. When I was born, we lived in a house in the hills over Stinson Beach. 1963. Close enough to ride a bike to La Honda, where Kesey began his parties and acid tests the same year.

When it was my turn to read I drank from the flask and looked out at the audience. My father's steely architectural gaze. His unforgettable hands. Then I looked at Kesey. He pinched his own nipples and smiled and made me laugh. At the end of the reading my father shook Kesey's hand and said "I'm a great admirer of yours." I knew it was true. I watched their hands press together.

When he met Kesey, my father's voice tremored. In parting, Kesey said to my father, "You know, Lidia can hit it out of the park." Having gotten as far as a tryout with the Cleveland Indians, that meant something to my father. The phrase, I mean.

The relatively crappy novel that came out of us, Caverns, was inspired by an actual news clipping, an Associated Press story on October 31, 1964 entitled "Charles Oswald Loach, Doctor of Theosophy and discoverer of so-called 'SECRET CAVE OF AMERICAN ANCIENTS,' which stirred archaeological controversy in 1928." Set in the 1930s, Loach is imagined as a convicted murderer who is released from San Quentin Prison, in the custody of a priest, to lead an expedition to rediscover the cave.

It isn't a very good novel. Whatever it was we entered, it wasn't a novel. And if we followed an ex-con priest into a cave, all we found was sea lion excrement.

I don't know if the posse would agree with me on this, but it seemed to me like what we'd entered that year was an ending. The most extreme part or point of something. Or a small piece of something that is left after it has been used. Or perhaps it was simply Kesey's last act – to further his own end.

Every Oregon writer has a Kesey story. I'm serious – go to literary readings in Oregon and 85 percent of the time his name will rise, whether or not whoever is speaking knew him. Sometimes it's about his house in Pleasant Hill. Sometimes it's about the bus. Sometimes it's about writing. Sometimes it's about his "wild spirit." Often, if I'm in the audience, it gives me a stomachache to hear his name used in such ... soft and impotent ways.

I think that everyone that knew Kesey knew him differently. Maybe that's true about all larger than life people, or it may be that no one really ever knows them at all – we just have experiences near them and claim them as our own. We say their names and wish that something intimate is coming out of our mouths. But intimacy isn't like in books or movies.

It wasn't until the following year, the year that was not the collaborative writing class, the year after the book we wrote that was not very good came out that made me feel like we'd utterly failed Kesey, the year after he'd ended up in the Mayo clinic for his affair with his lover, vodka, we met once at his coast house by ourselves.

That night he boiled water and cooked pasta and dumped a jar of Ragu on it and we ate it with bent old forks. We drank whiskey out of tin cups. He told life stories. That's what he was best at. Me? I didn't have any stories. Did I? When it got dark he lit some crappy looking ancient candles. We sat in two wooden chairs next to each other looking out at the moonlit water. I distinctly remember trying to sit in the chair older and like I had been part of history. Which amounted to extending my legs out and crossing one ankle over the other and crossing my arms over my chest. I looked like Abe Lincoln.

Then he said, "What's the best thing that's ever happened to you in your life?"

I sat there like a lump trying to conjure up the best thing that had ever happened to me. We both already knew what the worst thing was. Nothing best had happened to me. Had it? I could only answer worst. I looked out at the ocean.

Finally I said, "Swimming."

"Why swimming?" he said, turning to look at me.

"Because it's the only thing I've ever been good at," came out of my mouth.

"That's not the only thing you are good at." And he put his huge wrestler writer arm around me.

Fuck. This is it. Here it comes. His skin smelled … well it smelled like somebody's father's skin. Aftershave and sweat and whiskey and Ragu. He's going to tell me I'm good at fucking. He's going to tell me I'm a "tootsie" – the nickname he'd used on me the year of the class. And then I'm going to spread my legs for Ken Kesey, because that's what blond clueless idiots do. I closed my eyes and waited for the hands of a man to do what they did to women like me.

But he didn't say any of those things. He said, "I've seen a lot of writers come and go. You've got the stuff. It's in your hands. What are you going to do next?"

I opened my eyes and looked at my hands. They looked extremely dumb. "Next?" I said.

"You know, in your life. What's next?"

I didn't have a plan. I had grief. I had rage. I had my sexuality. I liked books more than people. I liked to be drunk and high and fuck so I didn't have to answer questions like this.

As I'm telling this I realize there is another way to tell it. Tenderly. Quiet and small. The question he asked me. It's what a loving father should ask.

Or I could lie. I could render an epic psychedelic love affair. Or hot older man younger woman sexcapades. I could write anything. Maybe there are a million ways to tell it.

Kesey was the best liar I ever met in my life.

When I got home I cut all the hair off on the left side of my head, leaving two different women looking at me in the mirror. One with a long trail of blond half way down her back. The other, a woman with hair cropped close to her head and with the bone structure of a beautiful man in her face.

Who.

Am.

I.

Back at U of O I went to classes. Once in the creative writing department a man big as a wrestler walked by me staring at my uneven head hair and kinda banged into my shoulder. Must be a writer. Who gives a shit about writers. Not me. Keep walking. But my heart nearly beat itself up in my chest.

I never saw Kesey again. His liver failed and he got Hepatitis C. In 1997 he had a stroke. Later he got cancer and died. But I'm of the opinion he drowned.

There are many ways to drown.

III. The Wet

A Happy Childhood

I AM SIX.

My friend Katie in the water my friend Christie in the water Phantom Lake Bath and Tennis Club and summer is every day every single day in the water we swim in the morning we swim in the daytime we swim in the afternoon we swim at night we swim every day we eat rainbow popsicles we eat fudgesicles creamsicles we go and go underwater laps hold your breath back and forth and back again three times no boys we stay underwater swim goggles look at each other blow your air out sit on the bottom we dive from the low dive we dive from the high dive we find pennies at the bottom of the deep end we laugh and laugh we race at swim meets in evening we race we win and win little gold medals beautiful blue ribbons we dive off of starting blocks we fly in the air we enter the water with the glee of girl splashing.

I AM EIGHT.

My sister my adoration my sister my awe my sister's room world of art world of music world of poetry and dried flowers and watercolor covers and long auburn hair.

I AM 10.

Vacationing at Salishan. My father calm, cigarette smoke curling around his head as he gazes out at the Oregon ocean. My mother humming. My sister and I swimming in the pool of a resort, laughing, like other peoples' children.

I AM 11.

    I play clarinet with my friend Brody and we tap our feet three-quarter time our mouths around the instruments our fingers between the struggle of learning and the dance of music our knees our lives nearly touching.

I AM 13.

    The family of my friend Christie my best friend my world miraculously take me on their camping trips with them in their big Winnebago at night in the little Winnebago attic where we slept in our sleeping bags I stare at her while she sleeps my skin hot and itching I have to pee I put my hands between my legs like an anxious little monkey I go to sleep I pee my pants hide my PJ's in one of the stow cupboards in the Winnebago and listen to her parents all day wonder "What smells like fish?" and Christie smiles and we run and play with frogs in the weeds knee-deep in the water of our lives.

I AM 15.

    In the women's locker room after swim practice and skin and wet. Little girls holding in youth in V-shaped torsos. Almost women shaving their legs. The bodies of women and girls safe in a room with heat and steam and let loose hair. My head swimming, swimming. I want to stay. I want to belong to something besides family.

Illness as Metaphor

KISSED A GIRL AND MADE ME CRY.

When I kissed Annie Van Leewan and got mononucleosis I was 11 years old. My skin took on a yellowish pale color and the blue veins in my own hands looked as if I'd colored them with one of my father's architectural felt tipped markers. I lost 10 pounds the first week and a half. My eyesight became slightly blurry. I had none of my swimmer strength – I remember wondering where it went – why couldn't I lift my own arms? What had happened to my legs? I could not get out of bed or stand without fainting. I could not eat, or walk, or go to the bathroom, or dress, undress, on my own. I could not bathe. I could not reach water.

My mother at that time was in the prime of her real estate glory. My father at that time had chosen to try his luck as a freelance architect. His office the bedroom next to mine – the room that had been my sister's. Before she left. In other words, it was my father who was home with me. For four weeks.

I'm trying to think how to tell you how four weeks can be years. It isn't possible, I know. But it happened. It's language that's letting me say that the days elongated, as if the very sun and moon had forsaken me. It's narrative that makes things open up so I can tell this. It's the yielding expanse of a white page.

In my sickbed my father removed my sweat soaked clothing. My father redressed me in underwear and pretty nightgowns. My father stroked my hair. Kissed my skin. My father carried me to the bathtub and laid me down and washed me.

Everywhere. My father dried me off in his arms and redressed me and carried me back to the bed. His skin the smell of cigarettes and Old Spice cologne. His yellowed fingers. The mountainous callous on his middle finger from all the years of holding a pen or pencil. His steel blue eyes. Twinning mine. The word "Baby."

Late at night, my mother would come home from selling beautiful homes to other people. She would come into my room and sing I see the moon. And kiss me. And say, "Don't you cry, Belle, everything's gonna get better. You'll see." And leave early the next morning.

There is only one other time in my life that I have experienced the delirium I entered during those weeks. Because there are times when a soul has to leave a body, times that are not death. Some people know this like a hymn. I knew she – my body – was still there, but I left her lifeless in the arms of a father.

I went into a white. Inside the white, there were sunflowers. And lapis colored glass. And deep aqua pools. There were beautiful rocks everywhere – but you had to find them. Small and exquisite journeys that took all day. Like in a very good dream. Inside the white too there were stories. As if written on the walls or floors or sky of the white. The words. You could see them. Reach out and touch them. Just like the rocks. You could pick up the rocks or words and carry them. Sometimes the wordrocks sang. After a while I believed in them more than my own life. I thought, it would be possible, even beautiful, to die.

But even girls whose strength has abandoned them are made to come back. And so I began to eat again. Taking the fork or spoon from my father's hand. I began to get up out of my bed and walk – wondering, is this what my mother felt like after all those months as a girl in a body cast, finally touching the floor and moving her legs, breathing in something called will? And mercifully. I again entered the water. To swim. Away from my father's house, every day I swam a tiny piece of self returned. And the strength of ... the strength of a girl.

Everything about him was in his hands.

A Burning

WHEN I WAS 13 I CONFESSED MY FATHER SECRETS IN the black box of catholic to another father in the house of our father who told me I should not tell lies.

Honor thy father.

Say seven Hail Marys.

It's wicked to make up stories.

For three days and three nights I prayed to the thing called god so hard I choked on the spit in my mouth. I clenched my hands until they went red. I dug my fingernails into flesh so hard little scarlet moons appeared. I shut my eyes so tight I thought my forehead would bleed. My head, my heart, everything on the inside was burning.

No matter how many times I entered the cool waters of the pool, I left the wet with a fire in me.

Mercy did not come from god the father. Mercy came from a book. That was the year I read *Saint Joan of Arc* by Vita Sackville-West. My sister gave me the book when she left our father's house.

At 13, I found most of the book terrifying. And I had to skip many words and pages that I did not understand. But I already knew who Joan of Arc was, because my sister had explained it to me. Girl woman with a war in her. Voice of a father in her head. And so I knew if I kept reading I would come to her burning. I didn't want to and I couldn't not.

Joan of Arc's burning scene is on page 341. Instead of a crown of thorns they placed a tall paper cap on her head. She did not die until the fire reached her head. People saw all kinds of things – one person saw a dove leaving her skull. Despite the oil, sulphur and fuel used, her entrails and heart would not go to ash. The executioner had to throw them in the Seine.

I could see her. How it looked. How it smelled. How her hair went to flame. How the bone form of her skull appeared, until her jaw and teeth shown, a terrible smile or a scream, before she burned to crap.

I'm 13 reading that. Honor thy father. It is wicked to make up stories.

I'm the rest of my life a burning girl.

That image of Joan of Arc burning up in a fire burned inside me like a new religion. Her face skyward. Her faith muscled up like a holy war. And always the voice of a father in her head. Like me. Jesus. What is a thin man pinned to wood next to the image of a burning woman warrior ablaze? I took the image of a burning woman into my heart and left belief to the house of father forever.

I didn't hate the fire. I hated the people who did not believe her. And I hated the father that let her burn. And I hated the men who … I think I hated men. The more I was around them, the more I came close to spontaneously combusting. Drawing them dangerously close to the flame.

The Hairy Girls

GIRL SWIMMERS ARE HAIRY.

I don't know how much you know about these things, but competition swimmers don't shave their legs unless they are preparing for the big meet, Regionals, State, Senior Nationals, for instance. So when I was a girl who barely had any hairs looking up at the towering corpus of Nancy Hogshead from the puny viewpoint of the pool, their leg hair was downright scary. And they had pube hair sticking out of their suits up at the top of their thighs and going into their business. Boy. Talk about terrifying.

OK that's a lie. It wasn't terrifying. It was mesmerizing. I couldn't stop staring. It made me into a mouth breather.

When Jo Harshbarger showered in the locker rooms, all I saw was her legs as something I longed to pet, and her stuff as a little furry special place, especially since as a girl I was afraid to look at tits or twats or even faces.

That's a lie too. I stared at tits and coochie as hard as a drunk eyeballing a fifth of vodka.

These hairy women – they were – they were mythic. As a kid, I had no idea what they were in real life – students, girl-friends of something, females who used hand-held hairdryers, people who shopped at the mall with purses and drove cars around – but at the pool and in the locker rooms they were mythic. I think that's why I remember so many of their names, these

larger than life to a kid women – Jo Harshbarger and Evie Kosenkranius and Karen Moe and Shirley Babashoff.

Lynn Collella Bell.

I used to walk around the locker rooms and toddle
dreamily out to my mom's car looking up at the sky with
LynnCollellaBellLynnCollelaBellLynnCollellaBell making song
loops in my skull. LynnColllelaBell with the broadest shoulders
and teeniest hips I'd ever seen. Making me hippoventate.

Is it any wonder that by the time I was 12 I could barely
keep from biting one of them? All that flesh and wet. Me standing forever in the hot shower staring and staring and I'm pretty
sure drooling … it's a wonder I didn't pass out in all the dreamy
steam and crack my skull open.

For a long time I thought there was something wrong with
me that I wanted to lunge at one of them and hump them like a
little monkey. At home, in bed, alone, I'd get on my stomach and
butterfly kick my bed to death. Or maul a pillow grinding my
hips and clenching my knees around it. Finally it got so frustrat-
ing – this whatever it was I had in me – I had to resort to hair
care items like brushes and combs and rubber bands. Snap.

Yeah? Have you ever tried it? Then shut up.

You know, now that I'm thinking of it, it didn't even occur
to me to put something UP IN THERE. I didn't get my period
until I was much older due to my athlete body, and no one, not
my mother, not my sister, not any of my friends, not my swim
coach bothered to explain the manwoman sex thing to me.
I mean of course I figured it out later, what with television and
film and so forth, and my slutty friend Kelly Gates who
explained it to me while I barfed a little in my own mouth, but
for a good long while, and you know, even today if I sit too close
to one, I thought I might die from wanting to rub myself raw on
a girl.

Look I'm trying to say I didn't have little girl crushes like
you are imagining. And I didn't have the cliché swimmers are all
dykes deal – though lots of swimmer girls regularly spanked

twinkies, I was to learn later – no, it was much more serious. I mean I was in pain. Whatever blue balls were, I was pretty sure I had them. Every day at practice, in the showers, with all that girl stuff right in front of my face. All the soaped up torsos and boobs, all the uninhibited washing of you know whats, the bubbles sliding down their asses and legs. If a kid could coronary from want, I'd be a dead woman.

No, I didn't want to have a slumber party. I didn't want to go to the mall.

I wanted to use my hair brush and rubberbands and make someone . . . whimper.

I did consider girls my age. Evie Kosenkranius had a kid sister my age. Tina Kosenkranius. I ... christ. Will you look at those names? I can't even look at those names today without going all porno in my head – hey, Evie Kosenkranius has a sister. I mean my god, why couldn't I just be a 16 year old blond boy with raging hormones and a spanky new flagpole that everyone wants to sit on?

But I wasn't. I was me, a painfully shy girl kid with a hidden girl bomb in her panties not knowing what the hell to do with it who really, really wanted to ... eat someone.

OF COURSE I tried the neighborhood girls my age. I'd invite them into my room to play doctor and they'd just lie there, letting me do anything, sometimes giggling, until they clamped their legs shut. The best I could get out of the deal was to put a blanket over us so the smell would intensify. Something like hay and apples. Then they'd get dressed and want to go do something dumb that girls do. Like ice skating or talking on the phone or mall bullshit.

What I needed was a girl who was older than me. Bigger.

Sienna Torres was a troublemaker young woman from a troubled household making trouble wherever she went. She broke the rules at school, she broke them at home, she broke them at Albertson's and Nordstrom and 7-Eleven, and she broke them at swim practice. She came late, she skipped laps, she got swatted with a kickboard in what was perversely known as "licks" for her rebelliousness.

I was terrified of her. The missing ingredient.

Sienna Torres was always late to practice but the much more important thing was that she was always the last one to get dressed. No matter how slowly I dressed, no matter how much I tried to comb and blow-dry my fuzzy white non hair (which took about 20 seconds), I was always dressed light years ahead of her. This meant that all I got was Sienna Torres in my Mom's rearview sauntering out of the building where a couple of boymen would be loitering. Sienna Torres getting smaller and smaller in the rearview until she was gone, and I was just a stupid kid in the back seat of a car I couldn't drive. My hands shoved between my legs. My face red.

Sienna Torres was 17 and came to practice with vodka on her breath. I knew it was vodka because her face and skin smelled like my mother's minus the Estée Lauder. Plus I'd see a flask in her swim bag sometimes. Also black lace panties and a black silk bra and a curling iron and mascara and car keys and cigarettes and Diet Pepsi and tampons and lip gloss and a Walkman and Certs and a very large ... hairbrush. I was 12. I was 13. I was 15. I was 35. See? I can't even remember just from writing about her. She made my breath jackknife every time I was anywhere near her. She made my mouth water. She made me dizzy.

Then a miracle happened. Coming out of the pool and on the way to the locker rooms one evening, I slipped and fell on my ass, spraining my ankle. Not bad enough to alert medics, but bad enough to get attention. A lot. Think about this. Not only did I have every girl swimmer in locker room heaven taking care of me, helping me to shower and get dressed, but when they finally believed I could handle the rest on my own, there were only two of us left in the entire locker room.

Uh huh, that's right. Me and Sienna Torres.

Sienna Torres was still in the shower, and all I had left was my shoes. So while I tied the slowest, like retard slow, most careful giant looped bow on one of my sneakers, over and over again, I watched Sienna Torres shave her pussy in the shower.

Soaping up the triangle, her hand making circles where I wanted to put my face. One foot up on the shower stand, her toes curled around the faucet, a palm sized peach peeking out from between her legs. A razor making paths through the white drifts of suds, then nothing but skin folding inward to that dark and daring other mouth.

I'm pretty sure at some point I went cross-eyed.

Terror takes strange shape in a horny girl. It weaves it way up her boy butt and up the V of her torso and settles in her shoulders and jaw so she can't act right or talk without twitching. After Sienna finished and dried off and put most of her clothes on and blow dried her hair and put rings back on her fingers, when I finished tying the one shoe and tucked the shoe laces in on the other and then pretended my swim bag had something confounded in it, I hop hobbled over to her. She was pulling her hoodie down over her black bra. She was running her ringed fingers through her blow-dried feathered hair. She was turning her head to look at me – only a few inches down from her. Her quadruple pierced ears staring at me going, what?

I may have been excruciatingly shy but I had a gushing in me the size of a swimming pool and I was smart – smart as any of those goddamned boys loitering outside the building – who I suddenly wished were dead – so I said, not quite believing my mouth would even work, "Um, can you help me?" Holding one foot slightly off the ground.

Sienna putting all her crap in her bag not looking at me.

Me waiting in the dead air like a little lost comma.

Sienna taking a hit off of her flask, then without warning, pushing it over at me, saying "This will cut the pain, I bet." Smiling her Sienna Torres smile. "Can you handle it?"

You have no fucking idea how close I came to lunging at her leg and humping it like a little monkey. You have no idea how close I came to sucking on her hip bone and crying "mamma."

But I didn't do those things. Sometimes you grow up in the space of a minute.

I quite calmly took a big old swig of vodka viper's flask just like my genetic code knew I could, and I never took my eyes off of her watching me, and I liked it, her watching I mean, because it certainly wasn't the taste of vodka, which though I didn't show it, like at all, tasted like what I suspected Estée Lauder must taste like if you drank it.

Then she said, "Being bad is good, huh." And laughed. I bit the inside of my cheek trying not to cough or barf. Trying to be bad, good.

And then Sienna Torres put her arm around my waist. And I put my arm around her shoulders and neck. And I could smell her skin. I didn't bite her or anything. I didn't hump her like a little monkey. And she helped me all the way to my mom's car which miraculously didn't kill me with embarrassment, bypassing the boymen waiting for her as always.

I was so happy in the back seat of my mom's car I thought I might make a water shit in my pants. I watched her in the rearview but this time she watched back. I was drunk with her touching me. I could still smell her: chlorine and vodka and Nivea and sh sh sh shaving cream and Suave conditioner. Nothing, nothing nothing nothing else went in my head all night, all week, all the next year. But that night, about halfway home, I reached down and felt something in my sweatshirt front pocket. I slyly put my hand in there behind the head of my driving mother.

It was Sienna's flask.

Nemesis

ANGER IS FUNNY.

It sits snarling in you your whole life just waiting for perfect ironic moments to emerge. Wanna know why I got a Ph.D. in literature? Because in the graduate fiction workshop at the University of Oregon Chang Rae Lee told me my story was "trite." I had infiltrated the writing workshops as a grad student in literature because I couldn't stop wanting to write stories after the Kesey thingee. When Chang Rae Lee told me my story and its sentiments were trite, know what I thought? I thought I wish I'd meet you in a dark Eugene alley out the back door of a bar so I could punch your smug face in you little prick.

I'm not saying I'm proud of that. I'm just saying that if the things we really thought showed up on paper we'd all be ... way busted.

All that day I stomped around fuming the fumes of a woman who doesn't know how to own her own intellect and blames it on men. I knew how to make a sentence hum. But my Kesey credentials didn't get me very far, I hate to say. Pretty much everyone at U of O who wasn't in that wild wonderful "class" hated everyone who was, and thus belittled the crap out of us. Punks. Plus our "novel" was a piece of crap so I simply had no literary currency. The story that had drawn such condescending mouth poo from Chang Rae Lee was from the point of view of Caddy from *The Sound and the Fury*. One of the last things I said to Kesey was how I wanted to write that story – probably every young woman who reads it wants to – so I did, and that's what I brought into the MFA workshop. And that's what Chang Rae Lee called "trite."

As I made my way through literary history as a graduate literature duck I also wrote a story from the point of view of Dora. Joan of Arc. Emma Bovary. Hester Prynne. Helen of Troy. Sade's mistress. Medusa. Eve. And the statue of liberty. Notice a motif?

In my story, Caddy is in the present. She lives next door to a tard neighbor boyman. Because she is sexually insatiable, and because he both scares her with his too white skin and his too big for his body head and his giant pants bulge and the sounds that come out of him instead of language and his pure physical brute force, she goes over to his house one day and takes her clothes off in front of him.

He bellows that Benjy bellow.

Then he attacks her and fucks her and nearly crushes her.

She loves it. She laughs until she cries and an ambulance comes.

Trite.

So after fantasizing about the dark alley and stomping around and cursing all things Chang Rae Lee that day, I decided to get a Ph.D.

Fuck all y'all "writers." Woo Hoo.

I took a break from creative writing workshops – though I have to tell you – I positively HAUNTED the halls of the creative writing department. I don't know why. I'd just find myself there, looking at bulletin boards, seeing what readings were coming up, grabbing random fliers from the office nerds. Twice I walked by a gorgeous tall guy with a ponytail who looked seriously like Marlon Brando but I didn't talk to him. Writing student.

Sometimes the choices we make come from jealous lame petty places. But they are as real as it gets.

I entered the Ph.D. program. I went on to gloriously immerse myself in Derrida and Lacan and Kristeva and Foucault.

In Homi K. Bhabha and Ed Said and Gayatri bad ass Chakra-
vorty Spivak. In Dickinson and Whitman and Plath and Sexton
and Adrienne you want some of this Rich and Ai and Eliot and
PoundBeckettStoppardDurasFaulknerWoolfJoyce (though he
kinda always made me want to piss on his grave) SyngeCortazar
BorgesMarquezClariceL'InspecteurHenryMillerAnaissexatious
NinDerekWalcottBertoltBrechtPynchonSilko WintersonDjuna
BarnesOscarWildeGertrudethemanSteinFlannerymotherfuck-
ingO'ConnorRichardWrightBaldwinToniMorrisonRayCarverJohn
CheeverMaxineHongKingstonSapphireDennisCooperKathy-
youmakemefeellikemyskinisbeingsheeredoffAcker – cascades
of authors kicking Chang Rae Lee's scrawny little ass. Take that.

Yeah. Up until he won the PEN/Hemingway Award in 1995
and it was his book I was assigned to read. I can't tell you how
great that felt. But what nagged at me no matter how far into the
literary intellectual pool I ventured, no matter how well I swam
its waters, was the story I had yet to write. Itching my fingers
like fire.

Two terms later, I tried again. Graduate fiction writing
workshop. This time the story I brought in wasn't about voiceless
women characters from literary history. This time the story was
about my life. About fathers and swimming and fucking and dead
babies and drowning. Written entirely in random fragments –
how I understood my entire life. In the language – image and frag-
ment and non-linear lyric passages – that seemed most precise.
The story I brought in was called "The Chronology of Water."

Something was coming out of my hands. Something about
desire and language.

Chang Rae? Sorry I thought those things. Thanks for piss-
ing me off all those years ago. Beautiful random nemesis.

Love Grenade II

WHEN I FIRST MET HANNAH IN GRADUATE SCHOOL I WAS a woman gone numb. I would do anything. Anytime. Anywhere.

I was using my body as a sexual battering ram. On anyone and anything available. In fact, you might say I sexualized my entire existence. It seemed to work a lot like alcohol and drugs. If you did it enough, you didn't have to think or feel anything but MMMMM good.

Hannah was one of those lesbians who looks like a beautiful boy – hazel eyes, that cool short curtain of hair hanging over one eye, broad shoulders, little hips, barely there titties. More like M&Ms. Hannah played basketball and softball and soccer when she wasn't being a Eugene lesbo and English grad student. She used to wait for me by my blue Toyota pickup truck between classes and hijack me and drive me to the coast, where we'd stay up all night getting it on in the back of my truck, drinking Heinekens and waiting for the sun to come up. Then we'd drive back and go to class. Or I would. Hannah thought grad school was kind of lame. She much preferred sex and club dancing.

So when Hannah captured me and my best friend Claire in the hall after our 18th-Century Women Writers seminar by grabbing our wrists and pulling us toward the wall, I already knew it would be something sly. She smiled her sly Hannah smile and whispered, "Wanna go to the coast? I got us a room."

Claire blinked so blankly her eyes looked like a doll's, and

I think I coughed academically. But I have to admit it. My crotch went messy pretty much that instant.

Listen, you probably think you wouldn't, but I'm telling you, if Hannah said get in my truck we're going to the coast, raising her little trickster eyebrow and putting her hand right underneath your breast and against your first couple of ribs, going, I dare you, you'd go.

Women go the See Vue Inn because of the themed rooms. The Secret Garden Suite (private garden). The Crow's Nest (nautical). The Salish (Native American). Princess and the Pea (weirdly medieval). Mountain Shores (rustica). Far Out West (cowgirl). The Cottage (you get the "house" to yourself).

We had The Cottage.

The little cottage sported a fireplace, so I said don't do anything without me and drove off to get firewood. When I got back, the door was open. I went in. The two of them were in bed with the covers pulled up just underneath their tits – Hannah's M&Ms and Claire's glorious pendulous globes, smiling like Cheshire cats. Cheshire cats who had licked pussy. And in the middle of the bed was a little suitcase that Hannah brought – filled with toys.

I immediately dropped the wood on the floor, shut the door, and stripped, launching myself onto the bed like superwoman.

Whoever was staying in the Princess and the Pea or the Salish or the Far East, they must've gotten an earful. Hours of woman on woman on woman whose regular lives didn't allow for such wild abandon. Sometimes Hannah's fist up my cunt Claire's mouth on mine or me sucking her epic tits. Sometimes Hannah on her stomach me up her ass with a strap on Claire behind me giving me a reach around – a skill she intuited. Sometimes Claire on all fours me and Hannah filling every hole licking every mouth rubbing her clit making her scream making her entire corpus shiver her head rock back her woman wail let loose gone primal cum and shit stains and spit and tears. I came in Hannah's mouth, her face between my legs like some goddess in a new myth. Claire came with Hannah's fingers in her ass and pussy, her body convulsing and falling off the bed, me wrapped around her and laughing and hitting my head on the wall. Hannah came jamming a dildo up herself while I buried my face in the clit of her. She pulled my hair. She pushed my head. Claire curled under me licking and gagging but not not not stopping. I don't know how many times we came ... it seemed unending.

We ate each other we ate pickled herring we ate gruyere cheese. We ate the animal out of each other's bodies we ate steak we ate chocolate two women my chocolate. We drank each other we drank all the beer we drank all the wine we peed outside. We got high on skin and cum and sweat we got high on pot. We came in waves we ran out and into the waves.

I wanted to stay like that forever outside of any "relationship" I had ever had and inside the wet of an unnamed sexuality. The moon a grand spectator. As full of alive as the ocean outside the door. All the night it was difficult to tell whose body was whose. The woman of it drowned me. It nearly cleaved my mind. And again. Again. Waves.

I don't know why women can't make the story do what they want.

I don't.

When we got back to our ordinary lives, Claire told me she was in love with me. A sentiment I couldn't find in myself to return, hard as I tried. I wish I could go back and try. It was real, what she offered. But kindness wasn't something I even recognized.

A Body in a Kayak

WITH HANNAH, IT TOOK ME WEEKS TO FIGURE OUT IF she was attracted to me or just really pissed off – her jokes always seemed a little mean, always left me feeling like a female headed slow-poke. Sometimes she'd charley horse me good ones in the arm or thigh hard enough to leave a lump. It didn't weird me out. Unlike everything else, I could feel it.

Once she bit my cheek so hard I sat in my classes the next week looking like I'd been mauled by a chimp. When she bit my cheek? I laughed so hard I cried.

I never thought Hannah was hurting me when she'd do things like shove me up against a wall for fun hard enough to ache my shoulderblades. I felt like I had pain in me that needed to come out. More and more I wished for the force of her. She'd drink my vodka from the bottle and we'd go for long walks at night in the graveyard next to the college and fuck on the stones of dead folks. After she'd flip silver dollars in the air and we'd lay on our backs and watch bats dive at them. I'd talk about dead things. She'd let me.

A few months in to our whatever it was she walked up to me and whispered, I signed us up for kayaking.

?

The U of O pool is where I first made Jr. Nationals as a teen. The pool had not changed – a slimy chlorine hell with Disney ducks painted on the walls. We were two of three women in the class. The third, big red, was 6′ 2″ with a mane of red hair all the way to her ass. I had a hard time not touching her hair. In our giant fiberglass kayaks we learned kayaky things from our instructor, Jeff. In our cockpits. Things like the life-saving Eskimo roll. Hoping to master an ender. A pry stroke. A put in. A wet exit. Hannah learned fast because she was a tomboy woman, and I learned fast because anything in the water felt like home.

Our last class in the pool our instructor put each of us one at a time on the end of the diving board, kayak noses pointing forward, and then he grabbed the back end and heaved so we went in nose first and hard. The idea being that you'd immediately be upside down underwater and have to practice your Eskimo roll. I loved it. Not the life saving part. I loved being pitched over the edge and being upside down underwater. I asked Jeff to do it again and again. Harder, I'd say, and Jeff would shove me off the board. I'd stay under for as long as I could – sometimes until I heard Hannah or Jeff yelling my name.

At the end of the five weeks our instructor took us all to the McKenzie River for our "final." Little bit of speed in the alley, little bit of whitewater for excitement. I decided that day it would be a really good idea to get incredibly high just before I met up with Hannah at the river's edge.

On the forest trail to the put in I remember Hannah being annoyed with me, because it took me too long to put my life jacket on and too long to secure my paddle into my kayak and too long to pick my kayak up and trudge down the forest trail to the put in as I stopped and turned to look at things and got the kayak tip caught in bushes and w o w look at my own magnificent red converse sneakers a step at a time in front of me making a rhythm and cottonwood blowing around like summer snow and look at the intriguing hats in the branches no wait those are BIRDS and stopping and laughing until she came back for me going WHAT ARE YOU DOING, EXACTLY? My kayak in the dirt.

Eye to eye, she saw it. Christ Lidia, you are high. What the fuck? You have to go in the water. To my huhuhuhuhuhuh.

So she slapped me hot and hard right on the cheek.

Time stopped. I'm pretty sure my pupils pinned. I saw stars. I liked it. For a split second I felt alive. I wanted her to do it again. Harder. But I didn't say anything.

Hannah turned and picked up her kayak and left the trail in the trees, making for the rocks near the river's edge. We could see the rest of our class up ahead – some on the rocks, some in the water. Still stunned into focus, at the point where the rocks met the water I saw a dead steelhead, half in water, half out. Even dead, she was something. The silver and black and blue sheen of her body, the white of her underbelly. She smelled like ocean. "She" because of her split open belly, and the dried up jelly of sunburned eggs on the rocks. I had a hard time not looking.

LIDIA. Hannah calling.

No one seemed to notice we were a little late, they just dipped in and paddled around like spinning ducks in a big pool of slow water, their shiny bright colored helmets looking like Easter eggs to me. Big red's hair briefly mesmerized me, as usual, and I reached my hand out to touch it, but Hannah pinched my arm where fat grows and I got clear again. In we went, Hannah ahead of me, me getting a little too interested in the black lines on the ends of my paddle. Huhuhuhuhuhuh. I had my bright blue tard helmet on backwards but no one noticed.

My feet and legs stretching out the front of the kayak seemed easy to forget existed. The slow water curled long left then slow right, around giant boulders that I knew had steel-head in the eddies. The tree leaves hanging over the water quivered. It smelled like river – dirt and fish and wet and algae. I put my instructional paddle across the skirt over my lap and let my hands trail in the cold dark wet. I closed my eyes. I leaned my head back, up toward the sun, the skin on my face hot, my hands in the water cold. I thought I might be touching bliss. A surface I'd not felt in years. Then I heard my name too loudly and looked up to see Hannah looking back at me: LIDIA. PAY ATTENTION. Too late, Hannah. Too late.

When we hit the whitewater, instead of the lane we were

supposed to navigate, I went down the one that was out of our league. Look at all the pretty white. Like lace. I smiled. I didn't make one paddle stroke how I'd been taught. Instead, I lifted my paddle into the air and laughed, and I heard Jeff's voice going LIDIA and Hannah's voice going LIDIA but I was laughing, so the power current took me into a spin and I traveled backwards for a bit and then down and sideways and then right over, my shiny blue helmeted head going down and down. I didn't have to think about taking an enormous gulp of air first. It's in my DNA.

Upside down underneath the water holding my breath things became oddly calm. You'd think you wouldn't be able to see shit, but the water is icy and green colored clear up where we were on the McKenzie. And the underwater blur isn't as pronounced as you might think. But it does make your eyes feel like ice cubes.

The boulders bigger than bodies rose up dark black jade and shimmered with the sun moving through layers of deep water. I could see the bottom of the river. Rocks, sand and plant life moving and moving by. More than one steelhead shaped itself, their dark shadow selves doing that thing where they water-hover in the current moving only their tails. The cold water made my temples pound. My heart beat me up in my chest and eardrums the way it does when you are running out of air. My lungs burned. My hands went numb. I closed my eyes.

Something – I think a rock – scraped my paddle. Oh. Yeah. My paddle.

I didn't think get yourself upright, dumbass. My arms simply lifted to position until I could see the lines of my instructional paddle – exactly as they should be. I definitely had the right grip to flip myself upright – I definitely had the right angle with my arms – up until I slowly and simply … let the paddle go.

Upside down I saw the sun and sky at the surface make silver blue electricity. The rushing water and strength of current pulled my arms, rocked my head. The upsidedowness of blood in my skull made my head ache. I closed my eyes. Still smiling.

The cold wet of my life. My body in deep water. Weightless. Airless. Daughterless void.

It's possible it would be impossible for me to drown.

After I shot through the rough and tumble of the white-water tunnel I pulled the skirt and made a wet exit not even bothering to hold on to my kayak. I somersaulted twice in the current and banged my knees and shoulder and something else on rocks and saw my own air bubbles furiously leaving my nose. But I popped up anyway, taking in the biggest breath of my life. Coughing. Snot all over. Something warm on my cheekbone. Blood. The cold finally making me shiver.

I saw the entire posse on the shore, some of them yelling and waving or pointing. Then my exasperated instructor paddled up alongside me and grabbed me by my life jacket. "Let's get you in – you gave us a scare – you gave us a goddamn scare, girl!" His voice controlled anger.

"Let go, Jeff," I said, "I can swim it. Let go."

It was true. I cut through the minor current easily. I swam upstream even though most of my strength had left my body.

Big red ended up swimming down my kayak and bringing it back to the exit edge. Magnificently. Hannah didn't say much. She sat near me and ate an orange. She looked pale. She fed me orange slices. She looked extremely serious and sooooooooo not high. I'd lost my high underwater. Jeff acted cranky – both because I nearly lost the kayak and paddle but also because he watched me enter the whitewater and surrender. It must be hard to know one of your students might drown. I wonder how often it happens. If at all. When we put our gear back onto the truck he pulled me aside. Were you trying to kill yourself? Jokingly, laughing the tight pitched nervous laugh of a man old enough to be one of our fathers.

Was I trying to kill myself. Letting go the paddle in deep water. Letting go the handlebars of the bike as a kid. Letting go the steering wheel. These are not questions I know the answers to.

Later at home Hannah put her arm around my waist at her

front door. She kissed my cheek lightly as whisper. She tried
to be womanish and caring, but it wasn't what I wanted. My eyes
stung. My chest hurt. I wanted to see stars.

She put her hands on my shoulders to gently usher me
inside. I stopped and turned my head back to look at her – no, I
said, harder. I put my hand on the door. She put her hand on
my hand. She pressed my hand against the wood. Harder. Let
lips do what hands do. Let hips.

I wanted to be pushed through her door and shoved to the
floor knees first, my elbows pinned behind my back, my hurt
cheek against the hardwood floor, my ass skyward, my good
cheek exposed to whatever was coming next. Her face close to
my ear: you could have died.

The truth is I was a woman who thought of dead things.
All the time. I couldn't help it. Dead daughters. Dead fathers.
Dead steelhead. I wanted her to somehow knock it out of me body
to body, even if it killed me, which it never did.

Maybe this is how the steelhead feels when it's caught –
thrashing itself against water, then land – a lifedeath fight. How
some get released and others get eaten and others just float
away, too weak to survive. All those body blows and wounds. Or
when they swim upstream to spawn then die. Are they killing
themselves? Or making life?

Inside her house, Hannah made me a cup of green tea.

But tenderness couldn't touch me then.

I went swimming in the river alone every night that week.
At a spot where hoodlums and teens got drunk and jumped
in to shoot the rapids. Nobody cared that I was there. Or that I
was older than them. Or alone. In nightwater, I didn't have to
feel what people are supposed to feel. There is a glooming peace
there. At the end of the rapids, there is a still.

In water, like in books – you can leave your life.

Writing

AFTER MY MOTHER TRIED TO KILL HERSELF WITH THE sleeping pills, we shared a strange dream-time together. Every day after school and before swim practice I sat with her in the living room while she watched television soaps and drank. She looked exactly like a zombie. But one day, she put down the giant vodka tonic she was drinking. She dug into her purse. She said "Lidia." She handed me a newspaper advertisement for a writing contest. Out of the fucking blue.

There was a prompt that required the story to include an important relationship between an adult and a child.

We talked for hours about what I could write about. I would say ideas and my mother would sit on the couch with her tumbler and southern drawl and say, "Yes. That's a fine one." Or, "And then what happens? Make it good, Belle."

I won a prize. Like she had as a young woman – a story she'd tucked into a shoebox with old photographs and a drawing of a redbird my father made when they first met. My photo was in the paper. The day they took the picture my mother took me to get a haircut. My mother and I went to the 7-Eleven to get the newspaper the day the story was supposed to come out. We sat in the car and stared at the picture of me and read the small story about the "writers" who had won prizes. My mother said I looked like a woman. When I looked at the image of myself I looked ... like a woman I'd never met.

The story I wrote was about a child who had witnessed a

crime in a city park – a pedophile has been stealing and molesting children. The only other witness is a blind man on a bench. The blind man has no children. No wife. Just a gentle man. The child and the blind man have to piece the story together to help catch the pedophile. When called upon by authorities to speak, because she is afraid, the child loses her voice. But she is able to talk to the blind man when they are alone together. Each without a sense, they make a story that saves children. The police find out that before the pedophile defiles the child, he whips them on the bare bottom with a belt. The police are able to catch him when they hear the thwack.

In the newspaper the judge of the writing contest remarked on how mature my story content was.

My mother and father took me out to dinner at the Brown Derby.

We didn't talk. We ate.

It was the first story I ever wrote.

About Hair and Skin

THERE IS SOMETHING ABOUT HAIR AND SKIN.

In a beautiful wooden box, I have the hair of people I love.

I have my sister's. My own when I was a kid. My son's. My dead infant's almost hair. The hair of my best friend in high school. In college. I have Kathy Acker's hair. Ken Kesey's hair. My first husband's hair. The hair of a longtime woman lover – several different colors of it. My second husband's hair. My third husband's hair. The hair of two of the dogs I owned. The hair of cats. The hair of – and this one is kind of random – my high school English teacher – who was over the top Christian – so I have Christian hair. I have Buddhist hair. I have atheist hair. Gay hair, straight hair, the hair of a post-op tranny who used to be a Scientologist. The hair of a white wolf. Seriously.

I have my mother's hair.

What?

I can't help it. When I get the chance to own the hair of someone important to me, I leap forward a little too zealously.

Ken Kesey's hair between your fingers feels like lamb's wool. If you hold it up to the light you can imagine shapes in clouds – like the touch of dreams kids have when they look up into the sky.

In anthropology the word fetiches was popularized by C. de Brosses' *Le Culte de Dieux Fetiches*, which influenced the current spelling in English, and introduced the obsessive desire part.

A nicey way to say it would be to say "something irrationally revered."

Fetishism in its psycho-sexual sense first cropped up in that swank sex writer's work, Havelock Ellis, around 1897. Have you read Havelock Ellis? Was that guy high or what?

Kathy Acker's hair is like blades of bleached grass – sharp and stiff – and smells like swimming pools.

It's not just hair.

There's the hair, and it's true to this day if I meet someone with beautiful hair I want to put my face in it and lose myself, and one other thing.

Scars.

I like to run my tongue along them like mouth Braille.

Buddhist hair smells like smooth stones taken from a river. Whereas Christian hair has a cross between new car smell, dollar bills, and after shave. Alternately like chocolate chip cookies.

There is a woman I want to tell you about.

Right after I tell you about my mother. Which is where everything gets born.

My mother was born with one leg six inches shorter than the other. In my life it meant something completely different than it did in hers.

In my life as a child it meant that the pearled gleam of her scar appeared exactly at eye level. So white. So beautiful. I wanted to touch it. Mouth it. When she got out of the bath I hugged her leg and closed my eyes and saw it and saw it and saw it. I saw the crossed white tracks, the too-white non-skin on her misshapen leg, the dark wire of her pubic hair. It made me dizzy enough to see stars.

And that's not all. My mother wore her hair wound in a never-ending spiral at the back of her head. When she let it down, it reached her calves. It smelled like fir trees.

Every desire that flickered alive in me as a child came from those two images.

My mother said that as a girl, she let her hair grow long enough to cover her body, her deformed leg, her scars. So that there would be something about her that was beautiful to cover a crippled girl.

When I was 13 my mother became an award-winning real estate agent. More and more she left the house. More and more alcohol entered. The bathroom closet full of vodka jugs. She cut her hair off in that 1970s real estate agent on the go way. The long trail of her hair sat curled in a box like a cat in her bedroom closet. Sometimes I would sit in the dark of her closet and smell it and cry.

Harder

"NOW ASK ME FOR WHAT YOU WANT."

Maybe it was because I only saw her three times a year. She lived in New York City, I lived in Eugene, Oregon. Maybe it was her stature – so high up in the academic echelons that it was like being awarded a very important prize to be with her. It could be it was that she liked my brutal and unruly stories. Or that I had no place in her daily life. Maybe it was her scar, her hair, my pathologics. But mostly I think it was what she taught me about pain.

When I was 26 a big time academic came to give a talk at the University of Oregon. I'll tell you right now, I wasn't prepared for it. I was being all grad student faux smarty butt. I was all Sontag and Benjamin and Deleuze and Foucault. I was talking the talk of Barbara Kruger and Roland Barthes and … who the fuck gives a shit. Point being: I was not prepared to psychosexually regress fast enough and hard enough to make me leave a puddle in my seat.

In the auditorium, when she walked out onto the stage, even though I was sitting fairly far from her, I could see that her silver and black hair traveled down the entire length of her back in a braided rope, past her ass. The skin on her face and hands was the color of Albuquerque. When she turned to face our jackastic applause, I saw something. Beginning just underneath the infant thin skin of her left eye was a tiny white gleaming. I had to strain to focus. I had to sit up and lean forward on the edge of my seat.

When they dimmed the lights, only a podium lamp illuminated her face from below. I saw then a web of thin white scars that curved around her cheekbone, cupped her jaw, and continued down her neck into the plunge of her shirt.

I went instantaneously deaf. I mean I didn't hear one word of her famous hour long photographer talk. It was like being underwater. Occasionally I was able to wrestle my eyes away from her to look at the stream of photos behind her, but not often. My breathing began to go wrong in my lungs. Sweat formed in lines underneath my tits and between my legs. My face got hot. My scalp felt as if it was leaving my head. My mouth filled with spit. I wished everyone in the room dead.

By the time her talk was over and I'd made my way down and through the idiotic academic sycophantic throngs, by the time I penetrated the clone army and reached my hand out to shake hers, to introduce myself, to look at what my body was begging for, I already knew.

She was the same age as my mother.

A few hands before mine I noticed that she wiped her hand off vigorously enough on her pant leg to create the beginning of what would be a stain when she got back to her hotel for the night. A stain on the thigh of her pants from the multitudes of greedy hands. I felt a tinge of shame.

I gripped her hand a little too tightly, as I recall. Desperately thinking inside my skull don't be desperate don't be desperate don't be fucking desperate.

When she looked at me she had that glazed look of a speaker handling the hands and faces of adoring morons. When she let go my hand I thought, that's that, I'm an adoring moron. Probably I'm drooling.

Her hand in mine was wet. Wet from the effort it takes to speak to a desiring crowd when you are meant to be off gloriously and unapologetically alone in the world with your

only beloved: a camera. Point and shoot. Wet with all of our slob-
bering projections of who we wanted her to be dripping from her
hands. Wet with the sweat of hundreds of numskulls just like me.

I don't know why I did it, I just know I couldn't not. While
I was holding her hand I leaned in close to her face and said my
name is Lidia. I am a writer. Which I said exactly to the scar
underneath her eye, letting my eyes and voice travel down her
skin. I saw stars as I let go. Her hair smelled like rain.

I remember leaving the campus feeling like I was exactly
like anyone.

But it would not be the last time I touched her.

I didn't know yet that desire comes and goes wherever it
wants.

I didn't know yet that sexuality is an entire continent.

I didn't know yet how many times a person can be born.
Mother.

Before I met her in that auditorium in Eugene, Oregon,
I'd been to exactly three s m play parties in Eugene. Wanna know
how? Because my former best friend who went on the little
beach excursion got me invited. At the s m play parties I saw some
awesome things happen. Once I saw a man wrapped in plastic
wrap with nothing but his mouth and dick unwrapped. Sometimes he got drops of water in his mouth. Mostly he got his dick
whipped until it was red as a screaming infant.

I saw a woman ample as a Michelangelo cherub with her
wrists bound and hung above her head get her twat whipped for
over an hour while her pussy swelled and reddened and purpled
until even the air shuddered and felt faint.

I went back.

I saw a woman's thighs pierced with tiny blue capped needles – 20 up one thigh and 20 down the other – her eyes streaming
with tears, her endorphin rush coming at those around her like a
tsunami, her cunt gushing.

I saw reddened welts rise on a woman's ass like swollen
railroad tracks from caning, I saw a tranny pierce her cheek

with what looked like a barbeque skewer all the way through to the other cheek without blinking, I saw a man hang from giant meat hooks carefully puncturing his back slabs. I saw bondage in 300 varieties, fistings, bloodsport, dungeons, crossbeams, strange wands shooting out electricity anywhere you wanted.

Some of which I began to let happen to me.

Watching pain and feeling pain mattered on my skin more than anything had since I was a child. Unlike drinking. Unlike drugs. I could feel it. I could more than feel it.

But I wanted to feel it more. Harder.

"Tell me what you want."

That's how it began. If I said something dumb like, I'd like a kiss, she'd say, "No, that's not right, Angel." And lightly sting my skin with a riding crop or this crop with thornish things dangling from it in a kind of tassel. "Try again," she'd say.

I'd try again. And again. Until I said what it was I really wanted.

What I really wanted was to be taken to whatever the edge of self was. To a death cusp. Maybe not literally. But maybe literally.

I suppose it's good I was in the hands of a professional. A calm sadist. An intellectual. Because she took my request and made it deeper.

"Can you take the pain and go somewhere? Can you make it a journey?"

I don't know why, but I thought of my mother – who was under hypnosis during my birth. "Dorothy? Do you have pain? Where is the pain?"

At first I didn't know what she meant by "journey." I just wanted to be with her. I just wanted her to hurtpleasure me. So when she asked me that, it was annoying. It involved thinking. Can't we just do it?

This woman though, she was 25 years older than me. For her, having sex – that anchor of heterosexual scripture – she'd left that behind more years ago than my age. So it seems true enough to say that in her hands I became again. I became a daughter again. I became a student again. An athlete. I became a sister again. A lover. And the most difficult: a mother. All the crucibles of my life were now available across the surface of my own body. With her.

This: territories that had caused me psychic pain were now available to recross physically through a pain that … cleansed me like water.

This woman unlike any other woman I ever met in my life didn't want to be in a relationship. If by "relationship" we mean living together with someone else and entering the social realm as two people you could point to and go look, there's a couple. Or any of the domesticity that comes with cohabitation or long term close proximity. In fact, my only option for seeing her and being with her and doing with her was to meet her when she came to the west coast or I went to the east. The longing in between? I could feel it in the bruises and cuts and welts left on my skin for weeks. My skin story.

Look I'm not trying to creep you out. Or shock you. I'm trying to be precise. I'm just saying maybe healing looks different on women like me.

She read every story I wrote. Where I placed my truths, just underneath the skin of wild girls – junkies and prostitutes and child thieves and girls with their hair on fire. And that is why the third year she told me to call her "mother." Because my real mother? She'd been a numb drunk folded into her own pain when I needed her. This one took action. This one could have killed my father. I wanted her to ravage me.

The cross beam was not in a dungeon – those remade basements in the homes of people you would never suspect. It was in broad daylight in her loft, bathed in white and golden light when the sun came in. Or hued black and blue when it rained. The crossbeam was lodged at an angle, not straight up. And there was a padded bench on it like on a weightlifting bench.

And a ledge for your feet. When she bound my wrists with thin black leather twine christ-like to the wood I started crying.

"Mother, I would like to be whipped."

Then she would present a long cat of nine tails – its dark red leather strips the color of blood. "Tell me where you would like to be whipped, Angel."

So I told her. And begged her. She whipped my breasts. She whipped my stomach. My hipbones. Late into the day. I did not make a sound, though I wept a cleansing. Oh how I cried. The crying of something leaving a body. And then she whipped me red where my shame had been born and where my child had died, and I spread my legs as far as I could to take it. Even my spine ached.

Afterwards she would cradle me in her arms and sing to me. And bathe me in a bubble bath. And dress me in soft cotton. And bring me dinner in bed with wine. Only then would we make love. Then sleep. Ten years to bring a self back. In between seeing her I swam in the U of O pool. I swam in the literature of the English Department. In water and words and bodies.

My safe word was "Belle."

But I never used it.

My Mother Demonology

IN THE END, THE BOOKS I LOVED THE MOST IN GRADUATE school were the deviant ones. The underbelly of literature. George Bataille and the Marquis de Sade and Dennis Cooper and William Burroughs. Which makes it easier to understand how I found a literary foremother in Kathy Acker.

So if you've never read Kathy Acker's books, then you don't know how often fathers rape their daughters. Without artifice or affect. Without any literary strategy to lyricise or symbolize or otherwise disguise. A father will show up on a page and rape his daughter, and the daughter will be the one narrating, and she will not be in any kind of victim position you've ever imagined. You'll be reading going, mother of god, that's some horrific shit, but the daughter won't be. The daughter narrating the rape by her father will be extremely articulate even if coarse, and the narration will be the jumping off point for radical adventures of a girl child or robot woman or she-pirate. Her rage will drive her. The transgression will write her very body.

When other people I knew in grad school read Kathy Acker's books they were shocked. Appalled. Particularly most of the budding young feminists. I actually began weeding out women friends by their reactions to her books. The ones that smiled and lowered their eyes with sly understanding and touched themselves, I kept. The ones that freaked out, well, they were idiots. Once I read a paragraph from *Empire of the*

Senseless in my theory of gender class and one of the women began to cry and ran out and barfed. No shit. Pussy, I thought.

When I read Kathy Acker's books, and particularly any section in which fathers sexually molested or raped or dominated or humiliated or shamed or abused daughters, all I went was yes.

I did not feel shocked. I did not feel appalled. I felt … present.

So it did not take me any time at all to understand that what she was deconstructing was the law of the father. Patriarchy and capitalism. More precisely, the effects of patriarchy and capitalism on the bodies of women and girls. Actually, you know what? I just cracked myself up writing this. If you've never read *Blood and Guts in High School*, you are in for a treat. Every year I teach it I expect to be fired.

You can count the books written by women that precisely articulate these themes on one hand; one hand that has four of its fingers shot off with William Burroughs' pistol.

But underneath that, what she was also writing was literal. A literal father and a literal daughter and the plainspeak necessary to name it. I'd read sections and stop and look around expecting to get caught or smacked a red blotchy one. You can say this shit? And it can be published?

In this way, her books saved me.

So you can imagine how large it was to meet her and hang out with her. Feminae a feminae.

Many many many people "knew" her better than I. I'm friends with lots of them. That's actually not the story I'm trying to tell. The story I'm trying to tell is quite a bit more ordinary than that. But sometimes ordinary things are staggering.

I swam with her.

When I swam with Kathy Acker it was at a Best Western shrunken indoor pool with too much chlorine. Trust me. I know chlorine. Her swimsuit was black and blue. Mine was dark red. Her body was decorated with tattoos. Her hair was platinum and

as short as a freshly mowed lawn. All kinds of sterling silver
sprouted from her face and ears. I had one side of my head close
shaven, and on the other side I had Breck Girl long blonde hair.
We must have looked like a pretty girl's wound.

How I came to be swimming with Kathy Acker was I
invented a Xine in Eugene – that's what you to do in Eugene –
called *two girls review*. One day when I was drunk and high with
my second husband, sitting on the floor of our next to the
tracks rental house I said to him, "Let's bring Kathy Acker down
here to read." And he looked at me all slow eyed and said, "OK."
Things seemed like they could go like that in Eugene.

It's not what you think to contact people you think of as
mega stars. I dialed information. He called. I wrote down what
he should say. He said it. And shebazz. I was swimming in a Best
Western pool with Kathy fucking Acker.

I know not all of you would do the tinkle dance to hang
out with Kathy Acker. In fact, some of you don't even know who
she was. But to me, Kathy Acker was the shit. She was the
woman who staged a break-in on culture and gender, on the
prison house of language, and blew it up from the inside out.
She was the female William Burroughs.

And after we swam, she talked about pussy spanking.

Pussy spanking, for the uninitiated, is not just foreplay.
Christ, most of the women I know now have never had the
pleasure, but the good ones have.

When we swam in that ghoulishly green colored Best
Western pool, we did laps. This was after she lifted free weights
for about an hour. She swam hard. She wasn't a superb
swimmer, but she was a solid swimmer. How she looked in the
water was like a human muscle beating the crap out of each lap.
And when she'd turn her head to breath, if I happened to
breathe her direction at the right time, her face with all that
hardware gleamed.

It wasn't in the pool that the pussy revelations happened.
And it wasn't later in my blue Toyota pickup truck after we went

to Rite-Aid to buy her sinus medication, where she asked me things about my body, having seen me swim. Though being asked questions about your body by Kathy Acker is definitely enough to make your car seat wet. It was later, at dinner, with 14 other people sitting around. Between bites of dinner and sips of wine she self narrated about how she didn't much cum from penetration and loved to be spanked into orgasm. I was sitting next to her. I've never been that wet sitting next to someone just talking in my life. I thought I might slide off of the seat and dribble to the floor right there, sucking her ankles and whimpering on my way down, begging her to go under the table with me.

I talked with her other times. People who knew her would agree with me – she was wide open mouthed about traditionally sexual things – she was precise and clear and fully descriptive. It was smaller, ordinary, human things she'd go all quiet or shy or girl about. Like an inside out woman. Like all the swollen red gushing salty complexity of a woman on the outside. Going THIS.

The night after we swam together at the Best Western, after her jammed to the walls packed reading, after the take the writer out to a bar so people can drool on her and crowd her into claustrophobic hell, at approximately 4:23 a.m. I think you know what happened.

I got the motherloving juice spanked out of my pussy until the bed flooded. It was not like with the photographer. I laughed. I laughed with pleasure.

I had a few other encounters with her. We exchanged two letters about sexuality. I talked to her on the phone once when I thought I might be in love with a transsexual person. That's it. And this. She read my writing and said: "You should keep doing it. Not everyone should. You should."

Kathy died in 1997 of breast cancer.

Kesey died in 2001 of liver cancer.

Sometimes in my head she is the good mother. He's the good father. Me swimming in words.

IV. Resuscitations

A Drowning Scene

MY SECOND HUSBAND WAS A CHARISMATIC NARCISSISTIC tender hearted frighteningly attractive artistic drunk. With hella black curls of hair traveling halfway down his back. And black eyes. It seemed. And a tiny zipper scar across his left wrist. My break up with Devin – poet, divine one – it took 11 years. Goddamn it.

I took an informal poll of all the incredibly intelligent, intriguing, beautiful women I currently know on the question of why we find ourselves driven like moths to fire toward men who fuck us up. They said things like: "Because in loving his darkness I found my own." Or "I learned from an early age that if it feels bad, it's good, and if it feels good, you are bad." Then there was the ever popular "Between slut and saint I choose slut." And this one's a classic of course: "Bad boys are more interesting than good ones. If you can survive it. And I still feel that way." Also: "Suffering makes a stronger bond than love," and "I'd rather feel alive and die than feel dead and live." This one nearly made me cry: "He made me feel like someone somebody would risk something to choose." But the one I personally identified with the most was, "He celebrated a death drive with me."

The first night I slept with Devin we consumed 25 bottles of Guinness and two jumbo bottles of wine. I barely remember the actual sex but I remember exactly what we drank. We listened to Jim Morrison all night in his bedroom. *Strange Days* and *LA Woman* until it felt like it was in our skin. When I woke up the next morning and looked at the desk across from the bed I saw as many bottles as I was old. I laughed and burped and went back to sleep, Devin's arm pinning me to the bed.

I didn't feel anything about myself.

It was everything to be filled with such nothing.

I first met Devin at the orientation meeting for new graduate students at the University of Oregon in Eugene. It was my second year, his first.

I looked around at all the earnest grad student folks at orientation and felt kind of like I had a big red "A" on my chest due to my checkered academic past. Flunked out of undergraduate school in Lubbock. Quit undergraduate school in Eugene. Went back with a pile of D's and F's and clawed my way up to the pretty people.

Then I saw a guy who looked equally out of place and very uncomfortable with astonishingly beautiful long black hair and eyelashes. I watched him. He kept looking at the door. And fidgeting like he didn't fit in the seat. I didn't hear an orientation thing. After the orientation I sort of sauntered up next to him and without looking at me he said, "I feel like I might get arrested here," and I replied without looking at him, "Do you think they can tell I'm not wearing underwear," and we went straight from the orientation meeting to a bar and didn't stop drinking for 11 years, so you might say I was perfectly primed to cross his path.

This man was gorgeous. I'm mentioning this because women live their lives secretly waiting for their lives to become movies. We act like men are the ones shallow enough to desire an unending stream of beautiful women but really, if a charismatic narcissist beautiful bad boy man actually desires us, seems to choose us, we go to pieces. We suddenly feel like we are finally in that movie rather than a life. Just what we always wanted. To be chosen by the best looking man in the room. Rhett Butler. Even though we are of course smarter and more mature and more together than to ever want that. Or admit it.

Honestly I remember feeling shocked every time he walked up to my Toyota pickup truck and got in. I always expected him to veer off at the last moment, get into someone else's vehicle. Or bed. Or house. Or life.

Our love, was liquid. Turned out we both loved drinking more than almost anything else. The anything else turned out to be fucking. Drinking in bathrooms and kitchens and alleys and hallways and bars and cars. Drinking all the way to the coast and all night at a bar and in the morning with eggs and oyster shooters in some crappy run-down motel and all the way back to Eugene. Drinking before, during, and after classes. Drinking in beds and in baths and at the rivers and in the rose garden and in the graveyard next to U of O and on top of Prince Lucien Campbell Hall.

We drank Guinness.

We drank cheap turn your teeth purple wine.

We drank Chivas, because he had a thing about Jim Morrison.

We drank vodka, because of … well, me.

We drank everything his favorite poet drank–Bukowski–and like Bukowski's women, I matched him drink for drink.

We drank each other blind.

Drinking our minds gone. Drinking our lives away.

In between drinking he said I want to be a painter. I said I want to be a writer. So we drank to that. And painted. And wrote. And celebrated every hour with booze. Dancing with lesbians. Tripping with hippies. Mushrooming with artists. Slitting the tires of Republicans. We drank with bums under overpasses and on the tracks. We drank with friends and enemies and ex-cons and tat artists and once a priest and bikers and once with a famous actress and with his drunk father and my drunk mother and all the people we'd never met. We dreamed in drink.

While we were underwater stories began itching at my fingertips.

While we were drinking he painted paintings of wild

faces – abstract faces so you could never say who they were or why.

While we were drinking the chaos of art came out of us. There was nothing we could do to control anything about us.

Always we were making. Making love, making trouble, making art. We made performance art together. He made paintings and I made stories. He made dinner and I made money. It seemed like all that making had a power bigger than our dumb lives. Making and making.

Art. The expression of human imagination. Or emotions that have been locked inside a body spilled out all over the goddamn place.

Always he made me laugh. I hadn't laughed since I was 10. It wasn't safe to laugh as a child, and later in life when I lost my daughter, laughter hurt too much. But a drunk man made me laugh. All the time. Sometimes I think that's the best of it.

I would have done anything for him. A love unto death. And …

Goddamn it.

I'm already lying. I'm making it all sound literary.

It was messier than that. A lot.

Like the image of him sitting slumped over drunk against the wall of an airport while I bought our tickets home from Reno, Nevada. How by then I was deadened with drunk. How I looked at him for a long minute. How I tucked his ticket in his pocket and left all our bags around him and got on a plane without him.

Let me start over.

Distilled

YEAR ONE WE DRINK GUINNESS MOSTLY ALL THE TIME and we ride Mountain bikes around Eugene at night and we go to the Vet's Club we go to the Vet's club we go to the Vet's club we go to the High Street Café hey I'll give you my student loan wad of $700 if you kiss the guy who joined us for a drink he does we laugh we drink we fuck. We rent a house together near the train-tracks we drink Guinness we paint each other's bodies we paint the walls we paint an entire room we fuck. We go crazy loving we go crazy fucking we go crazy drinking we do performance art in Eugene him naked on stage with a bloody pig's head me naked on stage wrapped in Saran Wrap we perform on stage we perform at school we perform a life his long black hair my long blond hair attractive dramatic people dramatically drinking we have our first yell fight me on one side of the bathroom door with a Swiss Army Knife him on the other side of the bathroom door with a kitchen knife we carve each other's names into our arms we do I fall and break open the body of the toilet water spewing everywhere he breaks down the bathroom door we bleed we fuck septic water. Year Two we drink Bushmills we ride our bikes in summer at night to the rose garden we steal all the heads of roses we strip and ride the current down the McKenzie river we road trip from Oregon to Florida we drink mushroom tea and hallucinate in the redwoods we see a guy die on the road some terrible wreck blood everywhere stretchers with corpse side of the road gorgeous ocean cliff view blood and road flares

and ambulances and bodies how you loved looking just like you
loved moving deathward so Jim Morrison I wanted to be in
your fire we eat ecstasy and ride our bikes on the freeway we drive
and drive all the southern states redneck fuckwads laughing
snakeskin boots and cowboy hats all the way to Alabama his home
to Florida my parents then turn around as fast as possible back
to the west to Oregon where we can be who we are the west we
get married in Tahoe at the top of Harvey's Casino with my best
friends lovers Mike and Dean and my sister and my parents
Oedipal fakers and his parents southern Baptist fascists and we
drink with the gay boys and a casino preacher with giant hair
groomed black as a record album marries us says a Native American prayer there on top of Harvey's Casino overlooking Lake
Tahoe we laugh all the way down the elevators all the way through
the year all the way to rings on our fingers and bells on our toes.
Year three love is a series of islands in Greece the Cyclades
rising from aqua ocean waters like stepping stones for dumb
naïve drunk Americans with back packs riding ferries we drink
Tsipouro we drink Mavrodafni we drink Retsina we drink Metaxa
Metaxa Metaxa white stone buildings endless rock beaches
mountains and olive hills and brown skinned people with dark
hair dark eyes open arms open hands fishermen breadmakers
winemakers women with giant tits and laughing until I'm drunk
dumb with love drunk dumb with Greece drunk dumb blond
sleeping while he goes out to sleep with Greece. Year four is London and Keats' house and laying on the tiny bed we're not
supposed to and getting kicked out drunk tourists and Hyde Park
naps and the Tate Gallery and Westminster Abbey choir boys
coming out from behind a giant wooden door my crying and
crying so beautiful these singing children but we didn't come for
London the food is shit the people are unattractive the Shakespearian tradition is all over everything until we fuck in a giant
tidepool near the Cliffs of Dover good really good pub with
no Americans but then some show up ugly very very very near to
giant fistfight he's drunk he thinks he's Bukowski run I say run

these are English pig dog thugs we escape to where we wanted
to be to Ireland. Becket and Synge and Joyce and at Yeats house
we fuck in the castle against the wall we fuck on the stones at
Innish Moore we drink and pass out in Joyce's country his shoes
washing away down a river my hair soaked with rain we read
books we wish we were part of history we wish we were part of
drinking we wish we were part of anything not ourselves we
walk and walk but why do the pictures we took of each other have
no smiles. Did we become a Beckett play? Year five a restored
farmhouse in France my beloved Michael with us his lover with
us we live there for a month we drink every French wine $5 to
$500 we drink champagne we eat rabbit we eat crepes we eat
escargot we laugh they taste like dirt we eat and eat and drink
restaurant with menus and walls designed by Chagall the
Louvre get lost and too high in all the art and high ceilings and
hide in a bathroom hunched like a little troll in the corner rocking until a French woman asks "sont bien vous? sont bien vous?"
Back out into the Louvre and even the Mona Lisa looks silly back
to the farmhouse which is not in Paris but on the speed train
taking speed on the speed train back to the farmhouse which is
near Normandy on the coast – stop – war and remembrance –
back at the farmhouse 100 year old restored house walk in fireplace cooking and drinking and fire. Next night nightmare
we become drunk people driving and getting pulled over and me
wishing wishing my beloved friend to talk to these police but
beautiful gay men stay in the car and Devin Bukowski begins to
fight with the French cop and a miracle we are not all taken to
prison. Gay men fight in the French farmhouse we feel less alone
when other people fight love. Year six yelling begins a rhythm
and me writing book begins and him painting paintings begins
and yelling gets louder and drinking gets louder and him
kissing women I know and him kissing women I don't know and
how do people last together how do they what is a couple over
time but a line and me writing more and more and him painting
and my first book and his first painting in a SoHo gallery but

nothing stops the yelling that is taking over the house and drinking and kissing that becomes animal and desperate and no travel too much reading graduate school too much writing me reading and writing and language and the liquor of intellectual fights the liquor of love no travel more writing just the distance of two bodies barreling through passion but barreling differently splitting apart into the flames one mind one body splitting. Year seven I start a dissertation he quits grad school drinking and yelling: cleaved. Year eight I get a Ph.D. I get a real job someone here needs to someone needs to take care of this couple gone haywire beautiful fucked up children so full of promise so full of self loathing so full with alcohol we keep on being married and married and married and yelling and drinking and he pisses drunk in the corner and he falls down the stairs and he passes out on the lawn and he passes out driving and how do you do this how do you where is my love going? Year nine here is a job at my job adjunct pretend grown up here is a trip with a drama colleague of mine I am giving you my love go to go to Vietnam here is a life I buy him a loft along the riverfront in Portland I buy him alcohol I try and try to buy our love back I try and try but no money stops him in Vietnam he falls in love Tu-Ha he lies and lies he comes home Tu-Ha he goes back I wait in bed for him night after night he stays in Vietnam Tu-Ha I stay in bed for days and days I don't eat I drink the drinking of alone I piss in the bed I don't move me urine and vodka and sad sad dead childless woman with her job and her house and her first book and her cat and her dog and her money no husband Tu-Ha. Year 10 we pretend. Year 10 we go back to Tahoe to try to remember pretend. Year 10 we drink on top of Harvey's Casino we drink in the elevator we drink instead of fucking until we can't see or hear or feel we drink even on the way to the airport in the cab we get to the airport I go to the ticket counter to go back to Oregon but I know I'm not going to get to go back to anything just Oregon I turn around with the tickets he's asleep against the wall snoring like drunks do all our luggage around him like children we never had I leave the ticket in his drunk sleeping hand he's pissed himself I can't take care of this man. Year 10 he sleeps with one of our mutual students she emails me and tells me she is a good person she emails me and tells me he is a good person she emails me and tells me I am a good person they fuck and fuck I come home from work she is on the black leather couch passed out he is passed out on the floor. Year 10 you said you would love me until I died you said we would die together in love you said when I was 75 we'd laugh our saggy skinned laughs and drink to our old ass love you said it to me you did every year until you stopped saying it where are you where is the man who would love a woman like me there are no men if not you there never were any men for me not even a father I stop eating lose 25 pounds everyone says everyone says you look so beautiful. Like a movie actress. Isn't she beautiful?

Am I beautiful?

Love is a lifedeath.

My Lover, Writing

I KIND OF DON'T WANT TO TELL YOU THIS.

I mean I was going to write this whole book not telling you. I left words out. On purpose. But I know why I was hiding words from you.

Ask me about my life as a sexualized, gendered body, and I can tell you tales. Endless stories of a woman who was me and is also all of us. Our bodies the flesh metaphor for all human experience. This. This happened to me. This is where I failed. Where I went blind. Where I opened my legs. Where I chewed off my hand. Where I tried to off myself, or offer myself up as useful, or deigned to ask for love, or ventured into pleasure or pain. Or just got drunk and fucked up. Again. Here are the scars. I am a swimmer. My shoulders are broad. My eyes, are blue.

Ask me about writing, well, that's a fierce private. Writing, she is the fire of me. Where stories get born from that place where life and death happened in me. She carries me and will be the death of me.

So when I tell you this, a little bit it makes me want to bite you.

Really hard.

Some people say that words can't "happen" to you. I say they can.

One of my last nights with Devin I got all hopped up on mushrooms and went for a walk by the train tracks. We lived next to the tracks in Eugene – in a neighborhood where you would find needles in the alley but also yuppies trying to buy and restore their way to better. I was supposed to be writing a dissertation. That night we sat down on the ground. We drank Chivas from a flask. Then a train slow rolled by, and I jumped up and chased it laughing, and then I hopped it. I have no idea why. I looked back at the image of husband getting smaller and smaller until I couldn't see him. I loved that receding him. Maybe it was our last good night. The wind felt excellent. The motion of a self riding to nowhere for all she was worth took my breath away.

Of course somewhere around five minutes later I snapped out of it and thought AHHHH what am I doing and thought JUMP IDIOT and so I did, I jumped off, and military rolled through some ground gravel until I came to a scraped to shit stop, laughing and laughing the high of organics and free. I walked home. Devin was exactly where I'd left him, kind of passed out like a giant drunk Caucasian Buddha.

The night after my gravel roll I sat at my computer with my fingers on the keys. My hands were all scraped up. My forearms and elbows, too. My chin and cheek. I was supposed to be writing my dissertation chapter on Kathy Acker, who by then I'd met. I stared at lines of hers I had typed and referenced as part of my critical discussion on the screen:

> *Every time I talk to one of you, I feel like I'm taking layers of my own epidermis, which are layers of still freshly bloody scar tissue, black brown and red, and tearing each one of them off so more and more of my blood shoots in to your face. This is what writing is to me a woman (ES, 210).*

When I went to write words over the top of hers, kind of I felt like I might throw up. Instead of the dissertation chapter, I began to write a story. The first line that came out of me was: "I am a woman who talks to herself and lies."

Please understand, I loved reading literary theory – I mean I devoured the primary texts as if they were romance novels – I dove into the discourse as if its waters were mine alone – my body song swam in between currents of language and thought. But trying to write critically, academically, hurt.

A lot.

Why would someone do that to novels? For what purpose, other than a sadistic impulse to hush, silence, incarcerate art? It seemed like a violence to me to write that way about literature. It seemed false at best and repugnant at worst – murderous even.

In my dissertation the novels I'd chosen were astonishing pieces of noisy art. *White Noise* and *Almanac of the Dead* and *Empire of the Senseless* – a book which I promise you, if you've never read it, will scrape your eyeballs. Books in which culture towered and collapsed, border identities defied the cult of good citizenship and revolutionaries turned back on their liberators with fire for hair. Wars of militarization and wars of race and wars of gender and wars of fathers and language and power and wars of just the human heart played out page after page, taking my breath away.

When I set my hands to writing literary criticism – that act of writing so legitimized by white male knowledge – I felt like I was a torturer. A killer. A Betrayer. An abuser. I slept with three of my professors – two men and one woman – I think trying to get the body back into discourse. HEY! What about bodies? The noisy, wet, rule-breaking body that seemed erased by all that lofty thought. It didn't work.

OF COURSE I considered quitting graduate school. I paid my ticket, I rode the ride. Right? Half the people I started with quit. I did not have to continue toward scholar. But something wouldn't let me. Some deep wrestling match going on inside my rib house and gray matter. Some woman in me I'd never met. You know who she was? My intellect. When I opened the door and there she stood, with her sassy red reading glasses and fitted skirt and leather bookbag, I thought, who the hell are you? Crouching into a defensive posture and looking at her warily out of the corner of my eye. Watch out, woman.

To which she replied, I'm Lidia. I have a desire toward language and knowledge that will blow your mind. And I'm here to write a dissertation.

Yeah. Right. Whatever. And anyway, where did you even come from?

Oh, I think you know. I'm from your father. Now open the goddamned door.

My father. Whose mind curled around art and architecture and classical music and film. Whose intellect I carried in my blood rivers. That's when my two mes had it out. The me I'd forged to leave a family and body batter my way into the world, and the me I'd never met, or even knew existed, except perhaps hidden in my hands, hiding like the crouch of dreams in my fingers. My father's daughter.

"I am a woman who talks to herself and lies."

The night after I jumped from the train of things, at the computer my heart raced. My first book came out of me in a great gushing return of the repressed. Like a blood clot had loosened. My hands frenzied. Words from my whole body, my entire life, or the lives of women and girls whose stories got stuck in their throats came gushing out. Nothing could have stopped the stories coming out of me. Even though my hands and arms and face hurt – bruised and cut from falling from a train – or a marriage – or a self in the night – I wrote story after story. There was no inside out. There were words and there was my body, and I could see through my own skin. I wrote my guts out. Until it was a book.

Until my very skin made screamsong.

Short Story

SO MY FIRST BOOK OF STORIES BEAT MY DISSERTATION to print. I got published by an independent press. One that did not care about how far I'd paddled outside the mainstream. I called the book *Her Other Mouths*. In every story, intense things happen to a body. Because, well, they do. Did. And I knew how to tell it. Words the body of me.

I did finish my dissertation though. It felt like walking through fire. A crucible. I called it *Allegories of Violence*. By some bizzaro twist of fate it got published too. I still think it happened to someone else. But something weirdly good came from it. The two mes? We began to get to know each other. Intellectual me and blood bodied me began to hang out. Brush each other's hair. Take bubble baths and draw soap pictures on each other's backs and clink glasses late into the night.

But there was a cost.

I was in my eleventh year of marriage with the Devin. I was a teacher of things, having achieved a doctorate and publications. But that woman I'd let into the house ravaged who I had been. Her zany brain force would not go. I didn't want to fuck. I wanted to read. I didn't want to go numb every night. I wanted to travel the country of ideas and feel thoughts and blast open the top of my head. I didn't want to drink until I dropped. I wanted to write. A whole other book. My husband became like a willful unruly child to me. A submerged one. And though my love did not leave, it went down into deeper darker places.

Devin's life moved bedward, fueled by alcohol and woman need. On one of his travels to another country for the first time without me, he found a foreign bed. While he was in Vietnam I waited for the word "husband" to come back. Days and nights. Then weeks. Then one morning I didn't get out of bed. Days and nights. When I had to pee, I did. When I was hungry, I cried. When I was awake, a white nothing. At night I ate small white sleeping pills. Something I learned well from my mother. More and more of them. When I slept, I hoped to die.

Finally a gentle friend broke into my house because he was worried about me. He and a bull dyke named Laurel broke down the front door of my house when I stopped showing up at work. He put me in the shower. Then he wrapped me in blankets. Then he fed me. Literally. Then we watched old movies for three days until I looked at him and said, OK.

I thought of Brody and his clarinet and beautiful black kid hands. I thought of my best friend in Florida, the one my mother had outed out of my life. Of my arch angel, Michael and how we both left the Lubbock and made up lives. There are many ways to love boys and men. Or to let them love you.

Devin did come back, but we were never again together.

He drank himself ever womanward. I entered my female family lineage – a suffering that once I again claimed it, felt as familiar as a mother. Daughter. Sister. Home. Her name, depression.

In that long thick underwater I lived the life of a devalued woman. Not a wife. Not a mother. No one's lover. No job or book gave me value to myself. I felt like a pointless woman sack. I lost pounds of flesh having no one to share a body with. My clothes began to hang off of my body as if I were someone else. Other women would compliment me on my supposed intentional feminine metamorphoses, and I'd smile, but I felt like an insect. In the morning I'd lose interest in washing my hair or brushing my teeth partway through, and find myself standing naked dripping in the bathroom staring at the floor or holding my toothbrush in the air, foam dripping from my mouth.

When I wasn't teaching or driving to and from teaching, I was at home. No, not home. An empty woman in a house. I'd sit in my living room alone grading student papers and stare out the large window onto the street. There were always more papers. I could picture a forever like this. Thoughtless and small and requiring me only to perform tasks with a pen. I'd drink only enough to not feel. Every day. About a bottle a day, roughly. Evenly. Sometimes wine, sometimes vodka. At night I'd watch T.V. until sleep saved me. Or didn't. This is my life is what I felt. It is slow like still water. There is a dull hum in the ear and a softheaded-ness best used for napping or making coffee. There is a neighbor-hood and a house and a refrigerator. The comfort of appliances and going to the gas station. There is a car in which I ride to work and then come home. There is a linear and accessible story to follow. You don't have to do anything. Or be.

But then there was another woman on the other side of the glass.

Staring numbly out the sanctity of the living room plate glass window one day I saw a woman with ashen skin and dirty blond hair walk by in denim cut-offs and a tube top and cowboy boots. Her arms looked like maps. The circles under her eyes weren't shiners but could fool you. She had a jerk to her right shoulder every third step or so. Walking by woman. Then I saw an emaciated man in jeans and a Lynyrd Skynyrd T-shirt walk after her. He hunched. He had darty eyes. He smoked. His hair hung down in a rat tail to the middle of his back.

The thing is, I'd seen them before. Lots of times. For about two years. She was a hooker. He was her pimp. This was their beat. The alleyway behind my house. We'd been living this way – me on the inside with my ever safening bouge life. Them on the outside with some trace of my past in their skin and hair.

This time when I saw her though, I felt something in my chest that hurt. It felt good to feel something for someone else.

Even pain. Maybe especially pain. Sitting there as they went out of view I tasted something warm in my mouth. Then I realized I'd bitten the inside of my cheek.

I didn't do anything but grade papers, that day. My chest and cheek aching. That night I threw up for no particular reason. Which was not eventful for that time.

But the next time I saw her, something very small and specific caught my eye. An important detail. A bruise at the bridge of her nose. It wasn't the bruise. It was the bruise that let me see ... her eyes, were blue. Like mine. I let the papers I was grading slide to the floor. I watched her walk by and wondered how much she weighed. I wondered her age – impossible to guess. I wondered what jobs she'd tried and failed, this walking woman in cut-offs with dangling maps for arms and a bruise and blue eyes. I tried to picture how much money I had in my wallet in my bookbag by the front door. I watched her ass hang-ing out of her shorts – it hung limply – two little flesh commas. Then she was around the corner. I waited for her dance partner to come into view. Without thinking I knocked on the window. Without thinking I got up and walked to my front door and opened it and walked outside and walked up to him and said "How much."

In the short story I wrote about what happened next I ask her in. I tell her to sit down. She sits down. In the story she smokes and bobbing machines her left knee. Her hand shakes. In the story I say this is what it feels like to be me a woman who teaches English looking down at a woman who sucks dicks all day and all night every night as she sits on my couch smoking. This is what me an addict upwardly mobile given something infinitesimally small to believe in called words thinks looking at her: she looks like Mary. This is what Mary must have looked like after jesus. No way for the body to bear the miracle, the bur-den, the unbelievable history that moves the world without her body. When I see an image of christ I picture a Mary so drawn and gaunt and tired and angry to the point of emaciation that she can barely wear her own face.

In the story I say, what do I think I'm going to do, teach her?

People are often asking me if the things in my short stories really happened to me. I always think this is the same question to ask of a life – did this really happen to me? The body doesn't lie. But when we bring language to the body, isn't it always already an act of fiction? With its delightfully designed composition and color saturations and graphic patterns? Its style and vantage point? Its insistence on the mind's powerful force of recollection in the face of the raw and brutal fact that the only witness was the body?

An exchange happened. Woman to woman. If she is still alive, she can back me up on this.

Was it possible I had something to give? Out of the nothingness that was my life? Really, what the fuck did I have to give? Woman with too many holes in her. And yet there was something.

Words.

With this woman in me I went to my teaching job and talked to students about ideas. The ideas got into my heart some. And then my heart began to pump. The talking with students about ideas had a pulse. Some of them cared, some of them could care less, but it didn't matter. I was so happy to get to stand in a room with words and ideas I would have talked to myself alone in a classroom. But I was not alone. I was with what youth should be. I was with artists and writers and scholars and bar-tenders and musicians and nurses and strippers and lawyers and mothers and some of them would become rich and famous and some of them would go to jail and some of them would become accountants and some would join the Peace Corps or move to France and some of them would fall in love and some of them would kill themselves and everyone who'd wronged us and everyone we'd been and everyone we would be all meeting in books. All touching the skin of words. What is a family.

Whatever it was or was not, there were words. Not just my own. I wrote stories, I wrote books, but the more I wrote the more I saw a door opening behind me, and I saw that if I jammed my motherfucking foot in it, more of us could get through. And that we could make things. Together. What we could make, was art. How that mattered. With other people I made paintings. With other people I made performances. With other people I made stories and readings and strange outsider art events like filling the trees with bras and little raw narratives or unbooting booted cars or hooking up free cable for poor people with a friend who worked for Bell or putting haikus about earthworms and cunts on the windshields of cars in corporate parking lots.

And I wrote my second book of stories.

The book that came out after the death of my marriage was called *Liberty's Excess*. If you pick it up, you will recognize the stories. They are the stories of people trying to perform the relationships we've been handed as scripts. Daughter. Mother. Husband. Wife. Marriage. They are the stories of women and men who try to love and fail. And fail. And they are the stories of people who live at the margins of this thing we call culture, mostly fucking up, but some of us, aren't we still here? For the ones who aren't? I wonder, is it us that fucks up? Or the stories we've been given?

It is not easy to leave one self and embrace another. Your freedoms will scar you. Maybe even kill you. Or one of your yous. It's OK though. There are more.

How many times do we die?

Words, like selves, are worth it.

Gray Matter

I MAY HAVE BEEN A BIG FAT FAILURE AT MAKING A HOME, but I made up how to make something else in its place. Out of the sad sack of sad shit that was my life, I made a wordhouse.

The first wordhouse I built was a literary journal. Now usually when someone says the words "literary journal," you picture something small and white and pristine like *Virginia Quarterly Review*. Not that. The thing we made was huge. Nine-by-twelve perfect bound four color in your face. Counter-culture. Every issue had a theme meant to deconstruct – my favorite thing I ever learned as a scholar – the "literary journal." Themes like Obscenitydivinity. Blow. Varieties of Violence. Alien. At the helm were me and my smart as crap talented as fuck friends, exactly like a garage band except with paper and comput-ers. We taught ourselves everything – editing, design, layout, typesetting – and then we took what we had learned and made every single page an event horizon. Image and text warred or danced with each other. Poems interrupted stories and giant photos of tits interrupted the white space and lyric line of poems. High art got under the sheets with low art – Yusef Komunyakaa's words right next to the words of some homeless woman, or a graffiti artist, or an unwed mom you never heard of before. The page made it possible to kill the distance. Writing, we decided, was everywhere. It was whatever we wanted it to be.

We put Annie Sprinkle and Andres Serrano and Kathy Acker and Andrei Codrescu and Joel-Peter Witkin on those big white pages. We put ex-cons and recovering addicts and drunks right next to them. And we destroyed the sanctity of the literary page while liberating the noise and heat of art. Everybody had day jobs. Everybody stayed up too late making the big books. Everybody spent way too much time cursing out the blue-aproned nerds at Kinko's. I spent my food and rent money on our big irreverent mouth. We won awards. We got grants. It really was something, though I don't know what, and that seems right, even today. It was a fast burning supernova.

I fucking loved it.

Why?

It was the first thing in my life I ever loved that I didn't spread my legs for. Maybe you believe that. Maybe you think it's a line. Either way it's true.

Something else happened through the wordhouse. Through the wordhouse I met writers who had somehow or other read my writing. Through the wordhouse I found voices and bloodsong exactly how it felt to me on the inside where I thought I was the only one. There were others like me. Um, lots of them. Breaking writing rules. Reaching for writing impossibilities. Taking their newly-found intellects into alien territories. Making things up. Maybe even a life. A self.

I'd meet these people at conferences and readings and performances and art shows. We'd huddle in corners and drink and laugh and plot our art secrets. We'd communicate like underground societies of people who read the outsider books, stared at the taboo art until we passed out, mouth watered in the presence of writing that tore your face to shreds even as it might never see the light of day. You wanna know what the two words are that describe what these people meant and still mean to me are?

Tribe.

Sacred.

I don't need anyone to explain to me why people join gangs or develop prison societies or only trust others of their rule breaking kind. I don't have any problem understanding why people flunk out of college or quit their jobs or cheat on each other or break the law or spray-paint walls. A little bit outside of things is where some people feel each other. We do it to replace the frame of family. We do it to erase and remake our origins in their own images. To say, I too was here.

And guess what? Turns out, I had a twin.

Did I mention I'm a Gemini?

When I say "twin," I don't mean biologically ... though who knows, the way genetics travel the superhighways of blood and cells. My twin in the tribe has blonde hair. Blue eyes. Unusual relationships with sentences. Weird views on culture and storytelling. Fire in his fingers and shooting out the top of his head.

I met my twin when I was miraculously invited to give a literary reading at San Diego State University. He had been invited as well. We had been invited together because our writing was, well, weird. There's never been a good word for it as far as I'm concerned. "Experimental" sounds dumb, and "Innovative" sounds strangely snooty. Whatever the word is for taking everything you ever learned about making characters, plots, and storylines and blowing them up like putting firecrackers in the heads of Barbies as I did as a kid, well, that's what we do. Whatever the word is for being more in love with words than with conventions and rules about words, that's us.

Lance Olsen and me, we are, and I say this with some authority, language bandits.

If you don't have a twin in a tribe I'm telling you – drop whatever you are doing in your life and go look for them. The twin and the tribe. I'm serious. Because having a bloodword tie and a tribe pretty much saved me from myself. If I had tried to live one more year trying to be like the people around me I wouldn't have lasted long.

If you Google Lance Olsen you will find that he's kind of a rock star within the tribal sphere we move through. But that isn't why I love him or why I have his back forever. It's this: his words make my words more possible. In his language my brain stops blow up and new ideas shoot out. In his books the moment of a kiss on Nietzsche's lips, or the seconds before a film begins in a theater in the Mall of America, or the instant before a blast that atomizes the very differences between warring hearts makes you forget the beginning, the middle, and the end as you knew it.

And you will find that he is a Fiction Collective Two author and editor. Like me. If you Google FC2, you will find their mission statement: "FC2 is among the few alternative presses in America devoted to publishing fiction considered by America's largest publishers too challenging, innovative, or heterodox for the commercial milieu."

I don't know about you , but "heterodox" sounds kinda brainy to me. So I will say this. I am a wrecker and maker of wordhouses. Me and my twin have each other's backs. And we're coming for your women and children.

Secular Miracle

NOT ALL MIRACLES COME FROM GOD OR LOOKING UP.

To say that what happened to me in the winter of my early thirties was a miracle is puny compared to what transpired. It started so small. In my hands. In that winter, I sent a short story out as a writing sample. The short story was called "The Chronology of Water." I sent the story four places: to the Admissions Committee for the MFA in writing at Columbia University; to the hiring committee for a tenure track teaching position; to Oregon Literary Arts as a writing sample for a grant; to *Poets and Writers* as a writing sample for something called the Writer's Exchange grant.

In the space of one month my mailbox presented me with letters exactly like the ones that had come to my home in Florida when I longed to swim to college. Only this time I was the only one who would read these letters, an adult woman who had put something of her busted up self straight no chaser into the world. They came one at a time – white and geometric and smelling of something like what if.

I was accepted into Columbia University.

I was offered the teaching job.

I was awarded a $3,000 grant for my story.

And I won the Writer's Exchange prize.

All in the same month.

NOTHING in my life had ever happened to me like that.

And most likely never will. Like the sea of my life waters had opened up. Like my wounds had something in them besides hurt.

Me being me, I chose the job over the MFA. This is important – the MFA was what I wanted more than anything. You have no idea. With all my broken little heart. But I couldn't choose it. I had to survive, is what I chose. I had to take care of myself. No one else would. And so I swallowed the desire to name myself as a writer who would go to Columbia. Like the swimmer who couldn't go to Columbia, either.

I took the grant money and bought a car. I wanted to go to Paris but I bought a car instead. A reliable car to get to and from work. I didn't take myself out to dinner, I didn't buy myself champagne, I didn't eat chocolate.

Thank god the go to New York Writer's Exchange prize didn't have a practical alternative for self destructive people or I would have let that go, too. Almost in spite of myself then, I went to New York. Where the writers are.

The "prize" of winning a Writer's Exchange grant from *Poets and Writers* is that you go from one state to another – in my case, Oregon to NYC. You get to choose writers you'd most like to meet and the *Poets and Writers* folks try very hard to arrange meetings. You get to give a reading at the National Poetry Club, you get to stay at the Gramercy Park Hotel and drink scotch into the night with smart cool people as if you are one too, you get to meet editors and publishers and writers and agents at very fancy lunches and dinners. How fancy? I kept the napkins and receipt scraps. From 1996.

The person who judged the contest on the fiction side of things was Carol Maso. I only entered because of her. Her writing was considered "experimental." "Innovative." "Heterodox." All I know is that her weird made my weird feel better. The writers I wanted to meet were Lynn Tillman, Peggy Phelan, and Eurydice. I don't know if you know them like I do, but to me they were the intellectual shit. I didn't actually think it would happen, I just got drunk, wrote the names down on the form they sent, laughed, farted, and mailed it back to them. I remember thinking, fat chance. My ass. But Frazier Russell collected them all. This is how four of the most humble happy nights of my entire life happened to me. Dinners that cost more than my rent. Food that tasted so good I thought I might faint. Wine that made your teeth melt. And women so intelligent, so creative, so gorgeous and present in their own minds and bodies ... I mean I nearly barfed, piddled, and orgasmed all at the same time. Fuck heaven. Puny cloud lie. These women were the loves of my brain life.

These four women wrote unconventionally. Intentionally unconventionally. Wildly, passionately, blood-bodied, unapologetically blowing up the house of language from the inside out, unconventionally. And all four of them insisted on the body as content. They were not mainstream writers. They were carving out astonishing paths of their own quite to the side of mainstream, quite in spite of the stupid mainstream, maybe the way water cut the grand canyon. I wanted my writing to go like theirs. Follow it. I felt like their writing had parted the seas for people like me.

I can't tell you how many times I choked up talking to each of these women. Looking into their eyes. Trying to see an I. I don't think I said much. It's possible I went mute. It's hard to remember anything about me. Though I remember nearly every word each of them said. Of this I am sure: I was never as ... happy.

More magic happened on that trip – there was a poet guy who traveled with me from Oregon. He'd won the poet side of the prize. Turns out, I knew him from the Eugene days. Incredibly wonderful man stunning poet named John Campbell. Among the poets he requested was Gerald Stern, who I will never forget eating and talking with because he'd dislocated his shoulder and wore this sling thing all evening – only able to gesticulate with one arm. Still, he was something. We also lunched with Billy Collins and Alfred Corn. The latter I adored. The former talked to my tits. But my poet friend also requested to go to a jazz club in place of one of his writer choices. So I got to sit about 15 feet from Hamiet Bluiett at one club and about five feet from McCoy Tyner at another. I'm pretty sure when I got back to the hotel that night my underwear was soaked to shit from glee. Thank you forever, John Campbell.

What an opportunity, huh? Oregon writers in the big city. Still makes me smile and get a piss shiver remembering it.

But there is a bittersweet in my throat too. A small stone I carry there. The small stone of sad that came from my inability to say yes. I was taken to meet an editor at Farrar, Strauss and Giroux. He talked to me about my life as a swimmer, and he suggested I had a nonfiction book in me about my swimmer's life. I don't know, say, like a memoir. I stood there like a numb idiot smiling and shaking my head with my arms crossed over my tits. He waited for me to jump at his suggestion. Nothing nothing nothing came out of my throat. He shook my hand and wished me luck. He gave me some free books.

I sat at dinner between Lynn Tillman and the beloved W. W. Norton Editor Carol Houck Smith – who sadly has since died – while Lynne tried to convince Carol to publish me at Norton. Carol Houck Smith, who leaned over and said well then send me something. Her bright fierce little eyes staring right through my know nothing skull. Most people would have stepped off the plane back in Oregon and run to the post office. It took me over a decade to even imagine putting something in an envelope and licking it.

After the reading at the National Poetry Club, the agent Katherine Kidde from then Kidde, Hoyt and Piccard came up to me and asked me if I'd like representation. On the spot. My small sad throat stone. I went deaf and smiled and shook her hand. I thought I might cry in front of all the dressed up people. All that came out of my mouth was "I don't know."

She said, "OK then."

All those open hands held out to me.

You see it is important to understand how damaged

people don't always know how to say yes, or to choose the big thing, even when it is right in front of them. It's a shame we carry. The shame of wanting something good. The shame of feeling something good. The shame of not believing we deserve to stand in the same room in the same way as all those we admire. Big red As on our chests.

I never thought to myself growing up, be a lawyer. An astronaut. The President. A scientist. A doctor. An architect.

I didn't even think, be a writer.

Aspiration gets stuck in some people. It's difficult to think yes. Or up. When all you feel is fight or run.

If I could go back, I'd coach myself. I'd be the woman who taught me how to stand up, how to want things, how to ask for them. I'd be the woman who says, your mind, you imagination, they are everything. Look how beautiful. You deserve to sit at the table. The radiance falls on all of us.

I knew even on the plane back to the west as the evergreens and rivers came back into view through the perfect drizzle of home that if I was a woman writer, then I was a broken kind of woman writer. I drank many tiny bottles of airplane feel sorry for yourself. I flew back to Oregon without a book deal, without an agent, with only a head and heartful of beautiful memories about what it would be like to be a writer, since I'd eaten with them and shared such perfect company. It was the only prize I allowed myself.

But something in me had been born, still.

Dreaming in Women

SOMETIMES A MIND IS JUST BORN LATE, COMING THROUGH waves on a slower journey. You were never, in the end, alone. Isn't it a blessing, what becomes from inside the alone.

With Marguerite Duras, you must lie down on a bed in an apartment in a foreign city – foreign to you – foreign enough so that you become the foreigner. Lose your name and your language. Lose your identity moorings. Lose your very thoughts. There must be shutters on the tall slightly open windows. The room must be blue. The floor made of stone. You must be naked. Her breath a whisper against your skin. Up the length of your body. Down. You must listen for the sounds of the city moving all around you. You must listen then beyond that, to the ocean and wind beyond all human motion. And then you must listen beyond that, to the blood in your ears and the drum of your heart and how a lover's skin stories over you. At night, it will rain. Open the windows. Desire wets. There is no inside out but the body. Love unto death.

With Gertrude Stein there will be eating and paper. Tea and money. She will say it gracefully. She will say it with ice-cream. Eating and paper. A flesh circle. So kind. And then again again.

Make quiet for Emily Dickinson. Sing gently a hymn in between the heaves of storm. Let the top of your head lift. See? There are spaces between things. What you thought was nothing-ness carries the life of it.

In the next room H. D. has brought the walls down, but look how the light dances across the floor of things differently now. Even your feet are new.

With Hélène Cixous you must close your eyes and open your mouth. Wider. So open your throat opens. Your esophagus. Your lungs. Wider. So open your spine unclatters. Your hips swim loose. Your womb worlds itself. Wider. Open the well of your sex. Now speak your body from your other mouth. Yell corporeal prayer. This is writing.

Jean Rhys came through the vast corpus of literature like water cutting canyon.

Adrienne Rich went down into the depths ahead of you. Her dive brought the possibility of language up to your surface. Breathe. And understand the broad shoulders you are standing on to reach the air. Take these objects.

With Margaret Atwood and Doris Lessing you will learn to stiffen your spine, when to laugh and throw the drink back, when to weep and with whom, when to pick up a rifle.

Jeanette Winterson will make a small thing enormous as the cosmos.

Toni Morrison will let you cry home the passage.

Leslie Marmon Silko whispers the story is long. No, longer. Longer than that even. Longer than anything.

With Anne Sexton and Sylvia Plath drink at the bar. Laugh the dark laughter in the dark light. Sing a dark drunken song of men. Make a slurry toast. Rock back and forth, and drink the dark, and bask in the wallow of women knowing what women know. Just for a night.

When you need to feel the ground of your life and the heart of the world, there will be a bonfire at the edge of a canyon under a night sky where Joy Harjo will sing your bonesong.

Go ahead – with Anne Carson – rebuild the wreckage of a life a word at a time, ignoring grammar and the forms that keep culture humming. Make word war and have it out and settle it, scattering old meanings like hacked to pieces paper doll confetti. The lines that are left ... they are awake and growling.

With Virginia Woolf there will perhaps be a long walk in a garden or along a shore, perhaps a walk that will last all day. She will put her arm in yours and gaze out. At your backs will be history. In front of you, just the ordinary day, which is of course your entire life. Like language. The small backs of words. Stretching out horizonless.

I am in a midnight blue room. A writing room. With a blood red desk. A room with rituals and sanctuaries. I made it for myself. It took me years. I reach down below my desk and pull up a bottle of scotch. Balvenie. 30 year. I pour myself an amber shot. I drink. Warm lips, throat. I close my eyes. I am not Virginia Woolf. But there is a line of hers that keeps me well: Arrange whatever pieces come your way.

I am not alone. Whatever else there was or is, writing is with me.

V. The Other Side of Drowning

Run On

IT'S YOUR SECOND EX-HUSBAND'S BIRTHDAY, YOU KNOW,
the one you divorced because he slept with not one but about
five gazillion different women, and he calls you at 2:00 a.m. all
drunk from Paris where you two used to rent apartments and
make art because it's his birthday and he tells you he's fallen in
love with a woman who reminds him of you at 23 – By the way,
I'm switching to second person because if I say "I," in your head
you'll just picture Heather Locklear or something so – YOU.
You are 37 on your way to the big 4-0. You are divorced for the sad
sad second time. You are in SoCal. Living alone. Making sure
your blonde is blonde. Waxed.

So your second ex-husband calls on his birthday and tells
you he's fallen in love with a woman who reminds him of you at
23 and that they've tattooed their ring fingers together and she
looks so much like you and acts so much like you and smells so
much like you at 23 so you calmly hang up the phone and
glimpse the 37 year old skin of your own hand and walk to your
writing desk and open the drunk drawer and pull out the bottle
and drink an entire bottle of scotch in the middle of the night
and drive your car out onto the six northbound lanes of the freeway in SoCal where you now live due to your great new job as
the Visiting Writer because you did the strong thing and left him
because you didn't want to be an enabler and so forth and you
wanted to rise above it and get on with your life so there you are
on this freeway in SoCal in a red car with your blonde hair and

your black dress and your stiletto heels to prove to yourself that you are still attractive like a fucking advertisement for Black Velvet and wait a minute, what's that shiny you see some pretty lights to the right twinkle twinkle little star and WOOSH you are cutting tracks through the thick ice plant between southbound and northbound freeway lanes at 90 literally carving through them with scars that will last weeks and be on the nightly news and spinning out big time and coming to a smoky stop – miraculously – pointed in the right direction in the southbound lanes.

You know what to do. You floor it. Laughing that maniacal laugh of a 37 year old divorced woman who should be dead but isn't.

A little soggy voice in your head goes take the next exit ramp and get your drunk ass home which you see as if you are looking through water up ahead you take it and you let go of the steering wheel like your hands are floating away from things until BAM you drive head-on into another car and your airbags deploy like two enormous fatty sagging breasts and the police come and you are sauced beyond belief and everything smells a little like gunpowder and scotch and it's ma'am get out of the car and ma'am stand on one foot and count backwards from 100 with your eyes closed and with this stick up your ass and balancing an egg on your left tit and what else?

You are cuffed and breathalyzed. You blow a number out of orbit. Don't even try. You are so beyond the legal limit you could power a car. Gimme a D to the U to the I. Oh and in case you were feeling any shred of hotness left in your bones, when you look pleadingly into the young male cop's rearview on the car ride to the facility and say, couldn't you just take me home? With what you think are pout lips and bed blond hair, he looks back at you with – you guessed it – woman, you are old as shit pity in his eyes.

Inside the jail the rerun begins. The first thing that happens that has already happened is that you are inside. You have been in jail before. You have a record. Not very many people know that since you look exactly like a Visiting Writer and anyhow you have always been a snappy dresser.

The second thing that happens that has already happened is there is another woman in the holding cell who is going through heroin withdrawal. She's drooling and she's in a tight ball arms choking knees and she's banging her head back against the wall and spitting about every eight seconds. Your left arm aches. Your feet go numb. You go sit next to her. You look a little bit like a martyr-ish crappy-ass too white benevolent Visiting Writer on the outside but what's not visible to the naked eye is that you haven't been clean all that many years, which suddenly has shrunken to the size of a human head. Weren't you getting a little cocky about it too, your beautiful recovery, your distancing yourself from yourselfstory.

Which takes you to the third thing that happens over again which is how quickly you become the Universal Caretaker when YOU are the sorry ass loser who needs the HELP, giving your socks to the black woman on welfare and holding the hand of the lumpy 50-year old woman who is actually maybe 28. You find yourself dialing the number of the boyfriend of the crack queen with the Alice Cooper mascara drool face. No really, you are on the payphone calling for her even though she has choke bruises around her neck, she begs you to call him so you do, you intervene, you become an objective outside resource, you tell him to call and drop the charges so she can get out since it is so obvious that he has abused her and later in life she will have one helluvuh case, one in which you will be a witness of course, watch out guy, you teach Women's Studies, and he proceeds to describe to you what she did to his living room and his cat and his motorcycle with a baseball bat and the house on fire before he calls you a fucking cunt whore ignorant bitch and hangs up.

Undeterred, you find yourself calling the guard to get the fat woman some Tylenol as you listen to the Christian chick with a silk scarf and a screw loose self-narrating her experience with the guy from the hotel bar who she believed was there for the Jesus on Ice convention. All of this activity suddenly takes its psychosomatic toll on you and your morning after green puke bellied nasty kicks in and you realize with a kind of brick to the lower spine feeling that you have to take an enormous scotch shit. Which you take, of course, in front of everyone, like cons have to, no matter how much the outfit they are wearing costs, no matter how beautiful a martyr they make, no matter how pretty the letters Ph.D. look after your dumb ass Visiting Writer name, you still have to shit in the presence of a crowd.

Weird, huh.

You close your eyes.

You breathe.

You are not sorry yet for what you have done.

You are simply an incarcerated woman.

Remorse, she came later. Lemme throw it into reverse.

Let me tell you who I hit.

Collision as Metaphor

THE PERSON I HIT IN MY HEAD-ON COLLISION WAS A 5′ tall brown skinned woman.

In the moment, this did not upset me. In the moment, I was drunk as a monkey, and so the entire scene that night looked a little like things were in slow motion and smeared over with Vaseline. And at a tremendous distance from my heart and whatever it might have said. Addicts have a problem comprehending gravitas. Everything just looks blurry.

My airbags deployed. Pow. If you have never had that experience, it's quite something. It's loud. Like gunshot loud. And everything smells like dynamite. If you were holding the steering wheel with both hands, your arms get heat and friction burns on the insides. Your head, because it didn't hit the windshield, smashes face first into the Michelin Man surface of the airbag; then your head jets back and knocks your noggin against the headrest. Afterwards, you just sort of sit there and wait for the dust to settle and your brains to recollect themselves. It helps to close your eyes and wait for everything to stop moving.

The person I hit in my head-on collision was a 5′ tall brown skinned woman who had no English.

I know that she had no English because, after I sat there trying to feel whether or not anything was broken or searing me with pain – which it wasn't, particularly since I had anesthetized myself with the bottle of scotch – I opened my car door and looked around. My car, a red Toyota Corolla, was weirdly angled

and had its face smashed in. Her car, a white … I'm not sure – it looked something like those old Gremlins – her car was smashed in on the left side all the way up to the windshield. Something warm and metallic filled my mouth. I'd bitten my tongue.
I saw the woman sitting on the guard rail, crying, saying things I didn't understand. Her hair was more black than the night around us. She had a lump the size of a golf ball on her forehead. No airbag. Her skirt was white and billowed out at times.

The person I hit in my head-on collision was a 5′ tall brown skinned pregnant woman who had no English.

How I knew the woman carried life in her gut is that her belly had the unmistakable mound of a child. Six, possibly seven months of child mound. At the time, this did not alarm me; as I said, I had the sensitivity of a drunk. Though I did feel a prickle of something far far inside my abdomen. I sat down next to her. She began to wail and hold her belly. I said, "Are you in pain?" She did not look at me or answer. Dumbly, I put my arm around her shoulders. I have no idea why she let me do that. She rocked. Inconsolably.

I didn't feel anything. No, literally. I couldn't feel my hands, my feet, my ass. I couldn't feel my own face.

The woman fumbled in her skirt pocket and pulled out a cell phone. I thought perhaps she was fingering 911, but she was not. I could see she was trying to dial a number. Someone she knew. Someone to help. I couldn't manage my own cell phone. I looked at it in my hand. I couldn't see any numbers, or how to activate the thing. It sat like a dead rodent. I noticed I smelled faintly of piss.

I don't know how long we sat there. The sound of cars whizzing by comforted me. After a while three cop cars and an ambulance showed up. I remember the sound of sirens trying to out-do one another. The cops blocked off the bit of road we were on – the overpass between north and southbound lanes. I cupped my ears with my hands. I remember the red white and blue lights flashing all around us. Something about the swirls of color looked like we were inside an underwater scene.

The cops immediately separated us. Her, they took over to the ambulance. Me, they asked me if I felt OK and I replied with a quite obviously soggy yes. They had a paramedic come over and "check me out" but no one was very worried about me since I could walk and talk. I hadn't a bruise or bump or cut on me, other than the airbag burns on my inner arms. My distinguishing characteristic: shit-faced. The emotions all went in the direction of the pregnant woman and her unborn child. Except mine. Mine floated toward nothingness.

While the cop put me through my paces, nearly all of which I failed in that ever so slight way that is inevitable given the amount I'd consumed, I thought of my mother. Literally – when the cop had me close my eyes and attempt that finger to the nose thing? I saw my mother's face. Puffy with drink and covered in sadness ... not a maternal, Madonna sadness. A sadness made from joy being siphoned from your life a year at a time.

I have a photo of my mother when she was a girl. It was between leg and hip operations. In this photo she was not in a body cast. It was probably taken a few years before my grandmother divorced my grandfather for molesting my mother's sisters. She looks to be about 13. It is the sweetest girl face you have ever seen, but something in the tilt of her head, something in the lowered gaze, you can already see the sadness in her.

I know this isn't true, but in some ways, I can see the woman who would pick up a bottle of vodka and never put it down. I can see the bottle of sleeping pills. The marriage that went so horribly wrong, and still she couldn't leave. I can see the mother whose children drifted so quickly away from her like fish cut loose. I can see the Cancer that came to the rescue, for as her sister said to me shortly before she died, "Every day of her sweet life she was in pain, of one sort or another. At least now she'll have peace."

Where does repressed pain and rage go in a body? Does

the wound of daughter turn to something else if left unattended?
Does it bloom in the belly like an anti-child, like an organic
mass made of emotions that didn't have anywhere to go? How do
we name the pain of rage in a woman? Mother?

I cannot see in her face that her children gave her joy,
though she said that to me the week before she died, and
I thought, looking at her milk white shrunken body, almost the
body of a girl, how?

When the cop hand cuffed me and told me to sit in the
back of his copmobile I was glad. Inside his car it was quiet.
It smelled like air freshener and leather. I closed my eyes. Somewhere, very far away inside me, I felt a tiny pang of pain for the
woman I'd hit and what was in her belly. But it was too much for
me, so I opened my eyes and watched the cop write things
down on a small clipboard instead.

Briefly and without any drama I wished I was dead. But
there were no other emotions or thoughts accompanying that.
It just sat there like me in the back seat of a cop car, flat and
plain and unevolved. Then he was driving me away from the
scene to the station to be breathalyzed.

In my head way back at the base of my skull near the top
of my spinal cord I didn't mean to I didn't mean to I didn't mean
to I didn't mean to I didn't mean to I didn't, did I?

Mean to?

The night stretched out long like it does when you fuck up.
It's like a night that lasts a year. Or like all the years of your life
are suddenly in your lap, wailing like needy children. You can't
take care of all of them. You don't even want to. You want to
abandon each yearchild on the side of the road and bolt. I am not
your mother.

After the autopsy of my baby girl, a doctor told me in his
office, "There is nothing conclusive to associate with her death.
The cord was not around her neck, and there were no identifi-
able physical problems of any sort. Here is a copy of the autopsy
report. I'm sorry. Sometimes this happens, and there is no

explanation." I stared at the white wall behind his head. He handed me a form that encouraged me to attend a special group therapy for parents whose babies died.

When I left his office, I went into the clinic bathroom. I pulled my pants down and peed. I kept sitting there. Then I began to shred the white form he'd given to me into tiny pieces of paper, and I ate them, crying without a sound.

The person I hit was a brown skinned pregnant woman who had no English. She sat on the dirty silver guardrail and cried. I watched her shoulders shake. She buried her face in her hands. She said words I didn't know into her own palms. She held her belly and rocked and wept. When they took me away I was so relieved I almost thanked the cops – strange saviors. In my head I thought take me away from this woman. I can't be near her. I can't look at her. I can't even accept that she exists. The image of a grieving mother is one that could kill me.

How to Love Your Mother After She's Dead

I FIRST MET MY MOTHER WHEN SHE WAS BORN WITH one leg more than six inches shorter than the other. A scar running kid-eye high up the length of her outer leg. From knee to hip. Stretching upward like wide pearled and waxen tracks. The eyes of a child fix on things. In the mornings while she dressed I would put my face so close to it I could feel my eyes shiver.

I first met my mother when I was born cesarean. Babies wouldn't fit through the tilt of her hips and birth canal without their skulls caving in. When they reached in to slice the caul – that amniotic membrane between her body and mine – my eyes were already open.

I first met my mother in her childhood. In the operating rooms and hospitals that were her home for years and years. Inside the body casts. Next to the ridicule of hordes of gremlin children. Hobbling atop a shoe with a four inch wooden block attached.

I first met my mother the day my father threw a fist intimately close to her head just missing her cheekbone and instead opened up a gaping mouth in the kitchen wall that stayed like that for years.

I first met my mother the day my father's mother said in her presence, "I don't know why you had to marry a cripple."

I first met my mother when she told me the only man who ever loved her right was gay, and he died "a death that laid waste to his body, Belle." Before anyone knew what AIDS was.

I first met my mother the day she told me she could see things that weren't there, except that they were, like armies crossing the freeway at night, like sea serpents over the side of the Golden Gate Bridge, like a UFO in the sky above her house in Port Arthur, Texas, like rabid poodles in the pear tree of our house at Stinson Beach. I was 12.

I first met my mother the night I had to wipe her smear of a 55-year old self off of the casino floor in Biloxi, Mississippi. The skin of her face was as soft and pelted as a baby's head.

I first met my mother the night before my first of three marriages, when she turned to me and said, I almost married a rodeo man. His name was J.T. The next morning at my wedding, out on a beach in Corpus Christi, in the stage of menopause wherein your periods go nuts, she bled, a giant red wound blooming behind her if she'd been shot in the ass.

I first met my mother inside the fury of our arguments – matching each other's rage all through my puberty and her middle age, how strangely glorious her never backing down, no one ever winning, just two women's voices like claps of thunder drowning out the world.

I first met my mother inside her lifelong leg and hip pain. Underneath the arm length scar where a steel plate masqueraded as bone. A body in pain for the duration of a life. Every hour of existence.

I first met my mother when she signed the scholarship papers setting me free.

I first met my mother her singing I see the moon, the moon sees me, the moon sees everyone I want to see, god bless the moon, and god bless me, and god bless everyone I want to see. Her voice carrying me to dream. The weight of father lifting, lifting.

If I close my eyes I can see her.

I remember the first time I saw her swim, joining me in the deep water, leaving my father standing impotently in chest high water. How powerful her sidestroke. The joy in her face.

How beautiful the gleaming white skin of her arms. The long glide of her. The water swallowing the fact of her pain, her marriage, her leg.

My mother loved to swim more than anyone I know.

Swan.

Your Tax Dollars At Work

Ernesto
Alejo
Angel
Manuel
Rick
Ricardo
Sonny
Lebron
Pedro
Jimarcus
Lidia

Notice anything about those names?

Six Mexicans, one Italian, one African-American, one Jamaican, one white dishonorably discharged Navy guy wound tighter than dynamite, and me. Compliments of the State of California.

The posse. All in day-glo orange vests on the side of the freeway picking up your trash with sticks that have "grabbers" on the ends of them. At least that was one of the week's assignments. The easiest and least humiliating. Who we were on paper:

Breaking and Entering (but not stealing anything. ?)
Possession
Possession

DUI

Domestic Violence

DUI

Possession

Driving without a License or Vehicle Registration

Fleeing a Crime Scene and Failure to Produce Identification

Public Intoxication and Indecent Exposure

And a big blond

D

U

I

Doing time on a road crew in the hot asphalt and suntan lotion world of San Diego makes you feel like you are in much crappier remake of the movie *Cool Hand Luke*. Everybody who is tanned and glamorous – the paid for whitey pretty smiles and the paid for bleached blonde color weaves and the paid for total laser hair removal jobs and the paid for body parts – drives by you like you are ice plant or oleander. The stuff in the divider between the zipping lanes of freeway life. When cars go by your hair blows up and hot wind brushes your face. The sound of all that driving and social surface life can make you feel nuts.

There's no Paul Newman challenging the man. You put your trash in shitty plastic bags and when you fill one you tie it off and leave it on the side of the road and move on. You don't get to stand around. If you stand around, officer Kyle comes over to you and reprimands you verbally. If you talk back it's simple – you go straight to jail. But you also develop ... strategies for moving as slowly as possible. Why hurry? There's only more trash. There's never-ending trash. And you are part of the trash – you are a trash advertisement.

Except for dishonorably discharged Rick, who had the kind of eyes that said I WILL BEAT THE FUCK OUT OF ANYONE WHO TALKS TO ME, me and my homeboys slowly but surely got along. You'd think not, right? Some middle aged bouge blonde woman with sagging tits getting along with a bunch of SoCal thugs? Au contraire.

People who have been to jail more than once can smell it on each other.

Men in groups operate through a series of male codes. Movements in the hands and eyes. Stances. Verbal exchanges with triple entendres. Little challenges and invisible battles and hierarchies worked out. So I rarely spoke and I never wore make-up and I wore baggy assed pants and I made goddamn sure my labor was not that of a woman. Luckily, I have the shoulders and strength of a swimmer.

The second week I lifted a big chunka railroad tie by myself. I hoisted it up onto my shoulder, and even though I knew my spine was crumpling up a vertebrae at a time like little wads of paper, I looked bad ass enough to be ... what's the word. A trusted body.

I've never been treated less like a woman in my life. I remember telling a colleague of mine – one of the only people who knew that by day I was out there with my posse while at night I had a fancy visiting writer job teaching budding young MFAs how to make their words more wonderful and she said: "Do they say lewd things to you? Do they do anything ... you know, weird around you or to you? Aren't you scared to be around those people?" I just stared at her. I tried to picture what she pictured. A bunch of male mostly minority small time criminals – those people – and a blonde woman who ... who what? Who did she believe I was? She taught World Lit. and drove a Beamer.

Who I was. I was the convict with the best English. The day Jimarcus asked me what I did for a living, and I told him I taught English at SDSU, he laughed.

"Hey mahn, check it out. We got a Professor with us," he broadcasted one day when we were scraping crap off of the walls of the county elections office.

A slow laugh made its way through the chests of the other men. And smiles. They'd smile like nothing you've ever seen before. All that dark skin opening. They slapped my back or put a hand on my shoulder and shook their heads, laughing, laughing. They laughed in a way that somehow felt good. "But you with us now, sistah?" Jimarcus would say, shaking his headful of dreads. After that they all started calling me "Doctor." You know what they wanted? They wanted me to teach them how to talk more like everyone else. They wanted more English.

On road crew my hands blistered so badly from hacking down sea grass with giant dull-bladed loppers near Sea World I couldn't hold a cup of coffee.

On road crew if there was heavy lifting my scoliosis spastic back hurt so bad when I got home every night I'd go straight to a bath and lay in it and cry.

On road crew we spray washed graffiti and painted it over with mindless gray paint. We laid tar. We carried concrete and wood and glass away from condemned buildings. Once Rick cut his arm and punched a hole in a wall. He got extra days for that. I surmised Rick was also in anger management classes.

Our assignments were mostly cleaning up the world so people can pretend it's not dirty, chaotic, out of control, a giant world-sized compost heap.

Once we cleaned toilets in day use area parks. You haven't lived until you have to pull tampons and needles and condoms and cigarette butts out of a john. Yellow plastic gloves just don't seem to quite make you feel better.

I got the closest with Ernesto. Ernesto played classical guitar. I never heard him or saw him play but I watched him air guitar it when he described it. I'd ask him about it on breaks and at lunch and he'd Spanglish it out to me – what I didn't need language for was how beautiful he looked talking about music. Or his hands. After a while he began to ask me to translate things. A word at a time. "Dr. Lidia. What is English meterse en líos? What is English un llamamiento a la compassion?" To get into trouble. To call for compassion.

All those weeks we labored. We sweat. It is a "we" I have

not been able to use as a word the same way since. There isn't a proper translation.

The eighth week of road crew we'd split up in teams under an overpass near Balboa park. The trees and bushes were thick and lush so we had the mercy of shade. Things smelled like water was near, but it was probably the highly advanced sprinkler system that helps keep Balboa park green and sparkly and fit for tourists.

Me, Jimarcus, Sonny the chubby Italian and Ernesto were shuffling trash with our sticks. Jimarcus yelled out hey mahn and pointed to a little path in the shrubs. So we followed him. After we were dumped off in a parking lot by officer Kyle, Jimarcus shared cigarettes when we finished each day that made you feel pretty good. To this day I've no idea what was in them. That's why we followed him. Because at the end of the day he'd ease us.

So we're walking down this little brush lined path and suddenly Jimarcus stops so Ernesto stops so I stop and chubby Sonny, who is last, kinda bumps into me. There in front of us, peaceful as can be, is a sleeping bum.

I think that's what some people call him, right?

I'm not sure what a good translation is. But I'm guessing some people would go with "bum" because of how he looked. And smelled. Our bum had an enormous Grizzly Adams beard. His hair shot out untamed and ratted – probably there were bugs in it, possibly worse. And his skin was red and pockmarked and puffy with drink. His nose landscape looked lunar. And he smelled like week-old sweet burned apple piss. Enough to sting your nasal passages and make your eyes water. I'd say he was about 5'8" and weighed maybe 210. His belly a smelly mound.

But what was most striking about our bum, and what made Sonny nearly puke on the spot, is that his pants were down around his ankles, and his exposed genitals were swollen. I mean like huge. I mean elephant man huge. His balls were the size of purpley croquet balls. His dick looked a little like a reptile had gotten loose. And the pièce de résistance? There was a giant pile of human shit about a foot and a half away from him. He smiled in his sleep. He snored. Sonny gagged.

Jimarcus said fuck mahn and Ernesto laughed and Sonny bent over how you do when you are going to vomit and I said "Shhhhhhhh! You'll wake his ass up!" So we backed up like kids who've seen something they weren't supposed to. The bum? He just slept the sound sleep of babies and puppies.

When we got back to the group none of us said a fucking thing about our bum. Rick would have popped a spring in that geared up little skull of his and beat the shit out of our bum. And look, there was no way we were going to tell the clean-shaven officer Kyle. He would have arrested our bum. We already knew what it felt like to be arrested. Multiple times. We already knew what it felt like to fuck up. To be passed out drunk. To stink. To not want to be alive. To wake up with your face on the pavement. To use words but find your sentences doubling back and betraying you. To stay in a hotel for a week when you hear on TV the police are doing a sweep. To have no one who understands. To be passing – leading a double life. Maybe we didn't yet know what it was like to have swollen genitals the size of Texas, but metaphorically – some body part out of control – some piece of you gone freakish – kind of we did.

So we just left him there. In a kind of peace. Next to his own shit.

Vagabundo.

The last week of my period of service we had to pull weeds along this giant paved road that led up to some fancy ass facility of some sort up on the hill. In a wealthy neighborhood filled with white people with Mexican and Filipino house cleaners. The "trees" that lined the grand lane were tiny, so the only shade you could get was on part of your face and maybe a shoulder. We went through the giant yellow plastic vat of water in the first two hours – I think it was something like 98 degrees that day. Goddamn those little paper cone cups.

By the last week my body had become used to the labor. I didn't get blisters and my wrists didn't ache and I'd stocked up on Vicodin so my back felt like anyone's. I didn't get dizzy in the sun and I brought enough food in my sack lunch and I smoked Jimarcus' cigarettes and Ernesto and I took our breaks together to practice English. I was not unhappy. I had a pretty great tan.

But really, I was going home, to my plush little bouge life. Half of them were going to jail. Ernesto disappeared part way through the ninth week. So that "we" I'm using? Well. It's just language.

At the top of the hill we got to rest. The shade of an enormous Torrey Pine tree umbrellad out and held us so we could feel the coolness of breeze. We drank water. We ate our pathetic little brown sack lunches. I thought about Ernesto playing guitar, but my guess is he wasn't.

That day though what I also felt was it's over. This small thing I did with these men I'll never see again. Something about that made me feel irrecoverably sad. But I was of course also thrilled to be "done" with my punishment. I closed my eyes and drank a Coke from a glass bottle. So simple. I wished Ernesto were there. Drinking a Coke. When I opened my eyes, I stared at my hands and how not Mexican they looked. My hands, they just looked … dumb.

Then I looked up the hill and saw the giant concrete and wood sign of the facility we had just carved our way up to.

The Cerritos Olympic Swim Center.

I'd competed there when I was 14. I'd won the 100-meter breaststroke. Sometimes I think I've been everywhere before.

Conversion

I'VE BEEN THINKING. MAYBE RECOVERING CATHOLICS turn to movies for salvation. I mean, in an informal poll that I took recently, a whole lot of ex-catholics seem unusually moved by film. The bigger and more epic the better. And we still really like sitting in the dark – if they ever get rid of movie theaters you are going to see a bunch of lapsed catholics wandering around in the street looking for a dark box to go sit inside so we can experience catharsis ...

Enter the Mingo, stage left.

Andy Mingo in a shitty ass Isuzu Trooper. After my head-on collision, an MFA thesis student of mine at San Diego State University walked into my life like a movie star, offering to loan me one of his cars. By the time I met him in San Diego, I was a woman who had to crash her car.

The first time I really saw Andy was at my SDSU job interview. He very nearly fucked my shit up – sitting there looking a little like Marlon Brando. I'm up there trying like crazy to sound cogent and smart, jawing it around postmodernism like someone a university should hire and he's zinging me with puffy lips and intense stares and is that a flattened spot just above his nose like in *On the Waterfront*? I swear to god the line "I coulda been a contendah" crept into my frontal lobe. I distinctly remember thinking, whoa. That guy is trouble.

When it came time for the question answer portion of the presentation, Andy Mingo raised his hand and asked, "What is your teaching philosophy with regard to what graduate students in creative writing should be reading?" All the grad students leaned forward at me.

I said, "Everything. They should read everything they can get their hands on. What they love, what they hate, all of it. You wouldn't jump into an empty pool, would you? Literature is the medium. You have to swim in it."

He crossed his arms over his chest. He glared at me. Pissed. It was not the answer he was apparently hoping for.

What I thought was, fuck you, Mingo. How many books have you written, big sexy looking guy? You've got a problem with reading? You can kiss my ass.

Miraculously, I got the job.

Every day I saw him in the graduate writing workshop Andy stared so hard at me I thought my skull might fracture. Or something in me, anyway.

After that eventful phone call from Paris that led to my carefully calculated drunk on and drive episode, Andy sauntered into my office and brought me a novel manuscript. A good one. And he offered to let me borrow one of his cars. Mine, was totaled. Like my life.

I borrowed the car.

When I drove his car around I could smell him and feel him. In the seat and on the steering wheel. In the holder thing between seats where I found cassette tapes he listened to. Bob Dylan and The Cure and Sublime. In the glove compartment where I found a lighter and rolling papers. On the car floor he'd so obviously worked hard to vacuum. The engine ran hot.

The kind of teacher I was, I'd meet the grad students to go over their writing anyplace but my office. I've never believed in institutional authority. So I'd let the grad student choose where we'd meet – let them name a place where they felt like themselves – and I would go there to talk with them about writing. With Andy, it was a Mediterranean coffee shop off the beaten track with an outdoor area where we sat under bougainvillea and orange blossoms and spoke of writing.

That sentence cracked me up. Immediately it was not about writing. Man-lust fucks a girl up.

We both wore sunglasses. Since neither of us took them off, I took it as a draw. We both threw out a few mock barbs. Neither flinched. We both executed a couple of low-level sexual innuendos. Dead even. And when I asked him about the references to Italy in his novel, he began to narrate his lifestory – so I came back at him with a bit of mine.

Andy grew up in Reno. And what was coming out of his mouth, well, it was a worthy backstory.

"My mother was a single mother. She taught math. I've always hated math. I grew up with a series of father stand-ins ... guys with names like 'Pidge.'"

I countered with "My mother was an alcoholic pathological liar. On the other hand, she was a great storyteller."

"I was once a bouncer at Paul Revere's 'Kicks' nightclub when I was 19."

"Paul Revere and the Raiders?" I asked, thinking about how when I was 19 I was in Monte's basement.

"The same," he said.

"I've been swimming with Kathy Acker," I said, trying quite hard to impress him.

"Who is Kathy Acker?"

Goose egg. Why had I said that?

"My father was in the C.I.A. He died of a heart attack when I was three. Well at least that's the official story. He was 33, so who knows."

That was a good one. I had to pause and pretend to drink my latte. "33. That was jesus' age." I have no idea why I said that. Why in the world did I bring up jesus? Idiot. Then I said, "My father ... my father ... "

"Your father what?" he asked.

"My father was abusive."

"Oh," he said. "I'm sorry," he said. "What did he do?"

To tell or not to tell. How did I get so quickly to the heart of my wounds? What had just happened?

"Sexual," is all I could manage. Then I wished I was a part of the shrubbery or tableware. Idiotidiotidiotidiot. Why don't you just slit open your own belly like a caught steelhead and spill it out on the table, moron.

"That sucks," he said. And then, "I hope something karmically fucked happened to him?"

Right answer. I laughed. I laughed kind of hard. "Kind of," I said. And we were able to move past the blood clot I'd presented between us.

"Excellent then," he said.

We switched from lattes to wine.

It wasn't just man thing that impressed me. It was his story. How he'd escaped Reno and moved to San Sebastian, Spain, where he briefly witnessed a series of ETA events – the armed Basque nationalist and separatist organization. How he later lived in Italy where he coached a not very good Italian American football team with guys named Mauro Sassaligo, Ugo Spera, and Giacamo Piredu. How he'd interview members of the Earth Liberation Front, how he'd cyber-pirated Bill Gates Microsoft.edu. How he came back to the states – the Northwest, to be exact – to be a writer. Then he said something remarkable.

"In Italy I read about Ken Kesey teaching at U of O. So I applied to the university creative writing program and was accepted. We moved to Eugene. But the Kesey workshop had already happened. I did meet some cool writing teachers though."

"Really," I said. No shit? I got kind of excited but played it smooth and nonchalant. This was my opening to impress. Ahem. "You know, I was in that Kesey year long workshop. Funny, huh."

"Yeah," he said, "I know. I think I saw you in the creative writing department hall after that. Did you have one side of your head shaved back then?"

"What?" I definitely needed more wine.

"Did you have ... a very unusual head back then?" He was staring at my hair.

Man alive. What are the odds? "Well, yes. Yes I did." I slugged what was left of my merlot.

"If you don't mind my asking, why the hell did you do that to your head?"

"Suave," I said, laughing.

"No, I don't mean to sound like asshole, your hair is beautiful. It's just, it looked kind of ... "

"Severe?" I offered.

"Severe," he agreed.

Why did I do that. Why did I. I got butkus. Then it just sort of came out of my mouth as, "I think I did it because I was hurting. I think I wanted to mark that hurt on the outside. I think I wanted to be someone else. But I didn't know who yet." It almost sounded aware.

"I see," he said, "and who are you now?"

Goddamn this guy just goes straight for the kill. Aren't guys his age supposed to be shallow insensitive arrogants? So I said, "I'm your teacher." We both cracked up. The kind of laughter that reveals a gaping fault line big enough to drive a U-haul through.

Then it just got ridiculous – I couldn't stop watching his lips move and I couldn't shut down the electricity creeping up my spine and then it became impossible to maintain the teacher student charade when he took off of his sun glasses for a moment and I took off mine and I swear he performed some kind of sly guy Marlon Brando like from Streetcar eye hoodoo on me. Still, I gave him my written comments on his work like a professional should and sent him away. But he already knew my weakness.

"Um, Dr. Lidia? Don't you need a ride home?"

I know you are not used to women saying this, but I wanted him to drive down into me and eat me alive.

Ecstatic State

OUR FIRST "DATE" ANDY SAID HE WANTED TO GO SWIM-
ming with me. He knew all about the swimmer of me from
reading my stories, which he'd apparently gone home and looked
up that night. Also from stories he'd been told. Now that I look
back at it, it was a brave move. He wasn't that great a swimmer.
He was great at other things – but not swimming. So that must
have taken some man guts. And he was mildly allergic to chlorine.
When he dipped himself in chlorine for long periods, his nose
ran. Non-stop. Still he asked to come swim with me. No one has
ever done that.

No one.

So we swam. In a little Y pool near my rented one bedroom
house in Ocean Beach a block from the sea. In the pool he
fought the water with all his might. Six foot three and built like
a tree his body was meant for land. But he swam with me. Lap
after lap. I lapped him a dozen times. Still he swam. His nose ran.
He stayed with me in the water. When I finally stopped, he
looked me right in the eye. Chlorine smell between us. His eyes
were bloodshot because he refused to wear goggles. He was
more present than anyone in my entire life had ever been. He
smiled. Snot running down his mouth. I smiled back. Fear in my
chest. You can't order a highball in the pool to calm the fuck down.

The second date he took me to a ratty little hole in the
wall Ocean Beach gym where he hit the heavy bag and did mixed
martial arts things I'd never seen, nearly making me cream my

jeans and pass out. I know. How not evolved of me. How not feminist and Ph.D. and university professor. I'm just saying. You could have hosed me down and carried me out on a stretcher.

Then he wrapped and wrapped and wrapped my hands and put the red gloves on me and took me over to a smaller weenier bag and tried to show me how to hit it. Everything smelled like man and sweat and leather and socks. I was the only woman there, and I was not young and hot. I was 38 and he was 28 and it looked that way. But I put my fists up. For him. For him, I tried to find some game. It was going OK, but mostly I bat at it like a girl. Not because I couldn't bring something harder, I was an athlete back in the day after all. But I was COMPLETELY UTTERLY STUPIDLY RIDICULOUSLY SELF CONSCIOUS. Middle-aged woman with hot guy in an O.B. gym.

At one point he tried to help me improve my jabs by having me put both gloves up in front of my face – I didn't realize I was supposed to protect my face, I was intently staring dreamily at his, hoping to look at least minimally sexy. So when he jabbed at my little red paws? I ended up punching myself out. My eyes watered and my nose went numb for a bit. But I stayed. And I hit the bag harder and harder. And when I hit it as hard as I could? It felt good. Um, really good. I hit it and hit it and hit it. I hit it like I was hitting my own past. Then he hit the heavy outdoor bag and knocked it off its metal moorings.

So, yeah. You know those illustrated Karma Sutra books? Here's a brief run-down: stimulations of desire, types of embraces, caressing and kisses, marking with nails, biting and marking with teeth, on copulation (positions), slapping by hand and corresponding moaning, virile behavior in women, superior coition and oral sex, preludes and conclusions to the game of love. Oh and it describes 64 types of sexual acts (10 chapters).

Upstairs in his house was a carpeted little attic room. And him. And me. And a bottle of wine. And pot. And no clothes. I don't know what the neighbors heard but I can tell you it must have been a startling interlude from the mundanity of their nightly televisions. One thousand nights in this first night of his mouth on the mouth of me my mouth on the cock of him his fingers inside my wet inside my ass my fingers around his throbbing inside his ass my legs on his shoulders my feet over my head then sideways like scissors then me on all fours then him underneath me riding and riding then him lifting me my whole body a muscle my back on his belly and chest me on top of him on my back his hands working my tits his hands working my clit my back arching up his cock so far up me my spine went loose my legs shook I screamed and screamed I bit his neck I scratched a self into the very flesh of him I pounded my body down onto him I made an ocean of bed. The sleep of lovers.

And then again begin.

In unending waves.

I don't know where my thoughts went. I only know for the first time in my life I felt everything about a body. Every day. There was nothing we didn't do, and I felt every moment of it in shuddering pleasure. More and more my stupid tumor of a life receded.

One night he put a blanket on the floor and told me to wait and when he came back he was a big 10 years younger than me beautiful man carrying a cello.

"Jesus," I said. "You play cello?"

He played Bach. The sixth suite.

I cried. Possibly the puniest sentence I've ever written.

I cried for the force and strength of his body brought to the brink of tender in his fingers straddling the strings. I cried for the violence of hitting as it fell away into the tremor of holding a note. I cried for the man of him – the size and shape of my father – the brutality of muscle and artistic drive – brought to the cusp of such beauty. Bach. But mostly I cried because I could feel something. All over my body. Like my skin suddenly had nerve endings and synaptic firings and … pulse.

On my birthday he bought me a Beretta 9mm FS and took me out to the desert to shoot. It's the first time in my life I experienced "glee." Shooting–I liked it. I liked the kickback going up my arm and shoulder. I liked the sound, drowning out thought. I liked aiming at a target–that could be anything. I shot and shot.

When Andy Mingo entered my life, I'd walk around at my job or the grocery store or the beach or bars or parties kind of wanting to tug on someone's shirt and say, "Um, I need to say something about men. Turns out? I was wrong. There's something ... I can't put my finger on it, but there's something sort of ... vital about them. Doesn't that beat all?" Or I'd be mid-lecture or mid-mouthful of food or mid swim lap and think "Hey–somebody–I want to note that I'm feeling something. It feels a little like my heart is breaking. Like breaking open. Do I need medical attention? Is there a pill? What should I do?" Or I'd be in medias res lovemaking, I mean mind blowing lovewaves with this ... this ... man creature from another planet and think "I really, really need to go get a different degree to understand this mutual respect and compassion and fleshheartmind hunger business. A Ph.D. just doesn't cut it. I'm quite clearly under educated. Can I speak to someone in charge?"

The one thing I didn't think? Drink it away. Possibly the only strong thing I've ever not thought.

That's why I say I didn't get god. Everything I ever loved about books and music and art and beauty all became recollected in the body of the man I met who hit the bag and played the cello.

After that we started arranging rendezvous all over town. Hungry. Frenzied.

Did I mention he was married?

Yeah. Well. What did you expect? I'm still me, after all.

We met on benches at the ends of piers in San Diego where he'd make me cum with his hands down my pants at the end of a pier while tourists and seagulls and fishermen stretched out behind us. We met on the beach with the surf pounding and the sunset cliffs and one night even when I finished coming and sang my siren song a bunch of hippies in the cliff shadows

put down their spliffs and gave me a standing ovation. We met
in bars where we sat next to each other on red leather stools
and pressed knees and shoulders and mouths together so hard
I'd find bruises in the morning. With my fancy job money
I bought us weekends back in Portland or San Francisco with
rich people hotel rooms and room service and porn channels
and 300 thread count sheets that we soiled and soiled. He said
"Sometimes love is messy."

It's true his almost not anymore wife chased me in her
O.J. white Ford Bronco. But our lovers story isn't the only story.
Though our affair was epic. And sordid. Narrative and passion
have that in common.

There's a story under that one.

In addition to loaning me his car, he began driving me to
and from my communist re-education drunk driver courses
every night for eight weeks. Bringing me a bottle of wine or vodka
on the floor of the car when he picked me up. You know, kind of
like a best friend would do. A kind, sly one.

He also drove me to and from my exhausting road crew
days for eight weeks. Cooking me pasta when I couldn't lift my
arms. He went to my mandatory AA meetings with me and sat
through the 12 steps and nodded and smiled in his black
leather jacket all the way up until we'd get home and I'd rage
rage rage at god and fathers and male authority and he'd
dismantle my rage with funny jokes about jesus and monkeys.

He treated this thing I'd done – this DUI – the dead baby –
the failed marriages – the rehab – the little scars at my collar
bone – my vodka – my scarred as shit past and body – as chapters
of a book he wanted to hold in his hands and finish.

But there's even a story deeper than that. After he moved
out of his wifehouse and into my little one bedroom seahouse
a block from the sunset cliffs in Ocean Beach, after he finished
his MFA and I filed divorce papers and he filed divorce papers,
after I had to go into the English Department Chair's office and
lie like a rug because his wife went in and spilled the shit, after

we both bit the bullet and said the "L" word out loud, something better than sexual and emotional zenith happened. I didn't know that was possible.

Night. Ocean sound. In my tiny seahouse. On the sofa. Both of us scotch handed. Mazzy Star playing all night all night all night. We'd been admiring his Karma Sutra book and he'd been explaining the Tibetan Book of the Dead to me. Sexuality and death. Home run.

He put his hand on my heart. I could feel the heat of his skin diving down into the well of me. He stared so deeply into me my breath jackknifed. I began shaking. Just from that. Then he said, knowing everything I'd told him about myself, he said, out of the blue, "I want to have a child with you."

.

?

.

Well you can imagine how many ways I tried to say "No." I wanted to pick up a phone. "Um, hello, human race? Can you connect me to the dreaded relationship department? I need to say something. I've got this man thing over here, and well, bless his heart, this man is confused. He's clearly mistaken me for someone else, and he needs rerouting. Different area code. Different address. Different woman. Is there a special number to call? I know. It's crazy. He thinks he wants to have a family. Yeah. With me. Nuts, huh? So can you just, you know, give me the number to relocate him? He may need prescription medication. I can stall him for awhile, but you may want to send someone out."

His argument against all my fluttering resistance? One sentence. One sentence up against the mass of my crappy life mess.

"I can see the mother in you. There is more to your story than you think."

The Scarlett Letter

FOR A GOOD SIX MONTHS BEFORE I WAS FIRED AS THE Visiting Writer at S D S U, my belly grew.

Listen. Happiness? It just looks different on people like me.

My belly grew in the halls of the English Department while colleagues tried not to look at or smell my ever enormous tits and belly bulge when they spoke to me about Cultural Studies or Gender Studies or Women's Studies. Then they stopped speaking to me at all, and simply nodded or half smiled as they passed me, like you might a mooing cow.

My belly grew when The Chair signed a paper saying I could never work there again, and I had to sign it too, and while I signed it, instead of looking at the paper, I looked straight into her motherfucking eyes. Old bag I thought. She coughed.

My belly grew every single class I taught, the undergraduates smirking and nudging each other's elbows, then turning strangely loyal like beautiful little revolutionaries against the man. My belly grew each week I taught the graduate fiction writing seminar, me staring them all down one at a time until they smiled, me helping them sew the colors of their words into magnificent tapestries no matter what the judgment, them not able to sustain their disdain in the face of my unapologetic radiance.

My belly grew too big for my clothes. Too big for my bath. My bed. Too big for my house. My former me and all her puny dramas. Bigger and bigger. My belly grew.

And each night Andy would put his hands on the mound

of me and whisper secrets to the little boyfish refusing any narrative but his own. Sweet hidden life in the water of me – the best thing I had to give. And he would suck the milkworld of me and our lovemaking rose and became enormous with my body, with our broken rules broken codes broken law love, every night our bodies making a songstory bigger than the lives we came from. The more my belly grew the more love we made.

At eight months I began to wear my enormity with a pride I'd never known. It is the pride of big bellied mothers who don't fit your story of them. If I glowed, it was with the heatsurge and flush of a sexuality that goes to bed in some other women when they are big with life. Our bodies forming more positions of lovemaking than painted in books from India. If I seemed maternal, it was the maternal grimace and fire of Kali – had anyone crossed me I'd have a head necklace. I'd go out of my way to wedge into elevators filled with condescending faced colleagues. In my head I'd think, I am the woman you teach from literature. But don't teach me as voiceless this time. This time, I am yelling. I am larger than you. I am not sorry. Do your worst. I'd sit in department meetings staring down the tenured women POETS and spit on their so-called feminism. I'd catch the cross glances of the philandering tenured literature old man balls and shoot shame eyes at them for turning on me when I had accepted their excuses for the line of women outside the academic doors of their lives.

My belly grew.

My belly carried me.

My belly carried our love, bulging between our shit faced grinning. The grinning of life and joy finally coming to you when all you knew was how to suffer.

When the time came I taught writing up until the day before I went into labor. I taught at that idiotic hypocritical place that had already fired me for the coming year two days after my son was born. I taught writing instead of pregnancy leave. I brought my little man with me to my graduate seminars in a carrier. I breast fed openly. I taught writing. I taught it well. Ask those students who graduated. Some of whom got jobs. And books. Sometimes his little man voice drowned us out. I laughed the laugh of mothers.

My thirst to go numb began to leave my body.

At eight months I married Andy Mingo at the courthouse. I wore a deep red vintage silk Asian dress, my belly enormous but stylish. It's the only marriage I have no wedding photo of. However.

That night after the knot tying business? We went home and staged a photo shoot. Me with a black satin ribbon tied around my neck and black satin panties in front of a deep red velvet curtain licking milk from a bowl. I don't know why. We just did.

God the sex we had from that photo. Big bellied sex.

Now that, ladies, is a keeper.

Because when love comes to someone like me? After all my black holes? You can bet your ass I'm going to grab it. I may be damaged goods, but I'm not an idiot.

And baby, lemme tell you. I'm no Hester Prynne.

Sun

LIGHT.

Life.

Beautiful alive boy.

The night my son Miles chose to come there was a thunderstorm. In San Diego in April a thunderstorm is a gift – as if your soul might be wetted for a moment between days of endless sun.

When my water broke I walked barefoot in a nightgown down the street a block to the ocean. Andy was asleep in bed. My sister Brigid was asleep in the house. I cried and the ocean within me made way for this boy and the ocean before me opened up. When I got to the water I said "Lily. He's here." Then I walked back to the house. In bed next to my sleeping love I counted minutes. It was 5:00 a.m. The contractions felt like sentences before they are born. It is the only time in my life I have experienced a purity of happiness. Because my head was empty of anything about me. Nothing else about my life in the room. Lightning lighting up the darkness. Water everywhere.

I've met many mothers whose children didn't come right or never came at all. We are like a secret tribe of women carrying something not quite of this world.

A Japanese woman friend whose infant son died seven days into his life – no detectable reason – just the small breathing becoming nothing until it disappeared, told me that in Japan, there is a two-term word – "mizugo" – which translates loosely to "water children." Children who did not live long enough to enter the world as we live in it.

In Japan, there are rituals for mothers and families, practices and prayers for the water children. There are shrines where a person can visit and deliver words and love and offerings to the water children.

There are no Western rituals for the water children. I am an American woman who does not believe in god. But I do believe in waters.

The day Miles was born, Andy cradled my body through its crucible. My sister Brigid stitched love in beautiful thread around the room of us – nothing wrong could have entered her fiercely sewn world. When he came I wailed as women do for the child they have carried and brought into the world. But my wail carried another soul in its song. My Miles' long body was brought up to my chest, the umbilical cord curling its milky grey spiral still connecting us.

He moved.

I felt the heat of his body.

His little mouth made for the mound of my breast and nipple.

So this is life.

The first thing Miles saw when he opened his eyes was a father who let out a sound I've never heard before. A male sob as big as space. A father with open arms ready for his child, ready to protect him his entire life, ready to love him above anything, ready to be the path of a man before him and hold his hand until the boy goes to man. A father who had no father himself rewriting the story.

My sister came to us and embraced the three-bodied organism. I do not know what she felt but her face is the word for it.

In my belly, before he was born, Miles swam. Back and forth and around and flip turns and kicks and such movement – so alive – watching the taught skin of my belly was a little alarming. The force of him took my breath away. And yet we felt inseparable. His body was my body was his was mine. When I went swimming with Miles in my belly, which I did often, people in the lap lanes would marvel at how I could be so fast. So big, so round, so breasted – but fast. But I knew a secret that they did not. We are all swimmers before the dawn of oxygen and earth. We all carry the memory of that breathable blue past.

It is possible to carry life and death in the same sentence. In the same body. It is possible to carry love and pain. In the water, this body I have come to slides through the wet with a history. What if there is hope in that.

In the Company of Men

THEY SAY EVERY WOMAN WHO MARRIES, MARRIES A
version of her father. My father fractured the hearts of all the
women in our home with his rage. And so when I go back through
and think about the men I have loved, or thought I loved, it is
with a split apart heart. If I have any idea what the love of family
means, if I have any sense at all where the heart of it is, then I
learned it first from the man I did not marry.

Do you remember where you were the day Kennedy was
shot? I don't. I was born the year Kennedy was shot. So I can't
remember anything about it. But I remember Michael. In every
part of my life.

The first time I saw Michael, he was standing next to Phillip
in the painting studio at Texas Tech. It was late at night.
I walked up to the floor to ceiling windows and looked in at them
from the outside. Two tall, thin, beautiful young men, standing
next to each other, painting on canvas. I held my breath. Staring
at the image of them … something happened in my heart.
It throbbed when I looked at these two men painting. My eyes
stung and my throat got tight. But I just took a swig of vodka
from a flask and walked up to the glass window and lifted my
shirt up and pressed my bare tits up against the glass and
knocked. Phillip turned and laughed, pointed. Michael turned,
and laughed, and our eyes locked.

Michael. My father's name.

Is that what my father looked like, I thought, as a man in

his early twenties? Tall, thin, beautiful, his hands making a dance against canvas?

I didn't learn to love men from anything I knew. I learned to love men from loving Michael.

There is so much I didn't glean from being a daughter in a family full of women.

I didn't learn to love holidays from my family. I learned it from entering Mike and Dean's house, beautifully decorated – as beautiful as you imagine fantasy worlds as a child – warm amber rooms and candle lights and ribbons and the smell of baked things and spice – with no father to smash it apart.

I didn't learn how to cook from any mother. I learned to cook from watching Michael – his hands, the patience, the artistry, the care, the joy of putting something into your mouth so filled with love it made me weep to chew.

I didn't learn how to be feminine from any women. I learned to take off my combat boots and comb my crooked hair from looking at pictures Dean took of me over the years, pictures where he showed me that someone like me could be … pretty.

Michael was at my first wedding on the beach in Corpus Christi when I said I do to Phillip on the white sand. Michael and Dean were with me at my second wedding with Devin on the top of Harvey's Casino in Lake Tahoe, where a strange casino minister with hair black as a record album recited a Hopi prayer while my mother waited to drink and gamble. Michael was not with me when I married Andy in front of a justice of the peace in San Diego, but my big belly was, and it carried something of him, too.

Once Michael came to visit when Philip and I still lived in Eugene. After the baby died. Philip and I were nothing about each other. I had already begun a new chapter with Devin in a house across town. Philip worked at Smith Family Bookstore by day, and by night he painted in a one-room efficiency somewhere else. The plan was that Michael would visit Phillip for a few days, and then spend a couple with me. But on the second day Michael showed up on my doorstep at three in the

morning. I opened the door. He looked like ass. He had his suitcase with him. He said, "I can't stay in that fucking efficiency.
It reeks. There's cat piss and shit and oil paint everywhere. The
guy doesn't live like a human." And I let him in.

It was then that I knew that we had both loved Phillip.
Together. Deeply. And that both of us left Phillip. Divorced him.
Forever. Unable to understand how to live with his brilliant,
passive hands. It was a sacred truth between us.

After Devin and I divorced, Devin went to visit Michael and
Dean in Seattle, I guess wanting to feel like they were still his
friends. I hated knowing he was there. My Michael and Dean.
Goddamn you, Devin. But then Mike called and told me, "All he
wants to talk about is how many times a day he fucks the woman-
child. I don't give a shit how many times he screws the infant.
GAWD. It's so juvenile." The next day he called again and said,
"Devin drank all the alcohol in the house while we were at work.
I think he stole one of our pans. And some of Dean's CDs. He's
never staying here again."

I know it's petty. Idiotic. But I loved him so much for telling
me that.

When Andy and I were first getting together, it was hard.
Andy was still married. So we had a couple of rendezvous out
side of San Diego. One of them was in Seattle where Mike and
Dean lived. They had moved there from Dallas sometime after
my baby died. They moved there for work, I'm sure – both of
them are astonishingly talented graphic designers. But to me it
seemed that Mike had moved to Seattle to be closer to me.
I mean I wished it was true. I wished the moment when he said
one afternoon "We should live closer together," the afternoon
we downed 12 beers in a row in my house in Eugene, was somehow why he was near. It's the wish of a child.

I called Mike in Seattle from San Diego to tell him about
my man situation. I didn't call my mother, or my sister, or my
father, or any woman friend. I called Michael. I called to tell him
that I thought I had fallen in love with a man who was not yet

untangled from a marriage gone bad. That the man was younger than me. A lot. That the man was big and beautiful and played the cello and could beat the crap out of pretty much anything. That the man had lived in Spain and witnessed some ETA stuff and that the man had interviewed people from Earth Liberation Front and that the man kissed me so hard in Tijuana I thought I'd swallowed my teeth. That the man was my student. All things that ought to have made another kind of friend go, Lidia, you are making a mess. But you know what Mike said? He said, "Jesus. Thank god you finally got with someone whose story can keep up with yours!" Then he said, "We're going out of town for a week. You should come house-sit and bring this guy up."

I did.

Our son Miles, my beautiful alive boy, was conceived in Michael's house. In Mike and Dean's bed. On the 600 count twill sheets. With Jake the dog loyally guarding our love. In his house, the only house I ever felt the word "home" in my heart, a boy was born.

In my head and heart I carry so many images of Mike and Dean. Me and Mike on the floor of a Baptist church at midnight, Dean playing Bach on the church organ. Me and Mike and Dean stripped to our underwear, running into the ocean on the Oregon coast. In December. Eating a Christmas rabbit with olives and capers that Andy and Mike cooked – snuggled up in Italy – me and Dean filling our mouths with more than food. Mike and Dean opening the door when I sent my sister to them – my sister whose lost tenure had manifested as a nervous breakdown – how they said, "You can come in." How they let her live with them until her self returned. Miles and Mike and Dean and Andy on top of the Space Needle. My god. How many ways are there to love men? It's enough to break a heart open.

The images in my head and heart. I know what they are. I do. They are a family album. It is possible to make family any way you like. It is possible to love men without rage. There are thousands of ways to love men.

A Sanctuary

THERE'S SOMETHING I WANT TO TELL YOU ABOUT THE miles.

When my son Miles was born we drove from San Diego to a place near Portland, Oregon. I'd been fired in San Diego and miraculously rehired in Oregon – back toward what I knew, and what Andy knew, the Northwest. Andy drove a U-Haul, and my dear friend Virginia and I drove a used Saab with Miles gurgling and pooing his pants in the back like a little road warrior.

Virginia. Everything that matters to me is a word. Slowly this woman grew in my life, a beautiful wetted stone turned over years. First she was my student, then my friend, then nothing I'd ever met before. Virginia became a friend who stayed near. She showed me intimacy is a word untethered from sexuality. Unconditionally, I drank.

The Saab broke down in Weed – yes, Weed, and Virginia and I sort of paced on the side of the road thinking, will he look in the rearview and notice we're gone? Will this man drive all the way to Oregon? No bars on the little cell of a bitch. We weren't scared, women like the two of us? That would not scare us. We'd have been excellent pioneers. Like Becky Boone.

But he did notice, because he's that kind of guy, and within 20 minutes here came the U-Haul on the freeway coming our direction. Then we all had to cram in the weird front space of the U-Haul and pretend we didn't have an infant stashed between the seats by the gearshift and cigarettes. Virginia and I sharing the passenger seat, our butts making sweat marks on the strange Burbury. We abandoned the Saab on the side of the road. Marking our exit like a scar.

When we got to Oregon Miles and I took a bath at a Holiday Inn. He lay against me, his back against my tits and stomach, his little monkey face smiling in between spit bubbles, and his arms and legs floating easily. I have a picture of us like that. My tits are as big as a human head, so it looks a little like a three-headed creature for a second, until you see his facial features. Then I picked his little bucket of baby weight up and turned him around so we were face to face, and he raspberried me a good one, and smiled, and farted, and I laughed my ass off and held him close.

With his head against my heart I suddenly felt his life-force – not the lifeforce of babies – a lifeforce bigger than a night sky. It was almost like thunder coming through us, just like the night I went into labor during a thunder storm. It was the exact opposite of the heart implosion I felt the day my daughter was born and died. The two of us in the water, thunderhearted.

At some point that night I walked out onto our little Holiday Inn balcony and Virginia was smoking a cigarette on hers. I looked over at her. My god. This person I had watched go from young woman to warrior beauty. It took my breath away. I never told her this, but what I thought … daughter. I almost couldn't breathe with the wonder.

"Those are death sticks, you know," I said.

"Yeah," she said.

"I love you, you know."

"Yeah. I do. Me too." Her eyes filling with tears across the distance.

We were driving to a house Andy had found and rented on the internet. Such a risky move – finding the next chapter of your life in cyberspace. But so gloriously risky. Because this was a hacker. A guy who had cybersquatted Bill Gates. When he was at the computer, whole geographies emerged you'd never thought of.

The house looked filled with light and space when I looked at the internet photos. I knew the value of light and space. And there were trees in the photos. Everywhere. The house was inside something called the Bull Run Wilderness near Sandy, Oregon. When I asked Andy "Why this house? Is it near my job?"

He said, "No, it's not near your job. But it is sanctuary." At the time, I didn't know exactly what he meant. But something in my skin trusted him.

The road to the house off of I-84 wound around forests and snuck alongside the Sandy River. I saw a few people riding the river on inner tubes. I saw fly fishermen. Kayakers. I saw the land rise and fall like it does in Oregon wilderness. Alders. Oaks. Maples. Douglas Firs. Everything it seemed, evergreen. I thought briefly of my father – how he loved the Northwest. I thought how maybe that feeling he had was something yet good between us. Then the word father left altogether, since it was nothing about my future. Up we drove. When we arrived at the house I began crying. Gut wrenching crying. A crying that must have taken years, pulled up from the depths.

The house was made from two octagonals. The first octagonal had the main room and wooden stairs made by a master carpenter leading up to a sleeping loft. The sleeping loft had 360 degree windows so that if you were, say, in bed, all you saw was trees. The second octagonal had a kitchen with cabinets you'd pay a fortune for in the city – the deep cherry and blond wood like inside trees.

Outside the house there was nothing but forest. The Bull Run Wilderness hid elk and deer and bobcat. Wild pheasants and coyote and eagles and great blue herons. A freshwater creek trickled at the base of our property – water that ran for miles. To the side of the house, a giant warehouse loomed that the owner had been using as a woodworking studio. The owner made wooden marimbas as beautiful as music sounds. He showed them to us. They smelled like life. The owner had built the house. Crafted the woodwork with the passion of an artist. Inside the warehouse was an enormous woodstove. Inside the warehouse I felt something stirring in me. Something about a self. Something about the freedom to make. The feeling felt older than me. Inside the house, I felt safety. All those trees protecting us. A river curling around us. Something up until that point in my life I'd only felt in water.

When Andy and I and Virginia and Miles sat down in front of the house, butterflies and dragonflies and a hummingbird accompanied our distance. As if to say, you are home.

We were 25 minutes from the city I would work in. From people. We were 45 minutes from Portland. Culture and the socius. Virginia walked off a ways to have a cigarette. Then it was just me, Andy, and Miles. I said, "Andy, I can't believe how beautiful it is here. It takes my breath away." I turned away from him. I felt small. Maybe like a kid. "I don't know how to thank you."

"You don't have to thank me," he said, coming up behind me with Miles on his shoulder like a little second man. "It's what's next." Andy has a weird way of making the impossible sound ordinary.

Our first days that ran into nights than ran back into days in that house in the forest were like what I understand Shakespeare to mean by the green world. Seriously. You know, where the action of a play starts out in normal world and then goes into green world where a magical metamorphosis takes place. Think *A Midsummer Night's Dream*. I always wanted to wear that donkey head thing or run around naked in the woods. Actually, Northrup Frye came up with the phrase. Sorry. It's the goddamn academic in me.

But my life with Andy and Miles in the green world really did magically change everything for me. For example. Christmas? At Christmastime we didn't trudge up any godforsaken mountain hill in the shoulder high snow to get a goddamn tree. No one yelled their head off. No one cried their eyes out. We simply went to a tree lot and bought the biggest fucking Christmas tree they had, like a 12-footer, strapped it to the car, drove it to our sanctuary, and peed our pants with joy – the open space of the octagons filling with the smell of Douglas fir and glee.

And there was no architect's office with smoke and anger pouring out late into the night while children hid in their bedrooms scared to sleep or dream. Miles slept in a bed 10 feet away from two giant writing desks Andy and I pushed together. So while the parents were writing, the child was sleeping, and art kept us well and space kept us well and trees watched over us so dreams could get born.

There was no mother you couldn't find in the house because she was out selling real estate, or locked in the bathroom with a bottle.

I used to watch Miles fall asleep from drinking boob milk late into the night. I'm guessing all mothers do this. But I bet not all mothers were thinking of Shakespearean sentence structures when they watched their babies drunkenly drift into sleep. I know, watching your boy suck tit doesn't seem very Shakespearian on the face of it. But when I watched Miles go from mother's milk to burp to deep and frothy dream, his body heavy in my lap, the blue-black of night resting on us, I thought of Shakespearean chiasmus. A chiasmus in language is a crisscross structure. A doubling back sentence. A doubling of meaning. My favorite is "love's fire heats water, water cools not love."

As a motif, a chiasmus is a world within a world where transformation is possible. In the green world events and actions lose their origins. Like in dreams. Time loses itself. The impossible happens as if it were ordinary. First meanings are undone and remade by second meanings.

I didn't sleep much the first two years in the forest house. Miles, bless his hungry little head, wanted more milk than any man alive. All night. I thought of my mother – and my own unquenchable, milkless mouth. If this boy wanted milk, I would give it to him. Maybe all our lives were being reborn in the forest.

My exhaustion was of course epic, but only in that way it is for everyone else, too. I taught full-time shooting for tenure so we'd have a shot at a life. Andy too exhausted himself. We taught in alternate waves day and night and parented by passing Miles off like a football between us. Thank god for breast pumps and bouncy chairs.

The exhaustion of new parents is absurd. Beyond absurd. But I'm not about to get all righteous about that. In fact, it's something else altogether I want to tell you. I think our exhaustion in the green world brought us to our best selves. Listen to this: the first two years of Miles' life? When I was supposed to be depleted? I wrote a novel and seven short stories. Andy wrote a novel and three screenplays. Read that again. How is it that so much writing happened inside the least amount of time or energy?

Green world.

We had no time. We had no energy. We had no money. What we had was making art in the woods. So when Andy turned to me one night over scotches and said "We should invent a Northwest press that isn't about fucking old growth and salmon," and I laughed my ass off, and then said, "Yeah, we should," we just ... did. Which is how the zenith of our depletion changed into the zenith of our creative production. Andy and me, we had another child. An unruly literary press, which we named "Chiasmus." Turned out, there were lots of writers in the Northwest who were tired of old growth and salmon. Our first publication was an anthology called *Northwest Edge: The End of Reality*. Because, you know, it was. Everything we were before we were this, utterly transformed.

Shakespeare.

In our forest we gave art to life, and life to art made us.

Angina

I KNOW. I'M MAKING ANDY SOUND LIKE A MAGICAL MAN-savior. You're going to have to forgive me. It's an effect of meeting someone who is your equal. It's an effect of an astonishment: that I love men.

And it's not like we have some relationship from a movie. For instance, in the beginning, we fought. Boy howdy. I fought like a woman whose father had betrayed her and whose mother abandoned her. He fought like a man who never had a father and whose mother's heart didn't quite reach him. Working out our childhood wounds at each other. Because ... because we could take it. Because there was something on the other side.

People – I guess I mean couples – don't like to talk much about fighting. It's not attractive. No one likes to admit it or describe it or lay claim to it. We want our coupledoms to look ... sanitized and pretty and worthy of admiration. And anger blasts are ugly. But, I think that is a crock. There is a kind of fighting that isn't ugly. There is a way for anger to come out as an energy you let loose and away. The trick is to give it a form, and not a human target. The trick is to transform rage.

When I watch Andy work the heavy bag, or work his body to drop doing mixed martial arts, I see that anger can go somewhere – out and away from a body – like an energy let loose and given form. Like my junk comes out in art.

Though like anyone else, our arguments are sloppy and dumb and artless. We look like cartoon adults, just like everyone. Like the time he put all our living room furniture out on the lawn. Or the time I grabbed his computer mouse and bit the cord in half. Yeah. Subtle. But I gotta tell you. People who never get angry frighten me.

Andrew: man-warrior. From the Greek.

Lidia doesn't mean jack-shit, by the way. Figures.

And then there are the little sufferings that make a bond as strong as love.

When I was 38 my Andy woke up to pee in the night. I heard him in that wife way, even as I was half asleep. Before we went to bed, we had heard some eulogizing about Ken Kesey's death on NPR. I'd cried some. Him too. Then we went to bed. When he got up to pee, he turned the bathroom light on and shut the door.

Then I heard him fall, like a tree landing on the roof. I ran into the bathroom and he had passed out. He was on the white tiled floor, on his back, his eyes wide open, his mouth in a grimace, making strange strangled sounds, white as death, seizuring.

I yelled his name at him. I put his feet up on the edge of the tub and held his head in my lap trying to give him a mini blood transfusion. He came to, dazedly. I called 911. I put a comforter around him. A firetruck full of paramedics came. I dressed my son while they hooked my husband up to wires and electrical machines. They put my husband in an ambulance and my son and I drove in our car – the ambulance took the freeway. I took the back roads. I was there 12 minutes ahead of them. At the hospital he lived. We discovered a triglyceride problem that scared the shit out of us.

The next week, driving to work in my car, I got an earache and my skull felt like a lightning bolt fracture had cracked it open.

My father's voice filled the ball of my head, curled around the lobes and through the canals of gray matter. It closed my eyes and clenched my teeth.

I began to not only hear my father again, but as clearly as you see the face of your husband, your wife, in front of you, I saw my father's face at the moment of his drowning. On his back, his eyes wide open, his mouth in a grimace, making strange strangled sounds, seizuring.

I nearly wrecked the car twice, unable to see the road or anything else, my ears gone crazy, the deep baritone of his voice making my brain ache.

How to Hold Your Breath

KID STORIES.

What sad little bobbers we all were.

Here's a pathetic little image: me at age two in a hooded baby blue parka and little red stretch pants jumping off a 25' dock into Lake Washington, yelling "WIM."

They say, and keep in mind the story comes from my now dead crackpot parents, they say I'd jump in any water I saw. Pools. Rivers. Lakes. The Shojita's carp-filled garden pond. That I was simply drawn to water, and I'd run and leap with one of those silly toddler glee smiles smeared across my face, and then I'd sink like a stone.

Somebody, usually my eyerolling sister, would have to jump in after me every time, and pull me sputtering to safety.

So when I was three my mother signed me up for swim lessons. But it was my father who put me in the car, drove me to Lake Washington, took off my little clothes and threw me in.

In November.

I was by far the youngest kid there.

I can't tell you I remember any of this, but I sure the hell can conjure up an image of my own skin bluing in the icy waters. And I feel pretty certain I have muscle memory in my mouth of my teeth nearly shattering from kid cold chatter. If I learned to swim that year I did it in a frozen zombie state, under the heavy weight of father, who, every time I came running out crying stuck his hand and arm out of the station wagon window like an angry god and pointed back to the water.

If there is more to that story it drifts away when I go near it – it's too far back, or too deep.

When I first began writing this story my son Miles was seven. So that means I'm seven too sometimes. I mean my seven year old me swims back during the course of an ordinary day all the time, whether or not I'm ready. Miles absolutely loves swimming pools. The thing is, Miles can't exactly ... swim. When Miles gets in the pool, there is no other way to say this, he's a spaz. And he's wearing more weenie water gear than a special needs deep sea diver. Don your protective gear: goggles, life vest. Then he wades in and has the time of his life, prepared for any aqua danger, looking like a water nerd. When he's in the water he laughs and laughs. He shows me all the things he can do in the water, things that amount to splashy little circles or pushing his way across the pool like a water bug, and says, "Lidia, look, I'm doing swimming." He throws his little arms around and kicks his unsynchopated legs and holds his head in this sort of strange crane upwards, his mouth in a little smirk nowhere near the water, his goggle-bugged eyes looking my way. It drowns my heart.

When I was seven I won 13 trophies with little faux gold girls leaning over for the dive on top. If my seven year old me saw his seven year old in the same pool? With all the gear? Well first of all my little posse of athletes wouldn't have gone anywhere near him. Gyawd they would have gone. What's wrong with that kid? Is he special ed? But the me inside the me would have adored him. I bet my current salary I would have been the one wishing I could swim over and try out his cool gear.

When I'm with him now, if any of the kids playing around in the pool near us who look like they were born fucking seals even GLANCE at him I shoot them a death look so sharp it slicks their hair back, reddens their smug little faces and ... well. Let's just say something a lot worse than water going into your brain. They're lucky to have brains at all after I shoot them the look. It's a look from my father.

Still, at my son's age, I was a racer. You know those little plastic wind-up bathtub things – contraptions with small flippers or limbs attached to internal rubber bands which, when wound, rotate at alarming speeds? Sending a little dolphin or boat or shark shooting across the tub? That's what seven year old girl racers look like. Heads down. Twenty-five meters. Maybe one breath. Maybe. Whoever we were on land, once freed in water, we grew dangerously alive.

My son's been in swimming lessons – level A – three times now. At the end of the lessons they always hand me the green card that says mamma of Miles, your son can barely float, he'll only hold his breath above the water, if he's in the water without supervision he'll sink to the bottom like a tire, and they smile, and I smile, and Miles beams, and then we go home and eat OREOS and I give him another one of my trophies.

When I work with him alone in the pool, he clings to me like a little sea monkey until I let him put his full regalia back on.

It's his head.

He doesn't want to put his head in. When I ask him why, he answers incredulously, "Because the water will go in my nose and ears and go into my brain. Duh."

I look at him for a long minute. He doesn't back down.

"I see," I said. "Where'd you get that idea?"

Quite convincingly, he responds. "Harry Potter."

Harry Potter.

Goddamn that little bespectacled twit.

I instantly know which Harry Potter scene he is talking about. It's the one from *Harry Potter and the Goblet of Fire*, where the five students have to compete in the Tri-Wizard's Cup. One of the trials is an ocean dive to save trapped friends and loved ones who have been suspended underwater by strange little sea witches with pitchforks. Each student must figure out a magical way to breathe underwater, or they'll die, and all their loved ones trapped underwater will die, water will go up all the noses and flood all their ears and drown all their brains unless they have special underwater gear. Total kid death fest if they don't find a way to breathe underwater. Neville Longbottom, the buck-toothed nerd kid interested in animals and botany and ichthyology, gives Harry Potter magic Gillyworms. Then he grows temporary gills and webbed hands and feet.

Christ. Why does anyone become a mother?

I look at Miles. I say, "Miles, you know when you see mamma swimming and swimming in the lap lanes?"

"Yes," he says, looking solemnly at the floor.

"Well, water has never gone into my brain. Not once."

He looks at me quite seriously. I can see from his eyes he's puzzling out an answer. He's a thinker, that one, so I already know he's coming up with a good one. He would have been all over Hogwarts. "Let's hear it then," I say.

"Then you must have had a waterhorse. A waterhorse who put you on its back when you were little and afraid of the water and then the water horse dove down underwater and taught you how to swim because the waterhorse loved you and you loved the waterhorse and there was magic." He rests his case, hands on hips.

Of course there was magic. Like in "The Waterhorse."

Goddamn American kid films.

The year I was seven the kid movies were *The Aristocats*, *Pippi in the South Seas*, and *King of the Grizzlies*. Nobody died from having water go into their brains. Wait. *The Poseidon Adventure* – 1972. That whole Shelley Winters thing. Man. That still gets me. That's some sad shit. I think I bawled for an hour when they took me to see that. I think we had to leave the theater. And I think my father said "If you're going to cry like a baby, you can't go to the movies. Crybabies have to stay home. For christ's sake." Pounding the steering wheel. My mother looking out the window with her endless denial. My sister half feeling sorry for me and half glad for another target in the family.

Now that I'm thinking about it, except for swimming, I was a big fat failure at many, many things. Being in public, for one, like at all, but other things too. For instance bike riding. Complete failure. I can still hear him. "Goddamn it! Every kid on this block can ride a bike but you. What are you, retarded or something?" Me pedaling, pedaling, weightless and mindless as air, nothing girl.

Miles and I spend a lot of time at the pool.

Him not putting his head under.

Me swimming the laps of the racer I was.

We're making our first progress, though. As long as I'm the waterhorse, he puts his arms around my neck in a near choke hold and, gasping for air and speech, I swim around and go, "OK, I'm diving down now," and we go down into the dangers and depths of public pools. He holds his nose tight enough to pull it off.

After we eat the multi-colored gummy worms, that is. You can't even think about going underwater without eating gummy worms.

My father never learned to swim.

Water

THERE IS A PLACE ON THE OREGON COAST CALLED Gleneden Beach. It's between Lincoln City and Newport, both tourist towns. The main thing that is at Gleneden Beach is a mildly well known resort called Salishan.

The resort is nestled up against a little saltwater bay and estuary. Beyond that, the ocean. It has a famous golf course, which I've actually played. When I was a kid. My father took us to this resort as a family. It is the only thing we did together as a family that worked.

I don't know exactly why it worked, but I'd watch my father sit out on the balcony of the luxury hotel room and look out at the ocean. At the windblown signature tree of the resort. At the birds and the way light changed over the water. He looked at peace.

At the resort there is a fine swimming pool and hot tub. As a family my mother, father, sister and I spent hours in the waters. My mother would side stroke her suddenly weightless swan body up and down the pool, smiling like a girl. My sister and I would swim the goof off way kids do – going under and up and splashing and racing and treading water and diving for coins. Despite our age difference. My father would wade in up to his hips, his chest, sometimes up to his chin. Since his feet were still touching the bottom, he felt safe. And though he'd only venture halfway down the pool to avoid the depths of the far end, he looked happy. Five years we went back to Salishan – until my sister left.

Of course, Salishan is not just a resort. The Salishan languages are a group of languages of the Native Americans of the Pacific Northwest. They are characterized by fusional and inflected language and astonishing consonant clusters. And all Salish languages are either extinct or endangered. That's not something I knew as a kid. But the word embedded itself in my head and heart differently than other words anyhow, and so it had a meaning secret from regular talking. Sometimes when I was hurt or angry or scared as I kid, I'd close my eyes and whisper, "Salishan. Salishan." Hoping it could work some kind of magic on the terror of family.

After we moved back to Oregon, when my son was about five, I took him and Andy back to Salishan. I did not know what would happen. Perhaps that kind of return would bring me nothing but sadness, and we were driving to the ocean of my childhood. But I trusted the ocean's pull. When we got to within a mile of the resort – when we drove past the estuary and around the corner where the Douglas Firs make a mound of forest in the heart of which is Salishan, my heart let loose. It wasn't the resort. It was the word. It was a space of ocean or peace that offered hope differently for a child. I rolled the window down and the salt air bathed my face. My son seemed excited but didn't know why.

My husband Andy said, "Is this it?"

"Yes," I said, this is the place.

My son had never been to a fancy place like that, so he spent the first 10 minutes running around the room in a little kid glee dance. Then he found the white terrycloth robes in the closet, stripped naked, put one on, went out on to the balcony, and said, "This is the life."

Then we all went down to the pool. The pool of my childhood hope. Miles kept saying the word Salishan. Words carry oceans on their small backs.

Joy.

A word. An act of imagination. Me, Andy, Miles. In the pool we work on Miles' water skills. My husband swims and floats and laughs, dives down like a kid, making his nose run from the chlorine. Not caring. He can swim the deep end.

When I am in the Salishan pool with Miles, I play. Usually we play water games Miles has invented, all of which involve him getting to keep his head above the water. This time he tells me he has a very important game. I say, "OK. What is it?"

"I'm going to put my whole head underwater," he says.

!

I nod and stay quiet, trying not to blow it. I move toward him to hold him so we can dunk down together quickly. Painlessly.

"No," he says, "you stay over there and do it and I'll do it over here and we'll look at each other and try to hold our breath as long as we can."

!

"OK." I say.

My heart.

He's got his goggles on. He's got a hold of his nose with one hand, and with the other, he's going to count off.

One.

Two.

Three.

And then he takes the hugest breath in like ever. And puts his head under. All the way. I do too. I can see him through the blue. His beautiful underwater head. For the first time. Holding his own breath. A magic.

When we rush up for air we are both laughing and I'm telling him how proud I am of him and he's splashing around and Andy comes over and we do a group hug. You know, like people goofing off on vacation.

"Again!" he says.

We do. We do and we do.

In this water with the two of them – the boy, the man. I almost can't breathe. I didn't know. It is a family. It is mine.

It's a small tender thing, the simplicity of loving.

I am learning to live on land.

The Other Side of Drowning

I WONDER. WHO WAS ROOTING FOR ME?

For the first time since I was maybe 14, I'm watching Super-8 films of myself swimming. Racing. My father took them. Many, many of them. They've been sitting silent and immobile in a cardboard box since 2003 when my father died – two years after my mother went. I knew about them. They've been down in the garage. I just never ... drug them up from the depths until now.

I don't quite know how to explain to you what it is like watching the little woman swim for her life. I mean from where I am now. Look at her go. Is she swimming away from something? Or to something?

On film I watch myself swim, and even though on the surface the plot is about winning races, or losing, there is something you will never see.

What you will not see is how far. How many miles I had to swim to come back to a simple chlorinated pool where I might... just be.

I swim laps three, sometimes four times a week now. At the Clackamas Aquatic Center near my home. It feels ... it feels like the closest thing to home I have ever had.

At the pool, the people who swim in the lap lanes next to me are not athletes. Though occasionally one will show up and my game will come alive in my body – I can't help it. I'll race them until they leave. We usually don't speak – just nod at each other when it's over, as if we've shared something intimate.

But more often there are regular people in the pool. Beautiful women seniors doing water aerobics – mothers and grandmothers and great grandmothers – their massive breasts and guts reminding you how it is that women carry worlds. When I swim by them I watch their legs and bodies underwater, and feel a strange kinship with a maternal lineage. You know you can smile underwater. You can laugh.

Twice in my life I have found myself swimming next to an albino. I felt lucky somehow. Like I'd found the right water.

At the pool near my home there is a woman who is missing a leg. She swims her laps with a prosthetic that has a flipper at the end. Very high-tech. Her workouts, I've noticed, are formidable. I love her made-up leg. I like to swim near her.

Sometimes kids and teens take up a lane – no doubt they are on swim teams – I can tell by their spectacular strokes and the kinds of swimsuits and caps and goggles they wear. They are in the sweet. Effortlessly.

Old men people the lap lanes too, most always extra friendly to me. Their skin hangs off of their backs in pale speckled folds. Their legs seem too thin to carry them – and they nearly all wear some form of white or beige boxer trunks. Sometimes with very thin fabric. But they wrestle the water anyhow, in all shapes and sizes, all forms of swimming. Once I stopped my laps to rest and two of them were staring at me. One said to the other, "Ain't she something?" The other one said, "And how." Then they clapped. It cracked me up. I still see them sometimes. We say hello, or goodbye, or keep up the good work.

Middle-aged women like me show up too – most of them do not have the stroke quality of someone who has competed – but I am filled with wonder at them anyway. They put their bodies in the water to swim the same way that I do. Maybe they are trying to shed pounds. Or maybe stress. Or lives. Or maybe it just feels good – being alone in water – no kids hanging on you, no husband to tend to, no one and nothing to answer to. When the pool is full I've noticed I'm among the first they will ask if they can share a lane. They must be able to tell I'm going to lap them and lap them. But there must be something more important that draws them to my lane. I think – I hope it is that the water is safe.

Gay men are there too, I can tell. Their legs will be hairless or they'll be wearing earrings and, well, the only other men besides athletes who wear Speedos are gay. I sometimes have to fight off strange impulses to crawl over the lane line into their lanes and hug them – to thank them for being the men they are – men who showed me love and compassion at every important moment of my life – even though we are strangers.

Occasionally a swim coach will show up. I always get the same question. "Did you compete?" I nod and dip back under quickly. It's not a conversation I want to have any longer, and they often ask me about joining Masters Swimming. I don't want to join Masters Swimming. I want just to be in water.

In the voiceless blue. In the weightless wet.

À La Recherché du Temps Perdu

SOMETIMES I THINK THINGS OUT IN THE TIME IT TOOK me to win a race. 200-meter butterfly: 2:18.04. How long it takes to walk from my car to my office. 100-meter breastroke: 1:11.2. How long it takes to brush my teeth. It's what swimmers do. It's muscle memory.

I remember things badly. When I look back, things are underwater, and when I pick them out and bring them to the surface they float around my idiotic attempts to drag them to land. I wonder what memory is, anyway. What writers are doing when they scratch at it. Usually I think of Proust, who tried to write a sentence about memory and ended up with seven volumes about nostalgia.

In psychology, memory is an organism's ability to store, retain, and subsequently retrieve information. It lives in the head, lights up with synaptic firings, and travels the waters of the nervous system.

400-meter individual medley: 4:55.1. How long to nuke a frozen Lean Cuisine.

According to recent neuroscience studies, the act of remembering triggers nearly the same activities in the brain and its circuitry as the actual experience. They found this truth in rats and lemurs. Little wires sprouting from their heads.

However, narrating what you remember, telling it to someone, does something else. The more a person recalls a memory, the more they change it. Each time they put it into language, it shifts. The more you describe a memory, the more likely it is that you are making a story that fits your life, resolves the past, creates a fiction you can live with. It's what writers do. Once you open your mouth, you are moving away from the truth of things. According to neuroscience.

The safest memories are locked in the brains of people who can't remember. Their memories remain the closest replica of actual events. Underwater. Forever.

When my father drowned in the ocean it took me the time of winning the 100-meter breast stroke. To reach his body. By the time I had dragged him to shore, I'd won the 200-meter butterfly. By the time an ambulance came, I'd won the 400-meter individual medley, the length of time it takes brain cells to begin dying. The length of time for his heart to fail. For memory to leave. Hypoxia.

The rest of his life, of what he did to us, there was nothing left. Of who or what his daughter were or became, nothing. Of my mother, their courtship – he did have images. In a loop. Like film. Of his greatest architectural achievement, a shopping plaza in Trinidad, and the steel drum music and warm wet air and white sand and dark skinned women he'd found comforted his rage and disappointment, nothing.

My father lost his memory in the arms of his daughter the swimmer.

My mother was his caretaker in Florida until she got cancer and died. So in 2001 there he was, all alone in a house he barely recognized, facing the prospect of the State taking ownership of him and depositing him in a nursing home for the rest of his life.

Have you ever visited nursing homes in Gainesville, Florida? I have. Let me put it this way. Walking in the door of one brings a disgust to your throat like someone grabbed it. They smell like urine and dead skin and Lysol. The creatures tooling around in wheelchairs or "walking" down halls look befuddled. Like hunched over zombies. In the dining room women whose hair and lipstick are not on straight and men who've wet themselves shove pureed gruel in their mouths. But what makes them particularly hideous in a Floridian sense is the heat. The humidity. The air conditioning that doesn't work quite right. The mold on the walls here and there. Cockroaches. Sometimes the old meat sacks sagging toward death in their beds are restrained.

Whoever I am, I am not a woman who could leave someone to rot in a place like that. Even him.

The grief I carried about my mother's death lodged in me like a baseball I'd swallowed whole. Inside my treehouse sanctuary with Andy and Miles, every night I would dream about her. Every morning I would wake up feeling vaguely like I had been crying. But something else wedged itself between me and my new life. A word. Father.

The man I'd pulled from the sea and breathed life into.

The man without memory.

And so I saved his life a second time, or Andy did, in act of unmitigated compassion and heroism. He flew to Florida to get my father. Then they rode a plane all the way to Oregon together. Briefly they were detained at the airport security arch because my father would not let go of the faux metal box containing my mother's ashes. He sat in his wheelchair and gripped them and shook his head no. Finally they let an old man through with what was left of his wife.

When Andy brought my father back to me I felt cleaved between two Lidias. A daughter, a tormented and damaged girl. And a woman, a mother, a writer whose life had just been born.

Andy and I found an assisted living facility about 20 minutes away from our sanctuary in the Bull Run Wilderness. The rooms were more like apartments than dungeons. His apartment had a giant window through which you could see fir trees and maple and alder – the Northwest. It was something I could give him that didn't hurt.

My father lived a quiet life there for two years until he died. In the morning he would watch T.V. In the afternoon too.

Sometimes he would just stare out the window at trees and smile. This man who took the place of the father I'd known before was sweet and docile and kind. Even his eyes were kind. Sometimes, I'd let him see Miles. I never saw the happiness that spread across his face like it did when he was with Miles. I mean in my life with him. Though I rarely let him hold my son, when he did, he looked like a miracle had happened. A boy.

A few times Andy and I brought him out to our house in the trees. He marveled at the architecture – muscle memory, I guess. He spoke of the way the light cascaded down the hand crafted wood stairs quite eloquently. The forest took his breath away. He said, "I love it here so much. I wish I could die here." I think he meant to say "live" here, but I let it go. It was not something I could give him anyway.

I'd ask him about things when I'd drive him to do errands or to lunch – I'd say, "Daddy, do you remember being an architect?"

"I was an architect? No. No, I don't think so. Was I?"

Or I'd say, do you remember the time when ... and I'd try to choose something happy. Like the time he took my mother and me to Trinidad, where his greatest architectural achievement had happened. Steel drum music. A tortoise we saw lay eggs on the white sand beaches. Or living at Stinson Beach. Fruit trees in our yard. The ocean on the breeze. Or my sister singing in The Singing Angels Choir. Or classical music. Or baseball. To all of these he'd smile, sometimes he'd laugh, shake his head yes, maybe a glimpse of something. Mostly he'd stay quiet and look out the window of the car. Once he looked over at me driving and said, "Marilou?" His sister's name.

"No Daddy," I'd say, "I'm Lidia."

"I know that," he'd say, and laugh.

Among the meager boxes of things he'd brought with him – old photographs and miscellaneous "papers" and a drawing pad and a very fine assortment of pencils and pens – was my first published book. I found it in his room one day. I picked it up and said, "Huh. What are you doing with this thing?" The cover was worn.

"Oh, I've read that book many times."

"Really. Do you know who wrote it?"

"You," he said, looking up at me with transparent blue eyes, twinning mine.

"Yeah, daddy. Me. Have you read all the stories?"

"I think so. I can't remember."

"That's OK. It doesn't matter."

"There's one about swimming."

I looked at him hard. Sometimes – I couldn't help it – I wondered if the other guy was in there somewhere. Some people will know what I mean. There were moments when he looked more knowing than he should. In those moments I almost …
I almost wanted him back. My father was one of the most intelligent men I have ever met. My father was an artist. My father loved art, and nature, and the life of the mind. He gave me those things.

He was talking about the story "The Chronology of Water" I'd written. In it, there is a father who abuses his children and then loses his memory. A father whose daughter pulls him out of the sea. A swimmer's story.

"I like it. It's a very good story."

"Thank you," I said, knowing not to say more.

"Not very flattering of me though."

I smiled and looked down and crossed my arms over my chest. "Fair enough. You know, I won a prize for that story. I got to go to New York."

"Isn't that something," he said, and whistled, and looked out at the trees.

That's the only thing we ever said to each other about anything that had happened.

A father. A daughter.

Recollected.

I have an image of him from that time. He appears in a

film short Andy made based on the same short story. My father agreed to let us film him for it. In the segment in which he appears, the film is black and white. You cannot tell from looking at him that he has lost his wits or memory. You cannot tell from looking at the square jaw and broad shoulders and intense stare that he abused his wife and daughters. You cannot tell he was an award winning architect, and before that, he had the tender hands of an artist. You cannot tell he is anything but a man who looks intense on film.

I'm in the film too. In the segment in which I appear, the film is black and white. I am walking out into the ocean of the Oregon Coast. In November. I walk in waist high, and then I dive into the oncoming waves, and I swim. How I swim.

My father died less than two years after my mother. His ashes were in a plastic bag about the size of a loaf of wonder bread. The ashes were white. I went to the funeral home to get them, but that's not all I got. I had asked for his pacemaker and defibrillator. The two mechanical things attached to his heart that had kept him alive after he drowned. How strange they looked, without a body. Eventually Andy helped me smash them on the garage floor with a mallet.

I drove my father's ashes up to Seattle pretty immediately because I didn't want them. I didn't want them in my house, or my garden, or any waterway near me or my son.

My sister and I dumped them in the river next to her husband's boathouse office under a bridge. That Seattle bridge in Freemont that has the cement troll underneath it at one end. We just parked the car, got the ash, opened the bag and dumped it at the edge of the river, where it mixed with river refuse and bird shit and the oil of passing boats. The white ash got on both our hands, and at one point, my sister sneezed. Without thinking, my sister reached up to rub her nose and mouth. White ash was on her face. Possibly in her mouth. We stared at each other. Then her eyes got big and she said "GET IT OFF!" So I splashed her whole head with crappy river water until she sputtered and laughed.

We laughed so hard walking back to the car we couldn't breathe.

We laughed so hard our sides ached.

We laughed the laugh of women untethered, finally, from their origins.

A Small Ocean

MORNING. I'M SITTING IN MY CAR WAITING FOR THEM to unlock the doors of the swimming pool nearest to my home. I can feel the years of training like a DNA river running through me. All those years of 5:30 a.m. Then I see my mother, sitting in a car just like I am, her long gray winter coat with the faux raccoon fur collar, smelling a little like last night's vodka and day-old Estée Lauder. How she waited for me every morning when I was too young to drive a car. How she sat there quietly, the engine purring alongside her middle-aged misery of a life. What did she think about sitting there in the dark? Who was she besides the mother of a swimmer and the wife of a jerk?

In Port Arthur, Texas, where my mother is from, the trees rise only a little off of the ground. The sky is the main thing, resting heavy and blue and hot on miles and miles of dirt. Heat singing like a fever in you. Making you forget water and that breathable blue past. Making you think the southern song was meant for you, the twang thick like syrup up your spine, cradling you like lemon drops in that hot dry always. The front porch. The cool of tile in the basement. Panties in the freezer. A breeze at night like prayer. And the land is filled with the up and down black steel heads of oil rigs hemming their way across dirt.

Where I was born the trees bear fruit and the ocean hugs the shore, making you believe in things like sea serpents and mermaids and Disneyland. When I was five, California had a smell. Orange trees, their waxen leaves like crowns studded by fruit. Marin County. Stinson beach. Warmth whispered around my skin, I could breath it into me, I was tanned like children get. My hair white against the whole sky. My eyes blue as lapis. In our front yard, orange trees, plum trees, and apple trees. The front of the house keeping its secrets, the hands of a child rubbing bark, or grass, or dirt; child's games. But the back of the house gave way to ocean and the edge of things – a girl's thoughts rose and fell as tides, drifted like the smell of orange blossoms through the windows and doors, out, across, beyond vision, beyond daughter. The house is of a man's hands, and I was not a swimmer yet.

Maybe there's another reason I went to Texas beside escaping to college. Maybe I was looking for something – something of her. Where in that dirt is she from? Is it from a damp place miles down, a place where dead things have composted? The wet at the back of the neck, a woman's hand wiping sweat away, her eyes closed? Or is she in the heat itself, the dry whisper of wind pushing everything out and away ... a woman's imagination burning a hole in her skull to get out? Did she nearly die waiting? Wanting? Is she in the sound of a southern drawl out the mouth of a woman, its dips and ahs making words go strange, beautiful?

My mother was an alcoholic manic depressant borderline suicide case with a limp. All of that.

In 2001 my mother went to the doctor because she was having trouble breathing. I was in my ninth month of pregnancy in San Diego. She'd been taking care of my memoryless father for over 15 years by then. I know what kind of toll that caretaking takes. It must have drained every drop of her. My mother didn't visit doctors much, having spent her childhood years in body casts and hospitals. So there were no chances for early warning. Cancer had already invaded her lungs, her breasts.

She called me in San Diego the day before I went into labor to tell me she was dying. Miraculously, Andy answered the phone, and hung up, and lied. He said, "Your mother says she loves you." He waited for our son to be born. Then he waited a little longer. He told my sister and me in our living room in San Diego a week after Miles was born. The three of us cried in my little seahouse, Miles asleep in my arms.

It took six months. The rest of her life. One of the more difficult parts of her hospitalization was her intense withdrawal from alcohol. You will hate my saying this, but it will be true nonetheless. If I hadn't had Miles, I would have moved back into her house of pain. And I would have brought her a bottle to ease her suffering, her journey. Every day if that's what it took. But my Miles – there was a deathmother, and there was his life.

That is all.

When she died I was not with her. I tried to help her during her illness but she had so clusterfucked her life up by then there was almost nothing I could do. Andy and I flew to Florida to see her. To comfort her. To show her Miles. She looked so happy to see the little baby boy with the lifeforce larger than thunderstorm. She said, "Belle, take him – I don't remember how to hold a baby right." She said, "A boyah! We've never had one a those!" Clapping her hands together and crying. But she had almost no life left in her.

Once when I was alone with her in her hospital room, I asked her a question. She looked so small and still. Her face was shrunken and wrinkled, and her body so pale and slight. She almost looked like a girl, except for the lines a sad cartography across her face. I asked her, "What's the best thing that's ever happened in your life?"

It was the question Kesey had asked me. It's what I could think to ask.

She said, "Oh. Well, Belle. That's easy. My children."

Though I couldn't imagine how, I believed her.

They called me from a Florida Hospice all the way in Oregon when her skin became ashen and her eyelids began to flutter. They put the phone to her ear. She could not speak, as she had starved herself and hadn't the energy by then. They said when she heard my voice on the other end her eyes became very wide, and then her breathing became very loud and urgent. Then the nurse took the phone back and told me she was gone, and that she looked peaceful, and that she believed my mother had heard me.

You probably want to know what I said to this woman. She was not a good mother. She did not save us from my father, and she taught us things that we have spent our entire lives trying to unlearn. But sometimes all I can remember is the way she rode with me to have my third abortion, the way she sat in the little room where they vacuum your insides out and call it a procedure, the little life disappearing into a glass container – and more specifically, I remember her face as we sat in the parking lot of Denny's because I didn't want to go home, or anywhere else, yet. She didn't say anything. She simply parked the car in the back near the big metal refuse bin. She petted my hand. She cried a little. She smelled like day old vodka and Estée Lauder. Her real estate signs were in the trunk. Nothing happened, she didn't ask me anything, she didn't tell me anything, and after that I was able to move.

Or I think of all the mornings she drove me to swim practice at 5:00 a.m. Or the sound of her voice singing I see the moon. Or the day she brought the shoe box out and showed me the story she'd written, and the redbird drawing my father had done – the lives they could have lived. Or her face when she told my father she'd signed the scholarship letter, and that I was going to college, that I was leaving.

Or I think of Israel and Becky Boone.

So when I tell you what I said to her maybe it will sound deluded or trite, since this woman is where my trouble started, since she let us down so terribly, and birthed an unforgiving darkness into us forever.

I said thank you mamma. I love you so.

And then she died.

It was 2001, the year my son was born. Her urn was a faux

gold box about the size of a coffee pot. My father wouldn't part with it – brainbird that he was by then – and so I didn't try to take it until after he died. Then I put it in our garage on a shelf for two years. I didn't look at it, I didn't talk to it, I barely thought about it. It just sat up there with nails and cans of paint and summer storage items and garden tools.

But one day I was in the garage hunting for corner braces to build a frame for a painting and I saw it on the shelf looking all …well. So I called my sister and asked, uh, do you want to do something with mother's ashes? My sister who had been estranged from my mother from the time she was 16.

Oddly, she said, I guess. So I drove my mother in a box up to Seattle. She sat in the passenger's seat.

Sitting in my sister's living room on her brown leather couch that smelled vaguely of cat piss, we stared at the mother-box between us.

She said, "You wanna open it?"

"Sure," I said. Then I examined the edges more closely, and I jammed my fingernails into the joints, and saw that there wasn't a clear way to do it. So I said, "Do you have a knife?"

My sister left the room, went into the kitchen, and came back with a butter knife. I stared at it in her hand. Then I took it and tried to pry my box of mother open.

No luck.

"You have a flathead screwdriver?" I said.

"I think so," she said, and went off in the direction of her garage.

"And a hammer," I yelled after her.

I put the box on the living room floor. My sister knelt next to me. "Hold the bottom of it," I said.

"Don't hit me with the hammer," she said.

"Move your head," I said.

I placed the flathead screwdriver at the line where the box edges joined, and then I whacked it with the hammer. The box shot across their hardwood floor. "Look at it go!" Came out of my mouth before I could stop it. Then we both nearly died laughing, rolling on the floor like kids.

I swear to god we tried everything to get that goddamn motherbox open. At one point I even dropped it from the roof of her deck hoping it would sort of break open, but no. I briefly considered running over it with the car. There was no way into the motherbox of ash.

After I left, my sister told me she buried it in her backyard, but I visited her a month later and saw it in the back of her mini-coop with all her life shit and dog hair and car crap. I never confronted her about the lie. But I never saw the box again after that, either. It could be in the ground in her backyard.

Or it could be someplace else.

I can still see my mother sitting in her car as I'd come out of swim practice as a kid. The heater running. Whatever else she was, she was there.

Morning. I'm sitting in my car waiting for them to unlock the doors of the swimming pool. They open, and I enter. I shed my clothes. The water is the color of my eyes. The chlorine smell is more familiar than anything I have ever known. When I dive in, all sound, all weight, all thought leaves. I am a body in water. Again.

Mother, rest. I am home.

Wisdom is a Motherfucker

YOU DIDN[1]T ACTUALLY THINK I WAS GOING TO LEAVE you inside marriage and family in the regular way, did you?

Listen, I love my family. Like gonzo. And it's true enough Andy and Miles have pretty much rebirthed me. And yeah. I'm married. With family.

And I love women. Sue me.

But there are other wisdoms.

Unfortunately, I am not wise. I don't have a special look back on your own life wise voice. More often than not, all I have is a wise-ass voice, and people get tired of that, I can tell you. Although I am fairly skilled at creating lyrical passages when needed.

Up until the place in my life where I crashed into a pregnant woman head-on and met the Mingo, I thought the whole story was about me. A me drama. All these things that have happened to the Lidia.

But what happens to you when you swim back through your own past is that you find an endwall. The endwall for me is my mother and my dead baby girl. I learned it at the surface of my skin where it is written now through rituals of pain and pleasure.

So here's the deal. About family, you have to make it up. Seriously. I know amazing single women and their children who are families. Gay men and women with kids who are families. Bisexuals and transsexuals who family up all over the place.

People who don't have partners create families in everyone they touch. I know women and men from a multitude of sexual orientations without any children just doing their lives who create families that kick the can down the street. The heterosexual trinity is just one of many stories.

If your marriage goes busto, make up a different you. If the family you came from sucked, make up a new one. Look at all the people there are to choose from. If the family you are in hurts, get on the bus. Like now.

I'm saying I think you have to break into the words "relationship" or "marriage" or "family" and bring the walls down. Don¹t even get me started on the current BAR PEOPLE WHO LOVE EACH OTHER FROM MARRYING fiasco. Annie get your gun. Jeez. Anyway. The key is, make up shit.

Make up stories until you find one you can live with.

I learned it through writing.

Writing can be that.

Writing to bring the delicate dream to the tips of words, to kiss them, to rest your cheek on them, to open your mouth and breathe body to body to resuscitate a self.

Make up stories until you find one you can live with.

Make up stories as if life depended on it.

Though I admit my resurrection and transformation have been a little strange, I can say it in a sentence now: my mother did not protect me. As a girl, I died.

So when my child died in the womb of me, it was as if I'd done the same thing. I'd killed a girl I meant to love.

It's a big deal to make a sentence.

The line between life and death.

It took me 10 years to emerge from the grief of a dead daughter. You have to forgive women like me. We don't know any other way to do live than to throw our bodies at it. I was the kind of woman whose relationships were grenades and whose life became a series of car wrecks – anything to keep the girl I was and the girl I had – tiny daughter dolls – safe from this world.

So yes I know how angry, or naïve, or self destructive, or messed up, or even deluded I sound weaving my way through these life stories at times. But beautiful things. Graceful things. Hopeful things can sometimes appear in dark places. Besides, I'm trying to tell you the "truth" of a woman like me.

The things that happen to us are true.

The stories we tell about it are writing. A body away from us. Writing – with its forms and contortions, its resistances and lies, its unending desires, its on and on.

Listen I can see you. If you are like me. You do not deserve most of what has happened or will. But there is something I can offer you. Whoever you are. Out there. As lonely as it gets, you are not alone. There is another kind of love.

It's the love of art. Because I believe in art the way other people believe in god.

In art I've met an army of people – a tribe that gives good company and courage and hope. In books and painting and music and film. This book? It's for you. It's water I made a path through. I'm not speaking out of my asshole when I say this.

Come in. The water will hold you.

Interview with Lidia Yuknavitch

RHONDA HUGHES, PUBLISHER AND EDITOR FOR HAW-
thorne Books, conducted this interview with Lidia Yuknavitch.

RH : *Your memoir opens with the loss of your daughter and your
grief process. It is some of the most beautiful writing in the book,
poetic, rich imagery, lines that demand the reader speak them aloud.
Your ability to transform profound grief into art, into literature,
speaks to me. It's one of the reasons I wanted to publish your work.
You write, "Language is a metaphor for experience. It's as arbitrary
as the mass of chaotic images we call memory, but we can put it
into lines to narrativize over fear." Can you talk a little bit about
your experience recreating with words this time in your life?*

LY : You know Faulkner said, "Given the choice between grief
and nothing, I choose grief." The same quote has been attributed
to him about pain.

I'm not sure it is possible to articulate grief through language. You can say, I was so sad I thought my bones would
collapse. I thought I would die. But language always falls short of
the body when it comes to the intensity of corporeal experience.
The best we can do is bring language in relationship to corporeal
experience – bring words close to the body – as close as possible.
Close enough to shatter them. Or close enough to knock a body
out. To bring language close to the intensity of experiences like
love or death or grief or pain is to push on the affect of language.

Its sounds and grunts and ecstatic noises. The ritual sense of language. Or the cry.

Poetic language – and by that I mean the language of image, sound, rhythm, color, sensation – is probably the closest we bring language to experience – poetic language takes you to the edge of sense and deep into sensation. So after I name my primal grief, the death of my daughter the day she was born, it felt precise to move directly to poetic language. The metaphor of collecting rocks is more "true" to me to the experience of grieving than to say, I was intolerably sad. It feels precise to draw that metaphor of collecting rocks out, to extend it as long as possible, to let the reader feel the space of grief in the house the way I did. It's my hope that at least one person will find resonance in that extended language space.

I want you to hear how it feels to be me inside a sentence. Even if some of the sentences seem to lose their meaning. I want the rhythm, the image, the cry to remain with your body. You could probably go through this book and literally chart the moments of emotional intensity by watching where the language – to quote Dickinson – goes strange.

You have published both fiction and nonfiction. Can you talk about your experience with both genres as well as the role memory plays?

While I was writing this book, many things occurred to me about both memory and about the relationship between fiction and non-fiction.

About memory, after my father drowned and lost his wits – specifically his short-term and a good bit of his long-term memory, I became rather obsessively interested in how memory works at the level of neuroscience and biochemistry. I was trying to deal with the fact that the things he'd done had been "erased" from experience. Part of me didn't believe it – I'd look at him and think, is the dark side of him still in there? Tucked deeply behind the gray matter?

Turns out, according to neuroscience, the more you actively

"remember" something, the more the headstory you carry
around changes. Every time you recall something, you modify it
a little bit and that's because brains – this is very cool – brains
work through a mixture of images, pictures, feelings, words, facts,
and fiction – all "recollected." Eventually you are not remembering what happened at all, but your story or head movie about
it. The safest memories are probably those embedded in the
brains of people who have lost the ability to retrieve them.

In writing, every narrative and linguistic choice you make
forecloses others, directs the story a certain way, focuses on
a particular image, extends a metaphor that on another day, you
might have chosen very differently. Form has everything to do
with content in this sense. So what is "true" in non-fiction writing
is also always "crafted" given shape and composition and
emotional intensity – through our narrative choices as writers.
And that's in addition to the science of memory. So the true
story is always a fiction. This is why I have come to believe that
non-fiction and fiction are as inextricably linked as memory
and imagination – which, as it turns out, also use the same brain
circuits when they are active.

So much of memory is recollecting pieces. And that's what
writing is – drawing from language to recollect and shape
pieces of things. I am absolutely more able to reveal emotional
truths about myself or anything inside fiction writing. The
imaginative realm makes the most "sense" to me in my life – it's
everything else in life that is difficult. But I did find something
in the course of writing this non-fiction book that truly amazed
me. I could address my mother and father as characters from
parts of their lives that did not include me. I could imagine a pre-
story to them. I could feel compassion for them. And I can thank
them for this life I have, as bittersweet a process as that is to
move through.

*Earlier you mentioned the metaphor of collecting rocks. One of my
favorite chapters, "Metaphor," describes this as follows: "The rocks.*

They carry the chronology of water. All things simultaneously living and dead in your hands." Here also is your title. What does the chronology of water mean to you?

Yes, this title came to me long ago – when I was 26! Wait, was I ever 26? Man that seems like epochs ago. I was in a creative writing workshop with the wonderful Diana Abu-Jaber. My daughter had just died, and I was a mess – raging, grieving, self-destructing. But I did manage to make it into that creative writing classroom. I wrote a crazy short story made from seemingly random fragments. Diana looked at the rush of fragments and said Lidia, they all have something in common. Because I was a know-nothing, I said, what? Water, she said. She also said, I think this is a book. I think it's the story of your life, maybe.

But at that time I was busy. Busy raging, grieving, fucking up.

Later I pulled the story back out and looked at it. You know what? She was right. And I thought, if this is the story of my life, no wonder it's in fragments. It's got a messed up chronology be-cause that's how I feel about life – it's not linear. It moves in fits and starts, doubles back, repeats or extends an image. I thought if my life has a chronology, it's the chronology of water – the way water carved the earth, the way water carries us into the world, the way we are made of water, the way water retreats or comes. I had, in other words, with her help, found my central metaphor.

That story was eventually published in *The Northwest Review*, and as you know, all these years later, has become the spine and bones of this book.

In my house there are many rocks. What I love about rocks that you find in rivers or at the ocean's shore is that they are the sediment of all life on the planet continuously destroyed and remade. When you hold a rock in your hand you are holding everything in existence, even space dust, and it's traveled oceans to get to you. So fragile and yet solid – made from pieces of things – like we are.

Writing restored your personal narrative that was not allowed in your father's house while you were growing up. "My voice, she was coming. Something about my father's house. Something about alone and water." Does writing provide the same essential to Lidia the adult? Are the reasons you wrote then and now different?

Many people will know what I mean when I say that I can't seem to live without the process of making art. I mean I literally fall apart or go to shit when I'm not making something, I can't find the balance in my life or the center, I'm simply less of a person. Lost. Or worse. It feels like writing is the only thing I am any good at, but that probably isn't entirely true. What I mean when I say that writing is the only thing I am good at is that it is the place where I feel most present, most worth a crap, most able to give something useful.

But there is another thing about writing that may or may not be something I should tell people – ha. I do know that when I'm inside writing I don't want to be anywhere else. It's like being inside a song or a painting. Wouldn't it be something to be able to inhabit art? It's a little frightening though – to think about staying there – not coming out. Perhaps that is a psychosis edge. I have a painter friend who talks this way about wanting to stay inside the painting – trusting images and color and composition more than people – I definitely feel that way too. We joke about not coming out sometimes.

There are reasons to come out. My son, my family. Love. Animals, the ocean.

Too, it strikes me that in America we don't much have a "sacred" place or role for the isolate artist any longer. Everything has been sucked up into marketing and celebrity and the almighty commodity – so if you are a writer, you are meant to sell something. If it sells, it has worth. But in my heart of hearts I just want to sneak individual books into the pockets of sad people. Or stuff pews with them! Because writing gave me a place to go and be and grow when I wanted to give up. And I'd like to jam my foot in the doorway so that others might find this place too. And yes, that is still true. Maybe more than ever.

Swimming offered you water, respite from home, your life there. During your senior year of high school at the State Championships your relay team scored the best time in the nation. "Then Jimmy Carter took all little girl dreams of swimmer glory away from our bodies with a boycott – Randy's famous pool full of winners included – anyway. There was no world left to belong to. Not athlete, not daughter." Later you accepted a scholarship in Texas and once there left both the college and competitive swimming. Did the U.S. boycott of the Olympics have anything to do with this or affect your future relationship with the sport?

My sister and I have always had a little bit of a hard time distinguishing reality from fiction. We both escaped our childhood terrors in books and music and art, and those creative worlds were more real to us than the one that trapped inside my father's house.

Something could be "true" one minute, say, Christmas morning with presents and a tree, and rendered "untrue" within the first twenty minutes of opening presents if my father's rage got loose. Or you could get an "A" at school, and bring it home only to be shamed: "What, does that make you special?"

Once my sister crawled underneath her high school art lab table and refused to come home. Ever. I'd go to school or to swim team – my two great escapes – and be unable to tell reality from nonreality. At the pool, in the safety of water, alongside the beautiful bodies of almost women, was that reality? At school where teachers gave me books to read that forever took me to other worlds, wasn't that real? Or was reality back at home, where even breathing meant shame?

Reality lost its hold on me by the time I was 10.

Very good swimmers spend their youth trying to swim to an endpoint like the Olympics. A tangible goal you are living for. Training for. Year after year. Something to give you self worth.

Something to make you feel special. And if you were fast enough, maybe you could even swim all the way to a new life.

So when the Olympic Boycott happened, it proved what I already suspected was true. Reality could disappear in an instant – a man could take it from you forever.

I think the beginning of my deepest acts of self destruction often have something in common – a question that comes up in different forms over the course of a life – when the thing you are living for dies right in front of you, why go on? It's a sadness that enters us all, just differently I suppose. But that Olympic boycott was one of my earliest moments of consciousness with regard to the mutability of reality in the world. Something called "poli tics" could steal your personal life. Just like something called "father" could. And I'd already grown up through the Nixon years and survived early Catholic upbringing ... so even children understood to be cynical.

On the hopeful side though, swimming, books, art, and love – those worlds are still most real to me. In the best sense of that puny word.

You purposely divulge few details relating to your drug use and you don't declare whether or not you have a "problem" with either drugs or alcohol, although you mention going to rehab and jail both more than once. What was your thinking about this part of your narrative?

Over the years I have become very disappointed in the idea that there can be only one, monolithic narrative about alcoholism or addiction. What I mean is, we've come to a time in both capitalism and literary history where unless you tell the *right* story about drug and alcohol dependency, you don't get to tell it at all. And that one, right story is most often dictated by the market – by agents and editors and publishers and media.

What a consumer audience needs the story to be.

If you write outside of those lines, you will more often than not be coached back into the center.

I think of the writers and painters and musicians who have inspired me to not kill myself and keep going. Most of them did drugs and alcohol. All of them, really.

I never say in this book what happened to the woman I hit head on with my car. I have deferred that information purposefully. Because I want you to stay with me – me drunk driving across eight lanes of freeway traffic at midnight in my car – stay with me inside my own pain and grief and vodka breath and pee and barf – stay with me as the gunpowder smell from the airbags fills the car.

Sometimes we're just sad. And wrong-headed. And drunk. That's all.

There are so many stories to tell about what we do to our bodies.

There is a history to the mythos about addiction in the country – we've always burned witches – but I think the potent turning point was probably the establishment and codification of A.A. in this country. And the subsequent nationalized embrace of the general principles of the A.M.A. and the A.P.A. and the bible of the *Diagnostic and Statistical Manual of Mental Disorders* – how each of these defines illness and cures. Not to mention religion's role in the false narrative of redemption. Now a whole industrial complex exists to serve the addiction narrative, along with a handy pharmaceutical empire.

My mother was an alcoholic. But I never think of her that way. I think she was in pain most of her life. I think she was just trying to drown a sadness that wouldn't lift. I think if I had been her I would have killed myself like she tried to. I wish I had come conscious sooner. Maybe we could have talked about it. What drinking is. What it isn't.

The other thing I'd say is that if we didn't have drugs and alcohol, we wouldn't have art. I know that is not a popular thing to say but I believe it is true nonetheless. Our drug and alcohol excesses kill people. Yes. But they also are part of who we are as artists. Part of why cultural production exists. Whether we want to admit it or not.

You write about the night you mother attempted suicide and how it angered you so that you wrote, "When I came out of the bathroom I felt a little bit like a person who could kill her." It seems as if your relationship with your mother was more complex and complicated because while she angered you she was also the parent who was there for you in ways your father was not such as taking you to and from swim practice and setting you free to accept the swim scholarship from Texas Tech in Lubbock. As your mother was dying you told her that you loved her. Did this love include forgiveness? Can you say a bit about when and how this forgiveness developed?

You know Marguerite Duras once said "in childhood and the lives that follow, the mother represents madness. Our mothers remain the craziest people we've ever met."

My mother remains the craziest person I ever met. But I mean something quite complex when I say that, maybe even profound. Up until the death of my daughter I would say that I maintained an antagonistic stance with my mother. I fought with her – I chose to fight with her – to find my own edges. She let me. She fought back. I brought my rage and pain right up to the surface of her puffy with drink skin. She let me. Maybe she even drew it out of me. Though we never laid a hand on each other.

We raged by and through one another. Not the rage of the father or symbolic father. The rage of women let loose, uncontained, when no one but us was in the house. I remember how her blue eyes went to the color of steel. I remember admiring it.

How she let me down of course is that she never took my sister and me out of that house, away from our father. She didn't save us.

How she was there for me though was that she took me. She didn't flinch. She took the full force of my adolescence and young adulthood and all the hatred and rage I had stored up and she didn't move a muscle. I yelled. She yelled back. It's a survival skill. A skewed one, to be sure, but one that carries an unusual strength. Sometimes I think our fighting bore me.

The last time she tried to "spank" me I was 10. She broke several blood vessels in her hand. I already had a muscled up swimmer's butt. I just stared at her after she hit me as hard as she could on the ass. I think she knew in that moment what would rise between us. All the rage we carried to survive my father. Everything it would take to enter "woman" in this still dumb world.

When my daughter died I broke. Open. Into stories. For the first time in my life, I wanted to know what my mother's story was. Badly. So I asked her. When I explored what my mother's story had been all I felt was compassion for the girl of her. Someone should have done something to save her. No one did. It's a wonder she was alive at all.

Maybe forgiveness is just that. The ability to admit someone else's story. To give it to them. To let it be enunciated in your presence. It's your job not to flinch.

Another subject that you name, but don't go into detail is your father's sexual abuse. Throughout the narrative there are references to the narrator's experience such as, "Or all the nights I made him [Phillip] break into other peoples' homes the way my father had broken into me," and during a conversation with Andy after the narrator tells him that her father was abusive and he asked what the father did, the narrator's reply is simply, "Sexual." Your father moved to Oregon from his home in Florida so that you could help care for him. Did you come to find forgiveness with your father? Was it the same as with your mother or different? How so?

Another narrative that's supersaturated the literary landscape at this point in time is the incest narrative. Someone in my writing group actually called it "cliché" ... Though when she said it I went into the bathroom and cried, I know what she meant. She meant that the incest narrative has been marketed and disseminated to such an extent that it's running out of meaning.

That sounds so horrible to say but talk to an editor or agent or publisher and you will hear rhetoric about the incest narrative and how to sell it or what will prohibit your book from selling.

As if that's what matters.

So like the drug and alcohol monolithic narrative, there are so many stories of incest out there yet to be told. But if you don't tell the *right* incest narrative, you got butkus. My goal in offering my own story isn't to claim that abuse suffered from my father is any more important than anyone else's. Nor is it to "claim" the incest narrative to sell books.

My goal is to put the reader into the space of childhood and young adulthood where fear and confusion and rage get born – like they do in us all for different reasons. To put the reader in their body through language. Because when I teach or give readings or workshops, I meet a hundred people who know what it feels like to be shamed, or beaten, or molested, or just made small. We all move through the waters. Language helps us feel less separate.

When my mother died my father was stuck in Florida. Alone. With not much of his wits left. With major heart damage. With a lien on his house. Andy and I visited some nursing homes in Florida. I threw up. They were simply awful. Whoever I am, I could not leave him there. I couldn't leave Hitler there. It simply wasn't possible for me to purposefully kill him or torture him or neglect his body. Ironic.

I don't believe in god. I don't particularly believe in the cult of sin and redemption. But I do believe in energy. What I hold my father most responsible for is for not facing his own darkness – not acknowledging it as his. I think that is a flaw a great many of us struggle with. Like in *The Tempest* when Prospero says about Caliban, "This thing of darkness I acknowledge mine." We all have to claim that which we have created. For me it's a detachment that I have to watch out for every day of my life – else I become untethered from the ones I love, even from life. My father never acknowledged his capacity for cruelty. His uncontainable anger. His misplaced desires. Maybe I learned to forgive him from the language and poetics of Shakespeare.

But forgiveness isn't the best I have to give him. Even as a dead man, the best I have to give him is an acknowledgement that I came from him. And I did not kill myself. I am living beyond his life, his end and pulse. I am trying to put things into the world that alchemize the dark and turn it to something beautiful and smooth you can carry in your hand. A small mighty blue stone.

I've never met anyone who hasn't fucked up in their life a time or two. Royally. I'm pretty sure that's what keeps us connected to one another. Not so much the superhuman savior stories. It's called being human. It's the energy and matter. Words let us say that.

Language! What a thunderous mercy, huh?

Sexuality in The Chronology of Water *is a multilayered, multidimensional aspect of your emotional life. From the beginning you had an attraction to both sexes and later as an young adult your sexuality became both a source of power and an expression of grief. It seems that as you discovered your writing talent and continued your education, finishing with a Ph.D. in English Literature, your sexuality also underwent transition. Was this your experience? And, while your sexual life may have been considered unconventional by some, you choice to marry men and ultimately become a family with Andy and Miles is more in line with society at large. How have you incorporated all these aspects into your adult life?*

My sexuality is still very much in flux. But I would say that about us all. The limits we put on our own sexual development and exploration are partly cultural scripts and partly our own hopes and fears playing out skin stories. In other words, sexuality is always undergoing transition – just like our bodies and minds and souls and energies – always in flux.

So to be married *might* mean for some people that they shut down their sexual journey, or that they follow a wife/mother storyline, but I remain interested in explorations in between those things, at the edges, or beyond the regular orbits.

I do still think that culturally speaking there is a very narrow bandwidth available for women in terms of sexual development. Wife, mother, lover, other. Men too, of course, but I have lived the limits more in terms of women and girls. But if psychosexual development and corporeal development is lifelong, then I consider it part of my job in life to journey right up until the last. Even if I'm a dried up old raisin. Because I think bodies are about the coolest thing in ... ever. Your body. Mine. All the different kinds. What a glory bodies are. I hope to write a book about bodies in the near future.

Your scholastic achievements are admirable, especially given that you accomplished them without support from your parents and despite the emotional chaos of your younger life. What drove you to do this?

Survival. Pure and simple. I discovered early on that mobility for a woman in this culture is crucial. The ability to live and work on your own if you have to is vital. The ability to pursue the life of the mind is vital. The ability to journey the body's full story is vital. Volition. If you can find that in yourself you are going to be okay.

I have a picture of myself running away from home for the first time. I'm three. I have a small plastic suitcase and a big scary looking doll. My cat "spice" is in the foreground, probably wondering where I'm going. My sister is in the background, nearly out of the frame, in the most glorious red dress.

I went to the edge of the yard and sat on the curb for about 30 minutes.

The house is near Stinson Beach near San Francisco, where I was born. The yard was filled with fruit trees. The house was filled with anger. My sister and I were terrified most of our childhoods. My father bred fear into the bodies of his daughters.

And yet, in that moment of the picture, taken by my mother who no doubt thought it looked cute, like mothers do, I knew what to do. Volition.

There is art in that.

I believe in art the way other people believe in god. I say that because books and paintings and music and photography gave me an alternate world to inhabit when the one I was born into was a dead zone. I say it because if you, even inside whatever terror itches your skin, pick up a pen or a paintbrush, a camera or clay or a guitar, you already have what you are afraid to choose. Volition. It was already in you.

Just be that – what moves inside you. It's already there, waiting:

Hush for the line
Crouched like the touch of dreams in your fingertips
She is coming with a vengeance.